AF564447

# Srilanka Misadventure

India's Military Peace-Keeping Campaign 1987-1990

BY THE SAME AUTHOR

*Unlearned Lessons: An Appraisal of India's Military Mishaps,* New Delhi, Har-Anand Publications, 2007 (Reprinted 2010)

*China-Tibet-India, the 1962 War and the Strategic Military Future,* New Delhi, Har-Anand Publications, 2009

*Understanding the Sino-Indian War 1962,* New Delhi, Har-Anand Publications, 2009

*A Question of Pride,* New Delhi, Har-Anand Publications, 2009

*China India Border Conflicts,* New Delhi, Har-Anand Publications, 2009

# Srilanka Misadventure

## India's Military Peace-Keeping Campaign 1987-1990

Gautam Das and M. K. Gupta-Ray

Military Affairs Series
An Imprint of Har-Anand Publications Pvt Ltd

HAR-ANAND PUBLICATIONS PVT LTD
E-49/3, Okhla Industrial Area, Phase-II, New Delhi-110020
Tel.: 41603490
E-mail: info@haranandbooks.com/haranand@rediffmail.com
Shop online at: www.haranandbooks.com
@haranand_publications
Har Anand Publications



**Reprint, 2025**



Published by Ashok Gosain and Ashish Gosain for
Har-Anand Publications Pvt Ltd

Printed in India at Megha Enterprises

# Dedication

This book is dedicated to the infantry of the Indian Army— the nation's insurance policy and last resort for internal security, for upholding law and order, for aid to the civil authority in natural and man-made calamities, and, after all the diplomats and the missiles, whether threatened or used, have failed, the country's ultimate foreign policy enforcer in its immediate region—India's under-valued 'maid-of-all-work.'

Secondly, it is also dedicated to those disabled in the Sri Lanka operations, and to the everlasting memory of those officers and men of the Indian armed forces who laid down their lives in an unnecessarily messy and ill-conducted campaign, in the hope that the powers that be who are meant to plan and conduct politico-military operations learn from their sacrifice, by planning and conducting all future campaigns in such a way that the task is accomplished with the least unavoidable loss of life, at least on the Indian side.

Last, but not the least, the authors dedicate this book to their regiments, The Sikh Regiment and The 11th Gorkha Rifles, and to 16th Battalion, The Sikh Regiment.

# Acknowledgements

The authors wish to gratefully acknowledge the inputs provided for this book, from their first-hand knowledge, or from their access to such knowledge, without which the experience gained by the Indian Army in Sri Lanka from 1987 to 1990 could not have been narrated in as much detail as the authors have been able to put in. They are: Col. Anil Kaul, Vr.C. (Retd.), *65 Armoured Regiment,* Lt. Gen. S.C. Sardeshpande, AVSM, UYSM (Retd.), *The Kumaon Regiment,* Maj. Gen. Harkirat Singh (Retd), *Brigade of the Guards,* Maj. Gen. Ashok K. Mehta (Retd.), *The $5^{th}$ Gorkha Rifles (Frontier Force),* Brig. A. Sanyal (Retd.), *The $3^{rd}$ Gorkha Rifles,* Lt. Gen. P.K. Rampal, *The $11^{th}$ Gorkha Rifles,* Brig. Rakesh Sharma, *The Sikh Regiment,* Col. M.A. Siddiqi, *1st Bn., The $11^{th}$ Gorkha Rifles,* Brig. Govind Singh Sisodia, *The Sikh Regiment,* Brig. S.K. Lahiri, *Corps of Engineers,* Lt. Col. A.K. Sharma, *$12^{th}$ Bn., The Garhwal Rifles,* Lt. Gen. S. P. Datta, PVSM (Retd.), *Army Medical Corps,* Col. Gurdev Singh, *Intelligence Corps (formerly of $16^{th}$ Bn., The Garhwal Rifles),* Lt. Col. Sanjay Bose, *$19^{th}$ Bn., The Jat Regiment,* and Col. Sudhir Gautam (Retd.), *The Regiment of Artillery.* We also wish to acknowledge our gratitude to Ms Manju Lal of Parity Paperbacks, New Delhi, for kindly granting permission to quote extensively from Col. Anil Kaul's book, *Better Dead than Disabled,* 2006. We thank Saisuresh Sivaswamy, Editor, *Rediff.com,* for the quotes from their feature of 2000, *The IPKF 10 Years On.*

Without the direct assistance of the following the production of the book would not have been possible: Tapan K. Ghosh, our editor, whose contribution has been invaluable, Maj. Gen. S.K. Singh, *The $8^{th}$ Gorkha Rifles,* Col. Rajan Bakshi, *$11^{th}$ Bn., The Dogra Regiment,* Hav/Dtmn (Topo) Jaspal Singh and Hav/Dtmn (Topo) Rajinder Pal Yadav, *501 Field Survey Group, Bengal*

*Engineers, Corps of Engineers,* Abdul Ghaffar, Raul Chandra, Rohitash Tewari and Lutfur Rahman, *'STATE OF MIND' Brand Communications, New Delhi,* T. Janardhanan, Lt. Col. Anirudh Negi, *The 11th Gorkha Rifles,* Brig. S.B.S. Lidder (Retd.), *Corps of Engineers,* and Devi Prasad, *Indian Military Academy, Dehradun.*

Nalin Sharma gave valuable advice which the authors greatly appreciate.

The authors thank Narendra Kumar of Har-Anand Publications Pvt Ltd for readily agreeing to the idea of this campaign study twenty years after the event.

Gautam Das thanks Rani, a *Karwani* (a.k.a. Smooth Saluki/ 'Caravan Hound') bitch, official name "Hirni min Nadi," (KCI Regn. No. 2006/026532, Microchip No. 985120027837957), born in a cowshed in a hamlet near village Shingewadi, Madh Taluka, Solapur District, Maharashtra, who shares his daily life, for her patience and understanding when he has disrupted her daily run, toilet and play timings; no thanks to his trying to finish the manuscript of this book to a deadline.

Gautam Das wishes to thank Lt. Gen. S.C. Sardeshpande for teaching him both tactics and how to keep an open mind, commanding by example as the GOC of his infantry division, encouraging him in his writing, kindly sending him his detailed notes, and for permitting the authors to publish his 'Analysis and Lessons' in full.

Gautam Das especially wishes to thank Lt. Gen. A.S. Kalkat, SYSM, PVSM, AVSM, VSM (Retd.), for kindly taking the time and trouble to discuss broad aspects of the book in terms of its aim and its target audience and other generalities, and for explaining the highest-level strategic and political parameters which do not fall within the aims and ambit of this book.

# Military Affairs Series

The aim of the Military Affairs series is to add to a nationwide debate on the security policies of India. And the intellectual pluralism that stems from this could, in turn, provide India's politico-bureaucratic elite an idea of the national mood on military issues and enable them to direct the country's policies in the right direction. Until recently a large number of India's politicians, and the people they represent, were only interested in regional issues within India's border. But that has begun to change. Across India, the media, a number of academics and intellectuals have started to debate issues of national security and military affairs, specially so, in an era when India faces and fights terrorism unleashed by Pakistan. This is the start of a healthy tradition in a country, which only recently was said to be without a tradition on strategic thought.

South Asia is now perhaps the most heavily militarized region in the world, and nuclear India remains boxed between the region's two other nuclear powers—China and Pakistan—and, while both are in land contiguity with India, diplomatic relations with them are far from perfect. But despite this, India sadly lacks a national security establishment and its people remain inadequately informed about the military issues that concern every citizen. It is this shortcoming that the series will address.

**MAROOF RAZA**
*General Editor*

# Preface

This book is intended primarily for the younger officers of the Indian Army, today's Captains and Majors, so that they can read about the experience of India's campaign in Sri Lanka twenty years ago. The intention is also to put before them the mistakes made by their predecessors and their seniors of the previous generation and a half, so that they can learn from reading as to what can go wrong with the best plans and with the worst.

Towards this end, we have added as many vivid first-person accounts as possible, from various levels of participation, both to make the account more readable, and to enable the reader to get a feel of the action that is as accurate as possible, including 'the fog of war'.

A word about spellings would be in order. Some of the place names have been spelt differently in the various written accounts available. Where these have been quoted, the spelling used in the originals has generally been retained, but elsewhere we have tried to use the most commonly used form. The name of the LTTE supremo had been found spelt in various different ways, among which the one used most commonly in Indian accounts (in English) is 'Prabhakaran'. Like many names from the Indian sub-continental region, proper names can be transcribed in Roman (i.e. Romanised) in different ways, and thus there are two other commonly found ways of spelling the LTTE leader's name, viz. 'Pirabakaran' and 'Pirabaharan'. In deference to the man who is the most notable indigenous military leader produced by this region after Subhash Chandra Bose, we have tried to use the way he himself spells it English, which is 'Pirabakaran'. The other two versions have been retained in places, especially where quoted, so as to keep the reader informed that these spellings also exist, and that it is not some other person with a similar-sounding name who is being referred to.

Finally, the authors would like to place on record that they have had no access to any government documents on the subject, other than those in the public domain, such as, for example, the Indo-Sri Lanka Agreement. The phasing of the IPKF's operations as given in the book are as perceived by themselves, and are not necessarily in conformity with any such phase demarcations as the Government of India and its organs may have made, or as understood by them.

# Contents

# Chapter 1
# Introduction

India's first major foreign-policy-dictated overseas military venture, named 'Operation PAWAN' ('Op Pawan') to Sri Lanka, which is just a short hop away, is a good example of how not to conduct an overseas campaign. The initial phases of the campaign, the inductions and the opposed advance onto Jaffna town, were classic examples of the Indian tendency for an orderly and planned method or system to break down and to dissolve into disorder and often chaos.

It is often said about military operations that amateurs talk tactics while professionals talk logistics. Yet in 1987 it was the professional head of India's Army, its Chief of Army Staff (COAS), General Krishnaswamy Sundarji, who ought to have talked logistics, but didn't. Not once, but twice: the second time within a few months of the first. The Director-General Military Operations (DGMO) at Army Headquarters (HQ), Lt. Gen. B. C. Joshi, an Armoured Corps officer, who would have well known the importance of logistics, and who should have dissuaded the Army Chief from ordering a too hurried move of troops into Sri Lanka, without logistical backup, evidently either did not or could not.

To be fair to both of them, the fault was not entirely theirs. The reason why no detailed logistical plans were made for the inductions into Sri Lanka, on 29 July 1987, was because the planning for the Sri Lanka foreign policy exercise was confined to only two branches of the Government, the Ministry of External Affairs (MEA) and the external intelligence agency, the Research and Analysis Wing (RAW). Though some possibilities had indeed filtered down the Army's chain of command to HQ

1 Corps and to a divisional HQ not under this Corps HQ, viz. HQ 54 Infantry Division, the speculative possibilities did not permit of formal preparations by these two different formations. Though 54 Infantry Division was the obvious first choice for any induction into Sri Lanka because of its location in southern India and its new intended role of being converted into an air-transported and air-landed formation, neither it nor its superior HQ, HQ Southern Command, had been formally warned through the mechanism of the 'Warning Order,' as taught in the army's staff teachings, which starts off what is known as the 'battle procedure' meant to ensure smooth functioning at the start-up of any operation of war.

The Sri Lanka Civil War that began in 1983 is now almost a quarter-century old, and shows no signs of dying down, nor of any satisfactory political settlement being reached between the Sinhala-ruled Sri Lanka Government and the Tamils of North and East Sri Lanka. It continues to simmer, flaring up every now and then into intense military operations by one or the other side against the other. Till March 2007, only the Sri Lanka Armed Forces (SLAF) had an Air Force. Suddenly, the LTTE, or the Liberation Tigers of Tamil Eelam, to give it its full name, brought two light aircraft into action and bombed Colombo's airport, becoming the world's only guerilla-style force to clandestinely assemble and operate aircraft in an attack role. This ingenuity and ability to retain the tactical initiative through innovation has been one of the hallmarks of the Tamil Tigers, another descriptive name for the LTTE, the politico-military organization that is now the sole ruler of the Sri Lanka Tamils and that fights fiercely for the creation of an independent Tamil state, or *Tamil Eelam.*

The Indian Army was caught up in this civil war from 29 July 1987 to March 1990, as part of the Indian Government's effort from May 1987 to resolve the root problem between the two major communities of Sri Lanka. India was interested in providing respite to the Tamil populace from the Sri Lanka Army offensive, and thus also assuaging public opinion in Tamil Nadu, which wanted the Indian Government to do something positive, as it had in 1971 when the Pakistani Army had begun its repressive crackdown on its Bengali citizens in East Pakistan.

The Indian armed forces' involvement with Sri Lanka can be broadly divided into four distinct phases:

*Phase 1:* The induction of the Indian Peace Keeping Force on the night of 29 July 1987 with the aim of keeping the peace between the Sri Lanka Government and the Tamil rebels, ensuring the implementation of the Indo-Sri Lanka Accord signed that very day, and generally functioning as a policing force.

*Phase 2:* The advance upon and capture of Jaffna town and the clearing of Jaffna district after the breakdown of the Accord on 5 October 1987.

*Phase 3:* Counter-insurgency operations against the Liberation Tigers of Tamil Eelam (LTTE) in the northern and eastern provinces of Sri Lanka.

*Phase 4:* The pull-out phase ending in March 1990.

*India's Vietnam*

In March 2000, the online news-magazine *Rediff.com* wrote:

"In March exactly a decade ago, the Indian Peace Keeping Force returned from the Sri Lankan shores after fighting an alien war.

*Vanquished*

The IPKF should have been Sri Lanka's saviour in its dark hour. Instead it ended up being hated by the very people it went to save. Hated and condemned.

It suffered too. Suffered terribly in an alien terrain, fighting an enemy which had the full support of the people and the government, fighting a war which was not its. It killed thousands, lost thousands. And came home under a cloud so dark and heavy that it has cast a permanent shadow over the fourth largest army in the world.

*What Went Wrong?*

Totally unprepared and ill-equipped, that was the IPKF."

Modern India's military involvement with Sri Lanka was indeed born out of perceived political compulsions at the national level, as are all wars, and became India's longest war so far, with 30 months of operations between July 1987 and March 1990. It involved both the assistance of a latent and later ongoing insurgency, as well as direct counter-insurgency operations. But the comparison with the Vietnam wars, fought and lost by first the colonial French from 1945 to 1954 and later by the U.S.A. from 1960 to 1973, ends there. The political relationships involved were far more complex and involved both India's external relations and foreign policy as well had direct internal public and political repercussions in a major Indian state, Tamil Nadu, with an identical ethnic population with one of the warring parties in neighbouring Sri Lanka. Secondly, military comparisons would be entirely misleading; the protagonists were organized very differently in each case, and both the French and the American military systems, while very different from each other, had practically no commonality with the way the Indian armed forces are organized. Also, the French and the Americans fought two very different kinds of wars in Vietnam. The Americans fought, for the first time in their own history of wars, what has been described as a "circular" war and not a linear war. American troops were deployed in fire bases or base camps from which they would foray forth, often in helicopters, in search of the enemy, supported by a massive air effort in terms of close fighter-bomber air support, helicopter casualty evacuation and reinforcements including ammunition and food replenishment, as well as artillery fire support with Air OP fire control. Perhaps the only valid comparisons that can be made with the Vietnam wars is with the French counter-insurgency campaign in the pre-Dien Bien Phu period, i.e. before May 1954, leaving out the Indian offensive for the capture of Jaffna town from 11 to 26 October 1987, which is probably unique in the annals of military history world-wide. Any other comparisons of India's direct ground involvement in Sri Lanka with the wars in Vietnam and the simultaneous ones in Laos and Cambodia are totally invalid, and would be a case of comparing apples with oranges, and thus lead to arriving at the wrong conclusions.

India involved itself in the internal affairs of Sri Lanka for three main reasons:

1. To show to its own Tamil population that it cared for the plight of the Tamils in Sri Lanka.

2. To bring an end to Tamil secessionist violence, so that it could be seen as not encouraging separatist movements abroad while it blamed Pakistan for fomenting terrorism in Punjab and Kashmir.

3. To generate pressure on the Sri Lanka Government to fulfill its commitment to its Tamil citizens as envisaged under the Indo-Sri Lanka Agreement.

Militarily, the lack of success in Sri Lanka should have caused much introspection within the Indian Army, and far-reaching remedial decisions and measures taken. Modern India's first overseas foray turned into a politico-military fiasco of the worst kind—in spite of the fact that the strategic concept was sound. It failed miserably in the execution, both political and at the military tactical level. In fact, it was a much more serious politico-military failure than the 1962 debacle against China, but it did not have the same kind of emotional impact on the Indian public due both to its complexity, and to the fact that modern India had lost most of its early nationalistic fervour by 1987, and no one cared any more. As a case-study of politico-military ineptitude by the Indian Government, it deserves to be studied in detail.

### *Background to the Direct Indian Military Involvement*

From some time in late 1977 the Government of India had decided to get involved in Sri Lankan affairs in a covert fashion, and had begun to train Sri Lankan Tamil militants, as has been brought out in several books and other publications, both in print and on the internet. The Prime Minister (PM) then was Morarji Desai, the Cabinet Secretary was Nirmal K. Mukarji, and the Director, R&AW was N. F. Suntook, this being the period before Indira Gandhi's return to power as Prime Minister. The R&AW (or RAW for short) was under a bit of a cloud after Mrs. Gandhi's exit from power and the consequent installation of a new dispensation at the Centre under Morarji Desai. The position of the head of RAW was downgraded from Secretary (R) to Director, RAW, and made at par with the Director, Intelligence Bureau, and the organization was facing both a problem of faith and trust, and one of credibility, with the new top political leadership. Allocation of funds to RAW had been severely cut down, and thus both the parent organization, RAW, and its subordinate organizations, such as Directorate-General Security (DGS), which was also headed personally by the Director, RAW, himself, were facing the twin problems of coping with less funds and of having to justify their usefulness to the new and rather skeptical PM. Indian political difficulties with the Sri Lanka Government (SLG) and the opportunity created by the emergence of a Sri Lankan Tamil resistance to the SLG were one of the straws that may have seemed worth clutching at the time.

The Government of India continued thereafter, even after Indira Gandhi's return to power, to train and arm Sri Lankan Tamil militants, and this understandably led to considerable bad blood with the SLG. This was made even more so by the fact that the state government of Tamil Nadu was actively providing sanctuary, medical aid, funds to the militants, and allowing them to establish training camps within the state. Thus, for almost a decade from 1977 till the deployment of the IPKF in July 1987, both the Indian central government, through RAW and its subordinate agencies, and the Tamil Nadu state government were functioning as patrons to the militants. During this period, the SLG became closer to the Pakistani Government on a common platform of dislike for Mrs. Gandhi.

The Pakistani military dictator, General Zia-ul-Haq, promised the SLG military assistance in its increasingly severe military operations against the Tamil rebels. This in itself produced disquiet at top levels in the Indian Government, as increasing Pakistani influence, particularly a Pakistani military presence, was naturally seen to be inimical to India's interests in Sri Lanka. Pakistani closeness to the USA, with whom India did not have the cordial relations it now enjoys, brought up fears of an American presence or control over Trincomalee harbour, the best natural harbour in the northern Indian Ocean littoral. The USA was interested in obtaining repair facilities for their naval ships at Trincomalee and the use of the extensive oil tank farm there. It was also interested in obtaining broadcasting facilities for their "Voice of America" radio programme at Puttalam near Mannar, very close to India. The combination of domestic political compulsions in relation to public and political opinion in Tamil Nadu, and foreign policy imperatives in connection with Pakistani influence in Sri Lanka and American interest in Trincomalee created a 'push-pull' impetus and an urgency to Indian decision-making and discussions with the SLG.

In May 1987 the Sri Lankan Government forces turned back a relief supply of food and medical supplies being sent in small civilian boats across the narrow Palk Straits that separate Tamil Nadu from northern Sri Lanka. The Indian Government in response launched "Operation POOMALAI" on 4 June 1987, dropping relief supplies from IAF An-32 cargo aircraft escorted by Mirage 2000 fighters, to prevent interference from the Sri Lankan Air Force.

In May and June 1987 there was serious disquiet at the highest government levels in India regarding the situation in Sri Lanka. It was feared that the Sri Lanka Government (SLG) might invite either Pakistan or China to send in troops to help in their civil war against the secessionist Tamils. The closeness between the leaders of Sri Lanka and Pakistan, President J. R. Jayawardene and Gen. Zia-ul-Haq respectively, and Pakistan's growing influence in Sri Lanka's military affairs was worrying the Indian Government. So was the American interest in Sri Lanka, at a time when relations between the American and Indian governments was not so cordial. Indian Army HQ had therefore planned for an induction of troops into Sri Lanka for offensive operations against the Sri Lankan armed forces should the situation so necessitate. 1 Corps had been given the responsibility for these operations. Certain units of 36 Infantry Division, one of the formations under 1 Corps, had therefore been kept earmarked. Eventually, however, with the signing of the Indo-Sri Lanka Accord (ISLA) these plans were not needed to be put into operation and 54 Infantry Division was asked to go in as a "peace-keeping force" instead.

*Brief History of Sri Lanka up to May 1987*

The Tamils of Jaffna have a history going back to about 3,500 BC, the days of Mohenjodaro and Harappa of the Indus Valley Civilization, and consider themselves the last of the pure Dravidians. Their religion is Saivite Hinduism, and there are legends as well as archeological remains of cities and irrigation systems in northern Sri Lanka which link the people with history from the days of the *Ramayana* up to the Dravidian kingdom of Jaffna in 1,500 BC. *(For a history of the later Tamil kingdoms in Jaffna, as spelt out by the LTTE, see Appendix.)*

The "Aryan" Sinhalas arrived under Prince Shri Vijaya in 600 BC as colonizers from the Bengal, Bihar and Orissa region of India, having set sail from the port of Tamralipta (modern Tamluk in West Bengal), and occupied the greater part of the island. Speakers of Prakrit (later to be known as *Simhala-Prakrit*), they were Buddhists who had left the Indian mainland during a period when Buddhism was declining in India, and saw themselves practically as a "chosen race" colonizing *Dhamma Dwipa,* an island to protect the Buddhist faith, somewhat on the lines of modern Pakistan, where they established *Dhamma Shasan.* This arrival itself in its original concept led to a feeling of antagonism to mainland India, the land where Buddhism was vanishing under a Hindu revival, and particularly to the "non-Aryan" southern Indian Tamil Hindus. Even today the Sinhala people reject the history of Sri Lanka prior to the arrival of the Sinhalas, and view the Tamils as invaders who came with the armies of Chola kings and established themselves in Jaffna.

In southern peninsular India, the territory to the south of the Tungabhadra and Krishna rivers, extending to Kanniyakumari (Cape Comorin), forms the Tamil country, which in ancient times was known as "Tamil-akam" or "Tamilikam." It comprised the three principal Tamil states, viz. the kingdoms of the Pandyas, the Cheras or Keralaputra, and the Cholas. The Chola capital was at Uraiyur, and Puhar or Kaveripattinam was their chief sea-port and alternate capital. Lying south of the Chola kingdom, the kingdom of the Pandyas extended from coast to coast, and included the modern districts of Madura, Tinnevelly and part of Coimbatore district, as also the erstwhile state of Travancore and Kochi (Cochin). The Pandyas had their capital at Mudura, and Korkai was their main sea-port. Also lying north of the Pandyas was the territory of the Cheras, stretching right across the Palghat gap through Salem and Coimbatore. Their capital was at Vanji, and their main port was Thondi.

The Battle of Venni (modern Koilvenni, about 20 km east of Tanjore) in about 100 A.D. between the Cholas, who emerged victorious, and the combined might of the Cheras, the Pandyas and 11 minor chieftains, established Karikala Chola as the main power. He later invaded Sri Lanka (or 'Lanka' as it is known to Indians) and brought back many captives, whom he used to construct an embankment of over 150 km along the Kaveri river.

Intervention in the affairs of Sri Lanka from India thus dates back to very early times, probably starting with the history of the *Ramayana* period in the pre-historic era. The three principal southern Indian kingdoms, the Chola, the Chera, and the Pandya, besides their exceptionally ferocious and bloody internecine wars with one another, were also engaged in constant hostility with the rulers of Sri Lanka. Direct involvement with the politics of the south Indian kingdoms, was thus a constant feature of the early historic period of Sri Lanka. The Sinhala kings of Kandy were in conflict with one or the other Tamil dynasties during a period of 400 years of warfare in the early part of the Christian era. The Sinhalese played the Cholas against the Pandyas (one side against the other) and survived. Even though this is much more difficult in the case of a modern united India, the Sri Lanka Prime Minister/President in place of the Kandy kings did play this game successfully. In the Indian federal system and a multi-party democracy, they managed to pit the Tamil Nadu State Government against the Indian Central Government, and the DMK (Dravid Munetra Kazhagam), an ally of the opposition National Front, against the ruling Congress party.

The involvement of the common Indian people with events in Sri Lanka is also considerable, because Sri Lanka is intertwined in Indian mythology, culture, and history thanks to the *Ramayana* legend and the Emperor Ashoka, and to southern Indians in particular because of the long history of political interaction with the island. In fact, political and military events in Sri Lanka affect a greater number of Indians than similar events in, for example, the north-eastern state of Nagaland, or far in the north in Kashmir. Events in Sri Lanka thus have a great impact in southern India, with a close and inevitable identification in the case of the Tamil state of Tamil Nadu. Its emotional reverberations are similar to, and even greater than those felt in the north-western Punjab (in Pakistan) for events in neighbouring Kashmir, for example.

### *Increase in Sinhala-Tamil Tension in Sri Lanka*

The conflict situation between the Sinhalas and the Sri Lanka Tamils was almost natural, given the strong sense of legitimacy on both sides. However, the roots of Tamil insurgency can be found in the Buddhist revival that began from the celebrations of the 2,500$^{th}$ *Mahaparinirvana* or death anniversary of the

Buddha in 1956, and the sunsequent rise in Sinhala chauvinism. A complete distrust of each other began and a deep schism was created. The Tamils fear that the Sinhalese want to wipe them out from Sri Lanka or to reduce them to second-class citizens. An early defining moment was in 1981 when a pro-government Sinhalese mob burnt down the Jaffna Public Library, inaugurated in 1841, after the violent Jaffna District Council elections of July 1981, an act which was seen as a kind of cultural genocide by the Tamils. The library had contained 90,000 volumes, including the one surviving copy of *Yalpanam Vaipavama,* a history of Jaffna. Thus two primordial emotions continue to fuel the ethnic conflict in Sri Lanka–Tamil insecurity and the Sinhala sense of grievance at Tamil advancement during the period of British rule.

But the tension between the two communities has an economic side to it as well, being born partly of a sense of losing earning opportunities among the Tamils, as Sinhala chauvinism grew. For example, many of the Tamil-speaking Muslims of the Eastern Province sold poor land cheaply to Sinhalas, to find government-constructed irrigation projects come up later in such newly Sinhala inhabited areas, which greatly enhanced the output and earnings from the same land. Similarly, the movement for primacy to the Sinhala language for official purposes put Tamils to a disadvantage, both practically and, more importantly, in terms of employment opportunities. But northern Sri Lanka, particularly the Jaffna area, which at its closest point is a mere 35 km from the Indian mainland, is also dependent upon other areas of Sri Lanka. Its requirements of agricultural produce for food are met from the Vanni-Killinochi-Mulaithivu hinterland, which Tamil militants thus felt the need to control, but its sales of prawns are to Colombo. Disruption of commerce between the two parts of the island result in economic deprivation for the Tamils, with the only recourse then left being smuggling from the Indian Tamil Nadu, causing smuggling to become a socially sanctioned activity in the absence of better job opportunities.

# SRI LANKA

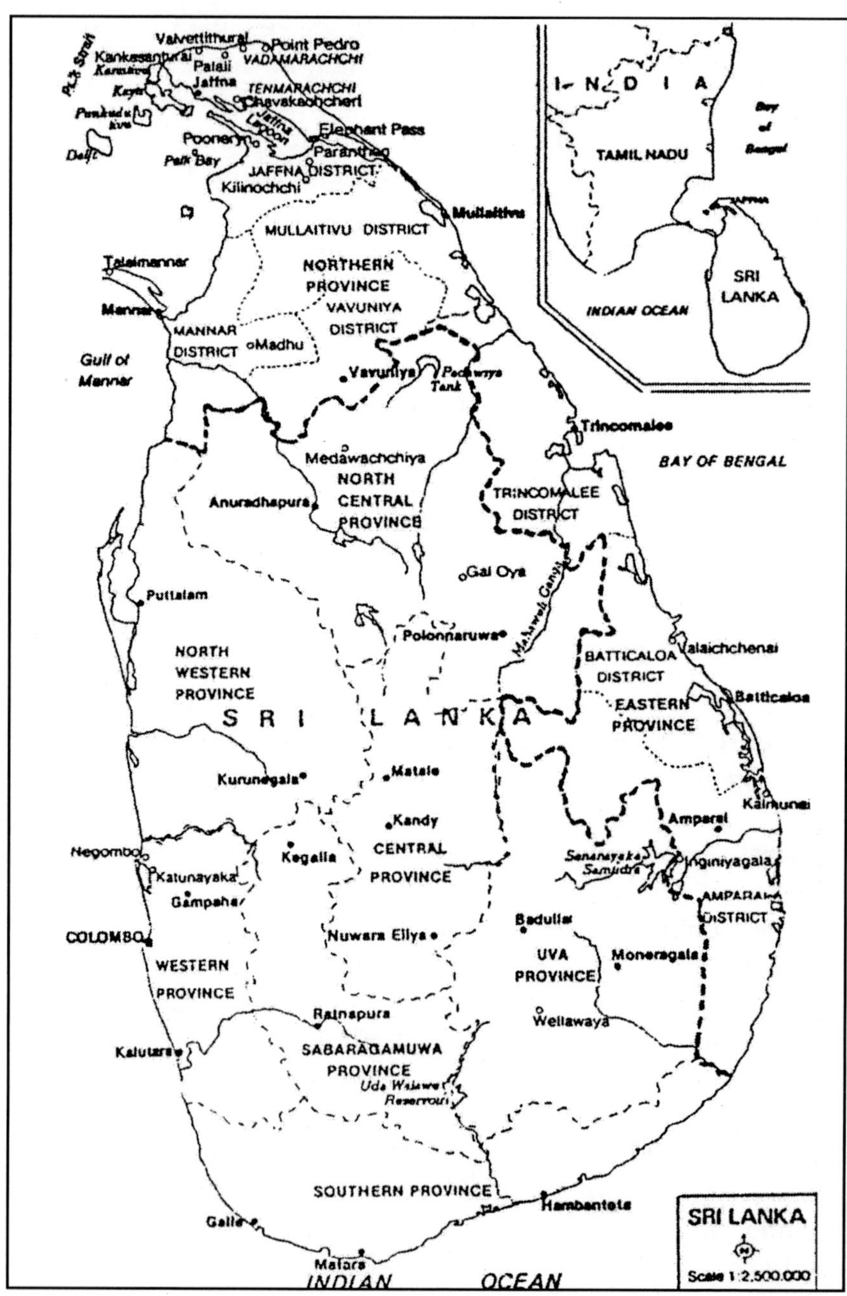
Valvettithurai
Point Pedro
Kankesanturai
Palali
VADAMARACHCHI
Jaffna
TENMARACHCHI
Chavakachcheri
Elephant Pass
Pooneryn
Paranthan
Palk Bay
Delft
JAFFNA DISTRICT
Kilinochchi
Mullaitivu
MULLAITIVU DISTRICT
Talaimannar
NORTHERN PROVINCE
VAVUNIYA DISTRICT
Mannar
MANNAR DISTRICT
Madhu
Gulf of Mannar
Vavuniya
Padawiya Tank
Trincomalee
BAY OF BENGAL
Medawachchiya
NORTH CENTRAL PROVINCE
Anuradhapura
TRINCOMALEE DISTRICT
Gal Oya
Puttalam
Polonnaruwa
Mahaweli Ganga
NORTH WESTERN PROVINCE
BATTICALOA DISTRICT
Valaichchenai
Batticaloa
EASTERN PROVINCE
S R I L A N K A
Kurunegala
Matale
Kalmunai
Kandy
Amparai
Negombo
Kegalla
CENTRAL PROVINCE
Senanayaka Samudra
Inginiyagala
Katunayaka
Gampaha
AMPARAI DISTRICT
COLOMBO
Nuwara Eliya
Badulla
WESTERN PROVINCE
UVA PROVINCE
Moneragala
Ratnapura
Wellawaya
Kalutara
SABARAGAMUWA PROVINCE
Uda Walawe Reservoir
SOUTHERN PROVINCE
Hambantota
Galle
Matara
INDIAN OCEAN
SRI LANKA
Scale 1:2,500,000
I N D I A
TAMIL NADU
Bay of Bengal
SRI LANKA
INDIAN OCEAN

*Sri Lanka Tamil Militancy and the Emergence of the LTTE*

Velupillai Pirabakaran, born on 26 November 1954, belonging to the fisherman-merchant Karaiyar community of Valveddithurai, formed a group calling itself the Tamil New Tigers (TNT) *(note the commonality of the acronym with that of the explosive)* in Jaffna in 1972 with 10 fellow-students. In 1975, its 18-year old leader came into the public notice with a bang when he assassinated the Mayor of Jaffna, Alfred Doraiappa. In 1976, the group changed its name to the Liberation Tigers of Tamil Eelam. It was banned by the Sri Lankan Government in 1978, along with another Tamil militant group TELO, because of their growing popularity among the Tamil masses.

The LTTE continued to grow in popularity and strength despite the ban. It carried out its first major act of terrorism on 31 July 1983 when it ambushed a police patrol in a vehicle at Tirunnelveli, north-east of Jaffna, killing 13 Sinhala policemen. Riots broke out throughout Sri Lanka, and over 3,000 Tamils were murdered and thousands of Tamil homes destroyed, sending 1.5 lakh Tamils fleeing to refugee camps. Of these, over 1 lakh Tamil refugees crossed over to the Indian state of Tamil Nadu, leading to an outcry from the state government and an immediate demand to the Indian Government to intervene in Sri Lanka.

The Sri Lanka Government first began military operations against Tamil separatists in 1983, starting the civil war. The SLAF launched its "Operation Liberation" in which it began a military campaign of conquest against the Jaffna Peninsula. The genocidal tactics of the Sri Lankan Army in their initial conflicts with the Tamil separatists groups led to the creation of the Tamil armed resistance.

The rise of Dravidian political parties in the Tamil-speaking Indian state of Tamil Nadu led to Sinhala distrust of the state government. The Dravid Kazhagam and its two later offshoots the DMK and the AIADMK (All-India Anna DMK) became vociferous and competitive supporters of the cause of an independent Tamil homeland in Sri Lanka, or Tamil "Eelam." M.G. Ramachandran, the Tamil Nadu Chief Minister, went a step further and linked Tamil survival in Sri Lanka with Indian nationalism. The Indian central government ruled by the Indian Congress Party realized the emotive nature of the Sri Lanka Tamil issue, and the requirement of appeasing the sentiments of its own nearly 55 million Tamils. Had Tamil Nadu not been part of the Indian Union, it would have developed into a straight armed conflict between the Tamils of the mainland and of the island together, against the Sinhala Government and its armed forces.

*Interview with Pirabakaran in 1984*

Sachi Sri Kantha, the erudite Sri Lankan Tamil chronicler and analyst of the Sri Lanka Civil War, whose internet series 'The Pirabaharan Phenomenon' is available on the website http://www.tamilnation.org, has placed an important interview of the LTTE leader's on the net, which gives an insight into his character and his thoughts in 1984. It needs to be read in full to understand the course of events that followed.

*Responses to Anita Pratap*

Anita Pratap was one of the Indian journalists who gained early access to Pirabaharan. She had first interviewed him for the *Sunday* magazine in 1984, when Pirabaharan was not yet 30. A few of the questions by Pratap elicited the responses related to his unusual development as a rebel.

*Pratap:* Could you elaborate on some of your personal experiences that compelled you to believe that an armed struggle was the only solution for the Tamils of Sri Lanka. Were you, your family members and friends, directly victimized by the discriminatory policy of the Sri Lankan Government?

*Pirabakaran:* The shocking events of the 1958 racial riots had a profound impact on me when I was a schoolboy. I heard of horrifying incidents of how our people had been mercilessly and brutally put to death by Sinhala racists. Once I met a widowed mother, a friend of my family, who related to me her agonizing personal experience of this racial holocaust. During the riots, a Sinhala mob attacked her house in Colombo. The rioters set fire to the house and murdered her husband. She and her children escaped with severe burn injuries. I was deeply shocked when I saw the scars on her body. I also heard such stories of cruelty. I felt a deep sense of sympathy and love for my people. A great passion overwhelmed me to redeem my people from this racist system. I strongly felt that armed struggle was the only way to confront a system which employs armed might against unarmed, innocent people.

*Pratap:* At what point of time did you lose faith in the parliamentary system? What precipitated this disillusionment?

*Pirabakaran:* I entered politics at a time—in the early [nineteen] seventies—when the younger generation had already lost faith in parliamentary politics. I entered politics as an armed revolutionary. What precipitated the disillusionment in parliamentary politics was the total disregard and callousness of the successive governments towards the pathetic plight of our people.

*Pratap:* How did you come to start the Liberation Tiger movement?

*Pirabakaran:* I originally formed the movement with a group of dedicated youths who sincerely believed that armed struggle was the only way to liberate our people.

*Pratap:* What was the reason for identifying yourselves as "Tigers?"

*Pirabakaran:* I named the movement "Liberation Tigers," since the tiger emblem had deep roots in the political history of Tamils, symbolizing Tamil patriotic resurgence. The tiger symbol also depicts the mode of our guerrilla warfare.

*Pratap:* When you decided to form the "Liberation Tigers," what was the reaction of your family members and those close to you?

*Pirabakaran:* As soon as the Tiger movement was formed, I went underground and lost contact with my family.

*Pratap:* When did you last meet your family members? Are they reconciled to your outlawed existence?

*Pirabakaran:* I have not seen my family members for the last 11 years. I do not think they regard me as an ordinary person leading an ordinary life. They are reconciled to my existence as a guerrilla fighter.

For an idea on how the LTTE grew, the LTTE's casualties in their actions against the Sri Lanka Government (SLG) are educative. The LTTE lost its first cadre on 27 November 1982, 5 in 1983, 36 in 1984, 123 in 1985 and 258 in 1986. By the end of 1986, its accumulated losses were 423. From November 1986 onwards, it was open civil war, and the losses increased dramatically. To understand the escalation of the LTTE resistance from the initial stages of civil unrest and strife, during which they could be said to be either a guerilla force or terrorists, depending upon the personal position of the describer, it is necessary to understand the defining nature of "civil war." Three words which are germane to the definition are: "unrest," "strife" and "war." The common dictionary explanations of these are:

"Unrest" is explained as: "trouble, turmoil, especially with regard to public or political conditions and suggesting premonitions of revolt."

"Strife" is explained as: "fighting; any contest for advantage or superiority."

"War" is explained as: "an armed conflict between nations or states; the science of military operations."

Sachi Sri Kantha quotes Roy Licklider, Professor of Rutgers University, USA, whose paper in the journal, the *American Political Science Review* of September 1995, has defined a civil war as any conflict that satisfies *all* of the three following criteria:

1. Some influential leaders must be concerned about possibly having to live in the same political unit with their current

enemies after the killing stops. This concern must be important enough to influence the kind of settlement they are prepared to accept.

2. There must be *multiple sovereignty,* defined by Charles Tilly as the population of an area obeying more than one institution. "They pay taxes (to the opposition), provide men to its armies, feed its functionaries, honor its symbols, give time to its service, or yield other resources despite the prohibitions of a still-existent government they formerly obeyed" (Tilly, 1978). This criterion differentiates civil wars from other types of domestic violence, such as street crimes and riots, in which there is no centralized control of the opposition. To distinguish civil wars from colonial wars, each side must have significant numbers of troops made up of local residents.

3. A civil war, by our definition, involves *large-scale violence,* killing people. I used the operational definitions of the Correlates of War project: (a) 1,000 battle deaths or more per year and (b) effective resistance, that is, at least two sides must have been organized for violent conflict before the war started or else the weaker side must have imposed casualties on its opponent equal to at least 5 per cent of its own (to distinguish between civil wars and political massacres). [*American Political Science Review,* Sept. 1995, Vol. 89, No. 3, pp. 681-690.]

By the above definition, the Srilankan Civil War began in November 1986.

*Interview with Pirabakaran*

In 1986, Pirabakaran gave two important and widely disseminated interviews. One was to N. Ram, of the *Hindu* group of newspapers. The other was to Sudip Mazumdar of *Newsweek* magazine. Sachi Sri Kantha has made both available on the internet. Pirabakaran gives the reader the benefit of his thoughts at the time.

*The 1986 Newsweek Magazine Interview*

Sachi Sri Kantha introduces the interview by saying: "Though few of the answers to the 13 questions posed by Sudip Mazumdar to Pirabaharan have lost their value with the passage of time and later unanticipated political developments, still this 1986 *Newsweek* magazine interview retains its glamor for the responses delivered and the expressed wishes of LTTE's leader, then aged 31. Since he was living in Madras then, he had been courteous to his host country. But in his responses Pirabaharan had shown that he is one who would not bend his knees to dance to the tunes of his host country. This interview is reproduced in full to show that, unlike the then parading Eelam militant leadership of other groups, Pirabaharan has matched his words with deeds."

*The Eye of the Tiger*

[*Newsweek* International Edition, Aug. 11, 1986, p. 48.]

For the past 14 years Velupillai Pirabakaran has led an armed struggle to create a separate Tamil state in Sri Lanka's volatile northeastern region. Pirabakaran, 32, commands the Liberation Tigers of Tamil Eelam (LTTE), the strongest of Sri Lanka's numerous Tamil separatist groups. It is generally acknowledged that peace negotiations with Colombo are unlikely to prove effective without LTTE's involvement. Last week, shortly before his group rejected Colombo's latest proposal for peace talks, Pirabakaran spoke with *Newsweek*'s Sudip Mazumdar in Madras. Excerpts:

*Mazumdar:* Your opponents charge that innocent civilians are often killed in your military offensive. How do you respond?

*Pirabakaran:* The LTTE has never killed any civilians. We condemn such acts of violence. There were occasions when we had to kill homeguards. But they are not civilians. They are trained [non-combat draftees who] carry guns.

*Mazumdar:* How many troops do you have under your command and where do they train?

*Pirabakaran:* That's a secret. I can tell you we are strong enough to take on the 51,000 strong Sri Lankan military and well enough equipped to carry on protracted guerrilla warfare.

*Mazumdar:* Why do you think LTTE has taken the lead among other guerrilla groups?

*Pirabaharan:* Discipline and order are most important. We emphasize personal morality and a sense of patriotism. Our cadres carry cyanide pills with them to avoid falling into enemy hands. Most of all, the people are behind us.

*Mazumdar:* Critics charge that you rely on drug trafficking to raise money for your military activities. How do you respond?

*Pirabakaran:* Our people support us financially. We capture arms and ammunition from the enemy and also buy them on the international market. We don't get support from any other country. Here in India we are living as political refugees and the Government of India extends moral support to our existence here. We have imposed a strict moral code on ourselves, not to use even liquor. How can one suspect us of drug trafficking which we condemn?

*Mazumdar:* Press reports say that you received military training in Cuba. How did you manage to acquire your know-how?

*Pirabakaran:* Through sheer personal training. I use my natural instincts and I watch war films and westerns by [American movie actor] Clint Eastwood. If I were trained in Cuba, I would have been a better fighter.

*Mazumdar:* What is your assessment of the latest round of negotiations between moderate Tamils and the Sri Lankan government on devolution of power to Tamils?

*Pirabakaran:* The proposals [put forward by Colombo] are insufficient even to start negotiations. We have enunciated four principles as the basis for talks; the traditional homeland of the Tamils must be recognized; Tamils should be [officially] recognized as a [separate] nationality; their rights to self-determination should be recognized, and the civil rights of stateless Tamils should be recognized. A framework should be worked out incorporating these principles. Then we will consider [negotiations].

*Mazumdar:* How serious do you think President Junius Jayewardene is in solving the Tamil problem?

*Pirabakaran:* This so-called peace initiative by Jayewardene is an attempt to hoodwink the world. That these negotiations are eyewash is clear from the fact that even while the talks were on the military killed nearly 150 innocent Tamils. Talks with Jayawardene? Possible, but only on the question of demarcation of our boundaries [as two separate nations].

*Mazumdar:* Why do you think India allows you to operate from here?

*Pirabakaran:* Purely on humanitarian grounds. There is genocide going on in Sri Lanka. India knows we are fighting against genocide and trying to protect our people.

*Mazumdar:* Opponents charge that India is abetting "terrorists" by giving you sanctuary, while New Delhi blames Pakistan for training Sikh terrorists? What is your view?

*Pirabakaran:* There is a fundamental difference here. Our people are facing genocide whereas the Indian Army is not committing genocide in Punjab.

*Mazumdar:* India favors a negotiated settlement of the ethnic problem and opposes your goal of a separate Tamil state. What is your view?

*Pirabakaran:* The world is constantly changing; so is politics. We rely on the hope that changing circumstances will finally lead to India's recognition of our struggle. India has recognized various liberation movements. At a later stage India may be compelled to recognize us as it did the PLO and SWAPO.

*Mazumdar:* What do you expect from the United States?

*Pirabakaran:* We want to appeal to the American people to realize that we are a nation of people facing genocide. And we appeal to the U. S. government to stop all aid to the Sri Lankan government which will be used for the destruction of our people.

*Mazumdar:* What kind of a political system do you envisage for an independent Tamil state?

*Pirabakaran:* We want to establish a socialist society. Ours will be a unique socialist model, neither Soviet nor Chinese nor any other.

*Mazumdar:* Have you ever considered calling for India's military intervention to stop what you call genocide?

*Pirabakaran:* India's military intervention is not necessary because we have a fighting force capable of facing the military. In fact, India's intervention may allow other international forces to meddle in Sri Lanka and create [chaos].

Sach Sri Kantha comments, "In retrospect, one can infer that Pirabaharan's answer to the second question that, "We are strong enough to take on the 51,000 strong Sri Lankan military and well enough equipped to carry on protracted guerrilla warfare" had stood the test of time. Even quite a segment of LTTE's non-combat sympathizers then would have felt that, without India's covert assistance, the chances of LTTE being neutralized by the Sri Lankan army (which had been receiving overt help from Pakistan and Israel) were considerable. But, as he had revealed in his 1986 interview with N. Ram a few weeks later, Pirabaharan had made his actions speak louder than words."

*Responses to N. Ram*

Two questions posed by N. Ram, then an Associate Editor of the *Hindu* newspaper in 1986, brought out from Pirabakaran, the formative influences on his character. His responses to these two questions are reproduced in full.

*N. Ram:* Could you give us an idea of your personal heroes in revolutionary struggles or liberation movements or in any sphere of life ... people and experiences that have inspired you? And perhaps thereby give us some insight into your own political evolution from the time you were a schoolboy?

*Pirabakaran:* From my boyhood, the struggle that attracted me most was the Indian freedom struggle. The role of Netaji attracted me very much. I was brought up in an environment of strict discipline from childhood. I was not permitted to mingle freely with outsiders. I used to feel shy of girls. Great store was laid by personal rectitude and discipline. My father set an example through his own personal conduct. He would not even chew betel leaves. I modeled my conduct on his ... he was a government officer, a district land officer. A very straightforward man. People say in our area: "When he walks, he does not hurt even the grass under his feet, but his son is so...."

Even while criticizing me, they marvel at the fact that such a son was born to such a father! He was strict, yes, but also soft and persuasive. In my own case, he reasoned rather than regimented and his attitude was that of a friend.... He would give me certain pieces of advice and discuss things with me. As I said, I grew up as a shy boy ... especially in the matter of mingling with girls.

The life of Subhas Chandra Bose attracted me specially. Even as a boy, I would delve into Gandhiji's books on Experiments with Truth, on celibacy and so on. Subhas attracted me particularly since even as a boy he went in search of spiritualism and, finding the life of a recluse dissatisfying, returned (laughs). Yet repeatedly, he retreated into spiritualism ... during moments of great difficulty and crisis. I followed this history and these stories with fascination. He became my special hero and some of his orations gripped me. For example: "I shall fight for the freedom of my land until I shed my last drop of blood." These words used to thrill me whenever they came to me. Then the story of Bhagat Singh fascinated me.

In other words, the biographies and histories of those who hit back at the perpetrators of injustice, those who counterattacked (the unjust foe) were my special favourite. Because in our land, the Sinhalese behaved so cruelly towards us ... we would hear stories about this and read about these cruel acts in books and newspapers.... Later I read about this particular episode that took place during the 1958 attacks on Tamils.... They broke into a temple, Panadura, found a Brahmin priest sleeping, tied him to his cot, poured petrol over him and burnt him alive. Ours was a god-fearing society and the people were religious minded. The widespread feeling was: when a priest like him was burnt alive, why did we not have the capability to hit back? That was one atrocity that made people think deeply. In another episode, they threw a child into a drum of boiling tar. This left a very deep imprint on my mind and in the minds of those around me. If such innocent lives could be destroyed, why could we not strike back?

In such moments, these heroic examples and models from the Indian freedom struggle came to me. Magazines retold these stories on special occasions such as India's Independence Day celebrations.... This practice continues. Consider another example of Tiruppur Kumaran—in his *ahimsa* there was a steely determination. If I was attracted by the experience of armed struggle against injustice, I was drawn by the moral force of *ahimsa* as well. I was inspired by examples of grit and determination. I began to think along these lines early in life. Why can't we follow their examples? Why can't we start an armed struggle?

I used to read books on the rise of Napoleon and his exploits. This kind of history held special appeal.... In the Mahabharata, the roles of Bhima and Karna were specially attractive to me ... the spirit of sacrifice appeared crucial. People respond to characters in the Mahabharata in various ways. I value the character and role of Karna the most, on account of his readiness to make the ultimate sacrifice.... I read some of Vivekananda's sayings and the urge grew in me to work towards a strong youth force. I plunged into this line of thinking.... At what age? These feelings and ideas began to take shape when I was 16 approximately.

I used to listen to the religious discourses of Kripanantha Variar ... I used to go to all these events ... those connected with religion. I would go and observe political meetings ... attend dramatic performances.... In my place, they used to enact plays on Socrates and so on.

So quite early on, we absorbed all these influences and the feeling grew in us that we must do something! Looking at our historical background, we had to take up arms to fight for our rights. The lesson was that they could do all this because we were defenceless and disarmed. Why should be remain so? We should take up violence to counter and overthrow their violence.... Only after that did I engage in this movement.

*N. Ram:* The impression among outsiders who have observed the development of the LTTE is that you—as its leader—have only recently begun to take a deeper or more detailed interest in politics ... whereas earlier, you used to live in mainly in the realm of military ideas. You were considered shy and did not meet people easily, which would make it difficult in politics. Now they find you speaking out on a number of political issues.

*Pirabakaran:* In reality, it has always been clear to me that an armed struggle takes shape only against a political background. If I had been a man without political clarity.... I went underground around 1973 and you know that leading an underground life is a very difficult proposition. I have led an underground life for a long time ... between 1973 and 1983, it was a very difficult period for us, with the army on the rampage ... to escape their net was very difficult. If we were able to go through this experience and are able to stand firm today, then surely you will concede that we could not have been political innocents or carried on without a political background!

But one thing is true, despite this political background, my natural inclination makes me lay less emphasis on words. In serious politics, it won't do to concentrate on talking; you must grow through action and then talk! You would have observed that only as we grew in our activities, in our activities in the field, did we come up to a position of meeting various people and explaining our ideas—only then did our words carry some value. Words must be matched and indeed preceded by content. This is crucial for our relations with our people.

If people respect our fighters more, it is because of this extra discipline. Certain exemplary personal attributes, a certain personal rectitude; that is why our people are attracted to LTTE fighters. When you speak of a political outlook, people will respect you only if you prove yourself in action. Action gives your programme a political content. When we say during this period, "They will use the army to attack us, we will resist and counterattack and we will protect you," well ... only when we actually do it, do we establish our political credibility and role.

That is why we have given due attention to military affairs in our organization. You know the character of your struggle. In a situation where the Sri Lankan state feeds its army on racism and chauvinism and through that army and through forced colonization, tries to displace and subjugate us. Only a political organization with military strength is capable of effective resistance. Look all around the world ... any real struggle has had a military background. Even if the Indian freedom struggle was conducted on the basis of *ahimsa,* Netaji's Indian National Army had a special place.... There is definitely a place today in Indian history for Subhas! His was an action-oriented political approach.

And take the Indian state today. If India is able to stand up in the community of nations, it is in no small measure due to the strength of the Indian armed forces; else, the Chinese would bring their frontiers up to Delhi!" [*The Hindu,* Madras, Sept. 5, 1986].

At this juncture, India started by deciding to have an overt official "Indian" rather than a "Tamil Nadu" policy towards Sri Lanka. Its main components were:

(a) India to firmly oppose the Sri Lanka Government's military operations against the Tamil public.

(b) India to exert more direct political pressure on President Jayawardene to implement the devolution package which the Sri Lanka Government had negotiated with the Tamils in 1985-86.

(c) Should these two succeed, India to persuade the Tamils to resume negotiations with the Sri Lanka Government.

(d) If solutions are worked out at these negotiations, India to directly guarantee the implementation through suitable agreements.

In addition to being a mediator, India was to be a guarantor of the solutions reached, so as to give a tangible sense of security to the Sri Lanka Tamils. Though the LTTE had been consulted, with its leader Pirabakaran kept practically under house arrest in Room No. 522 of the *Ashoka Hotel* in New Delhi, the LTTE itself was not a party to the accord. This was a major mistake, as the LTTE did not have any compunction about going back on any reluctant assurance given by Pirabakaran to the Indian Prime Minister that the LTTE would lay down arms. The other problem with having secured Pirabakaran's assent in this fashion was that there was another aspect to the deal between him and Rajiv Gandhi which was not officially made public, i.e., the promise that the LTTE would be given adequate money on a regular basis to keep paying the LTTE cadres once their power to extort money from the Tamil public in Sri Lanka was gone.

Thus, from June 1987, the Government of India began to prepare for the ISLA, simultaneously making its contingency plans for the induction of Indian troops as an Indian Peace-Keeping Force (IPKF), the entire military part of the exercise being named "Operation PAWAN." Neither the Government of India nor its military land-force component, the Indian Army, regularly rehearse or practice international peace-keeping methods, in spite of its numerous assignments as international peace-keepers under UN auspices in various parts of the world right from the 1950's onwards. This is in contrast to NATO, which has always practiced these even under peaceful, normal circumstances, so that some troops are kept mentally prepared and practiced in both the methods themselves, as well the various complex aspects of cooperation with foreign armies, both those of the host country and those of other NATO countries likely to become fellow-members. Such practices help resolve many practical problems of inter-operability, including language and local knowledge, BEFORE any requirement arises. For a modern example, a company group of the British Army's 4th Battalion, the Duke of Lancaster's Regiment (4 LANCS), a British TA battalion, recently took part in the NATO practice for peace-keeping, "Exercise STEPPE EAGLE," held in Kazakhstan along with the Kazakh Army and US Army troops at the Illiskiy Training Area near Almaty in Kazakhstan, from 9 to 24 September 2006. The soldiers rehearsed drills including urban and rural patrolling, vehicle checkpoints and riot control. Such practices exercises, which are known as "NATO Partnership for Peace" exercises, are held annually by different units in different countries around the world, and in the case of Kazakhstan, as a joint anti-terrorist exercise annually since 2003.

*Indo-Sri Lanka Agreement (ISLA)*

India's pressurization led to the signing of the India-Sri Lanka Agreement (ISLA) which provided for Indian troops, on specific request, being stationed in northern Sri Lanka to keep peace. It was seen by the Tamils in both countries as a measure whereby the Indian Army intervened to rescue Tamil civilians from being killed by the SLAF, as indeed it was intended to.

President Jayawardene had most reluctantly agreed to the Indian Government's persuasion. His immediate interest was to end the violence in the Tamil north and the re-establishment of law and order there. The agreement provided for the establishment of a North-Eastern Province in Sri Lanka, by merger of the existing Northern and Eastern Provinces, with a democratically elected provincial assembly and government with some powers that gave the Tamils a reasonable degree of autonomy. It showed to the Sinhalas and to the world that India was not interested in the secession of the Tamils, but instead in the integrity of Sri Lanka. In effect, the provisions, which included the laying down of arms and the cessation of hostilities by both sides in the civil war, were being underwritten by the Indian Government, and the agreement was thus welcomed by the world. The Indo-Sri Lanka Agreement was signed in Colombo on 29 July 1987 by Sri Lankan President Jayawardene and Indian Prime Minister Rajiv Gandhi. The Indian 9th Paras, a commando battalion, were on stand-by in Indian frigates in Colombo harbour to rescue the Indian High Commission staff in case chauvinistic elements within the Sri Lanka Armed Forces tried to take some form of precipitate anti-Indian action. The accord began on an inauspicious note when one of the Sri Lanka Navy personnel in the guard of honour for the Indian PM suddenly assaulted Rajiv Gandhi by swinging the butt of his rifle and striking the PM on his neck and shoulder. This incident clearly showed the extent of the Sinhala dissatisfaction with the Indian military intervention on behalf of the Tamils. This dissatisfaction was taken advantage of by the Marxist-oriented Sinhala party, the Janata Vimukti Peramuna (JVP), which had once attempted a violent overthrow of the Sri Lanka Government, and had its sympathizers in the SLAF.

President Jayawardene wished to make the best possible use of the ISLA and asked for Indian troops to maintain law and order in northern Sri Lanka, specifically the Jaffna area, where the government's Sinhala troops were over-stretched and tired, so that most of the Sri Lanka Army could be withdrawn from there, and used to fight the JVP in the southern, Sinhala-inhabited part of the island. Apprehensive of Indian military intervention from soon after the Sri Lanka Army's operations against the Jaffna Tamils began, Jayawardene reasoned that if an Indian military presence was thrust upon Sri Lanka it would be best used to relieve the Sri Lanka Army after a stalemate situation had been reached in its operations against the LTTE.

### *Lt. Gen. Sardeshpande's View of the ISLA*

Lt. Gen. S. C. Sardeshpande, AVSM, UYSM, (Retd.), was a key participant in the IPKF in two different capacities as a Maj. General. First, as GOC 54 Infantry Division (the division responsible for the Jaffna area) after the initial phase of operations there, and immediately thereafter as Deputy OFC. A highly respected, erudite, and very practical infantry general with previous counter-insurgency experience, his views on the ISLA are worth recording:

"The ISLA was the terrible infant – precocious and complex, with its own chinks. I highlight its soft spots:

"(a) The IPKF had to be prepared to use force to disarm militants; to confine the Srilankan Security Forces (SLSF) to barracks in the Tamil provinces; and to confront both militants and SLSF jointly if they joined hands. These threefold implications had not dawned on the leaders then, but all these eventualities came about as the IPKF bashed on for the next two years.

"(b) There was conspicuous underestimation of the Sri Lankan Government's intransigence in devolving power to the Tamils, and Tamil militants' obduracy to agree to anything short of Eelam.

"(c) India lacked the ability to persuade the two antagonists and the will to force it down them. This lack emanated from the peculiar dilemma that ate into the Indian political scene. As the overwhelming majority, the Sinhalas, who had done or meant no harm whatsoever to India, could not be antagonized beyond a point, in order to help the Tamils, if lasting peace was to be found. Nor could the minority Tamils, who suffered enormously and provided a strong lever to check Sinhala chauvinism, be ignored and forced beyond a point.

"(d) Lastly, what was missed out totally was the LTTE's hypnotic hold over the Tamils in Sri Lanka as well as India, its determination to fight on its own to the bitter end even with the IPKF, when necessary."

*The LTTE's View of the ISLA*

The LTTE was and remains critical of the ISLA. To quote its own internet news-site as of July 2007:

"To this day, it is being heralded as a goodwill gesture on the part of the Government of India to restore the Tamil rights, infringed over a 40 year period by successive Sinhala dominated government, and resolve the "war in Sri Lanka."

The accord failed to achieve its stated aim, unless of course, maintaining the "territorial integrity of Sri Lanka" and the "security of India," which were also affirmed as objectives of this accord (The Annexure), were the *only* intent of the exercise.

- The Tamil people, whose predicament it was professed to resolve, were *not* consulted in a meaningful way.
- No safeguards against future infringement of Tamil rights were proposed.
- Contrarily, greater attention was paid to weakening the Tamil status. e.g. referendum in some parts of the Tamil homeland. The accord, not unexpectedly, failed to restore peace in the island.

This failure was at a great cost:

- The Indian army lost nearly 1,200 of its soldiers.
- Over 7,000 innocent Tamil civilians (and an undetermined number of Tamil combatants) were killed."

*International Peace-keeping or Regional Power Projection?*

Though the primary, immediate, and overt reasons for the Indian policy decision to intervene in Sri Lanka's political and military situation was the Tamil factor and its immediate impact upon the population and politics of Tamil Nadu, there were other reasons too. As brought out earlier, India's desire to keep the Pakistani military out of Sri Lanka, and also to pre-empt any possibility of an American take-over of Trincomalee harbour, made the deployment of Indian troops an unstated regional power projection. This was clearly understood both by the LTTE and by the SLG, which therefore put the functioning of the ISLA in jeopardy right from the moment it was signed. It was the hapless IPKF, sent in without adequate mental and physical preparation, which eventually suffered the brunt of the resentment against the Indian government.

# Chapter 2

# 'Operation PAWAN' – Phase I: Induction of the IPKF

Northern Sri Lanka has a flat landscape and has a harsh, dry, and hot climate for most of the year, with a wet north-eastern monsoon period from October to January. The Vanni region is mostly desolate and almost barren, mainly covered with scrub jungle, while the Jaffna peninsula is cultivated and densely populated. The Jaffna peninsula has a number of shallow lagoons. There are a number of largely deserted islands which extend towards the Indian coastline of Tamil Nadu. These islands have flat open grasslands interspersed with shallow lagoons. Palmyrah palms, which produce both toddy and jaggery (*gur*) are the dominant trees and the most prominent vegetation, along with some plantations of coconut palms in the cultivated areas. Sri Lanka's Northern Province was expected to be the IPKF's main area of operation.

*Induction of the IPKF: July 1987*

Though the initial force levels envisaged for "Operation PAWAN" (Op Pawan) were quite substantial, the strength initially inducted into Sri Lanka as part of the IPKF was much less for three reasons.

1. The tasks envisaged for the IPKF did not appear to the planners to warrant more. As it appeared to them, the induction for the contingency that eventually had to be implemented was to be unopposed and on specific request. The main task envisaged by the GOC, staff and units of 54 Infantry Division was of the kind normally described as "Aid to Civil Authority,"

which lead at worst to "Internal Security (IS) duties on behalf of the civilian state government concerned. In layman's language, this means;

*Forces Originally Earmarked For "Operation PAWAN"*

*Army*

Headquarters Overall Force Commander *(This was NOT set up as a Joint Tri-Service Command, but was eventually created as an* ad hoc Army *organization)*

Headquarters 1 Corps
36 Infantry Division
54 Infantry Division
2nd Armoured Brigade
340 (Independent) Infantry Brigade Group

*Navy*

| | |
|---|---|
| Frigates | 5 |
| Landing Ships Tank (LST's) | 6 |
| Submarines | 2 |
| Patrol Boats | 12 |
| Fleet Auxiliary ships | 2 |
| Naval aircraft | 9 |

*Air Force*

| | |
|---|---|
| Jaguars (fighters-ground attack) | 24 |
| Canberras (light bomber) | 6 |
| Ilyushin-76 (Il-76) (transport) | 4 |
| Antonov-12 (An-12) (transport) | 6 |
| An-32 (transport) | 30 |
| HS –748 (transport) | 7 |
| Mi-8/17 helicopters | 22 |

(a) What are termed as "flag marches" to show the government's seriousness to deal with outbreaks of lawlessness and rioting, by being seen as the available backup to the civil police,

(b) Riot control if the situation actually gets out of hand for the civil police and armed police, and,

(c) Establishment of well-spread-out army outposts for "quick-reaction" tasks across a wide area. Such tasking is completely different to a deployment for a warlike, or possibly warlike, situation.

2. Out of the brigades and units actually inducted, some of the brigades were one-third to two-thirds under-strength because some units had proceeded to the field areas on the Indo-Pakistan border and had not yet been replaced.

3. The units themselves were under-strength by up to 50 per cent due to normal leave, courses, etc., since no mobilization had been ordered by the Government of India.

Two major areas of logistical support for a field force to operate overseas were not adequately catered for. These were:

1. Casualty evacuation and field treatment facilities and other medical support, as would be normal for warlike deployment, such as the move and establishment of field hospital units and Advanced Dressing Stations (ADS's), augmented by Surgical Teams and blood banks, were not deployed.

2. Ammunition storage and replenishment facilities, as would be normal for a non-"peace-keeping" deployment, were not catered for, as no ammunition expenditure was expected.

It is also important to note at this point that the infantry battalions that are routinely located in the Southern Command's geographical area, even though part of fighting field formations which have an operational responsibility, whether specific fixed "operational areas" or to be ready as a reserve on outbreak of any hostilities, are all units which are rotated through Southern Command. None of the regular infantry units within it at any given time are permanently part of the Command's Order of Battle (ORBAT). Infantry units are generally those which have been allotted these "peace-stations" after being brought back from hard field locations either in the mountains on the northern borders, or from operational areas where they have been engaged in counter-insurgency operations such as in Kashmir or in certain areas of some of the north-eastern states. After a hard tenure of field soldiering under tense conditions, "peace" locations in Southern Command are a necessary relief where the units carry out their necessary internal administrative requirements, retrain and refit, and many men and most officers are joined by their families after three or more years of absence. There is routinely less tension in Southern Command because of less local political unrest that often results elsewhere in intermittent "aid to civil authority" or "internal security" duties, and the expectation is that there will be ample time for mobilization for war if given a "warning order" and put on stand-by. Unless the field formations of the Command are warned to be ready for impending operations, neither the subordinate formation headquarters nor their constituent infantry battalions are normally standing by to plunge into action at the drop of a hat.

In addition; aircraft from Indian Airlines and Air India were to be made available on an "as required" basis. The Railways were to provide rolling stock for the overland move within India to the embarking port/airfields.

54 Infantry Division, the bulk of which is normally concentrated in the peace-time location of Secunderabad-Hyderabad in Andhra Pradesh, minus its heavy arms and equipment, was the only major formation initially inducted. Since the tasking of the IPKF had not envisaged any actual fighting, no counter-insurgency trained unit or formation was inducted. 54 Infantry Division was in the process of being slowly converted to an air-transported/air-landed formation, and was located in southern India, which automatically influenced the choice of formation. However, there was no detailed war-gaming of the possible situations that might arise, even though the policy group in Delhi, headed by the inexperienced Prime Minister, had discussed various

possibilities, such as the "hard option" of inducting troops in to the island, under differing contingencies, including having to fight the Sri Lanka Army to save the Tamils, or even to fight the LTTE and other rebel Tamil groups. The widely-divergent contingencies that had been discussed were:

1 Operations to re-instate the Sri Lanka Government in the event of a coup against it.

2. Operations against the Srilankan security forces with the assistance of the LTTE.

3. Operations against the LTTE to implement the ISLA with the assistance of the Sri Lanka Armed Forces.

Therefore, though basic planning for a possible induction into Sri Lanka had begun in the first week of June 1987, no detailed plans had been made by Headquarters 54 Infantry Division, and discussed in detail with their higher formation, Headquarters Southern Command, because no firm tasking had been given to the division. The division received no Operational Instructions, made no Operation Order, and therefore there was no logistical order or movement plan prepared, in spite of the fact that the Divisional Headquarters knew that they might be required to be inducted into Sri Lanka.

Worse, no formal Warning Order as prescribed in the Army's own battle procedure was issued to the division, which is specifically meant to facilitate operational moves by spelling out very the broadly the envisaged task ahead, any special administrative arrangements as would be necessary for the intended operation, thus ensuring both a smooth start and adequate preparedness from the start of the operation, as well as the "No Move Before" or "NMB," as it is routinely called in the Army's day-to-day language. This last is a very important piece of information to the recipients, as it tells them how much time they have to prepare and get organized, and they in fact have to issue their own Warning Orders to their subordinates, so that everyone down to the last man is organized and ready. The Warning Order procedure also allows married men living with their families in station to make the necessary domestic arrangements. Maj. Gen. Harkirat Singh, GOC 54 Infantry Division, who had been a Senior Instructor at the Defence Services Staff College as a Brigadier, said later that it seemed a case of the Army believing that its own Staff College teachings were meant to be applied only at the Staff College itself, and not in real life.... Or at least not if there was a "flap" on, which is actually when a formal Warning Order is needed most, since it is the formal start of the battle procedure, and thus actually starts off the operation.

The actual order to move came at extremely short notice, 54 Infantry Division being put on "Six-hours Notice" with just a day to prepare before the first units started being air-lifted. Infantry units were pushed out willy-nilly in a very unprofessional fashion, leaving behind essential requirements which are part of standard mobilization drills and orders, all of which are necessary for a unit being ready and capable of fighting at a new location, should it be required to do so. The chaotic move was responsible for a great deal of the army's initial weakness in Sri Lanka, when the "political task" of implementing the ISLA by just physically being there turned suddenly into a military task of fighting highly-motivated urban guerillas on their own home ground. A great deal of this misplaced over-confidence was due to the Indian civilian intelligence agencies, who had assured the Prime Minister and the army that the LTTE and other Tamil militant groups would never attack the Indian Army because, they were 'our boys,' trained and equipped by them.

The Army Chief's "Order of the Day" received just prior to the departure of 54 Infantry Division from Secunderabad for Palaly airport, Jaffna, which was to be read out to all troops before they left, laid down certain norms of conduct, as under:

"For the success of your mission you will have to ensure the following code of conduct:

- The highest standards of personal discipline and integrity.
- Tact and impartiality in dealing with various ethnic groups.
- No harassment to the civil population.

- Respect for the women, old people and children.
- No involvement in any local grouping/politics.
- Ensure justice to all."

There had perhaps actually been no need for such a great and unprofessional hurry, but the Army Chief himself was doing the pushing through his senior staff officers at Army Headquarters in Delhi, and he would brook no resistance from the Southern Command Headquarters at Pune (Poona), or from the division itself. There was no Joint Tri-Service Command established under one senior commander of any of the three armed services, since the move was undertaken by air and by sea, and thus no joint movement and induction plan. The infantry of 54 Infantry Division were sent in piece-meal, disorganized, under-strength, with none of the supporting weapons of the division which might be needed if a fight broke out and they suddenly found themselves with a war on their hands, as, of course, actually happened. They also landed without maps, practically no tentage, and with very little ammunition, a criminal negligence on the part of the formation headquarters all the way up the chain of command to Delhi, since every unit being embarked had brought up the issue, but had been hustled on to aircraft and shunted off to Sri Lanka. They had been given no operational briefing, and no 'Operational Task'!

A great deal of the confusion was caused by the unseemly hurry, which added to the problem of having to get adequate troops initially to the Jaffna area, where the only locations they could be landed were at Palaly airfield, or at the small jetty at Kankesanthurai (KKS), built to land stores for a cement factory. A large harbour with docks where large forces could be landed was available only at Trincomalee in the east, and so more forces actually arrived there, even though actually required for the Jaffna area, where the induction capability was extremely limited. The induction itself was handled as best could be under the circumstances, with military professionalism doing its best to re-assert itself on arrival at the Sri Lanka end. 54 Infantry

Division, the designated IPKF, started arriving in Sri Lanka on the night of 29/30 July 1987, by a variety of means and routes, with the divisional HQ and most of two brigades being airlifted into Palaly, and 76 Infantry Brigade from Pune being moved by rail to Chennai on 30 July and then by sea to Trincomalee. 1st Maratha Light Infantry of 47 Infantry Brigade was moved from Chennai to KKS. The mounting bases used for air induction from India were Dindigul, Begumpet, and Tiruchirapally. Sea induction was from the Indian ports of Vishakapatnam and Chennai. All heavy equipment had to be inducted by sea to Trincomalee harbour. No defence stores for the construction of field defences were moved, and the fighting echelon troops had no tentage since they had moved with minimal "operational" loads. Troops had to bivouac in the open, sheltering as best they could during the heavy downpours of the prevailing monsoon period. A proper logistical nightmare!

14th Sikh Light Infantry from Hyderabad received orders on 29 July to mobilize and be ready to take off to Sri Lanka the next morning. The same night further orders from HQ 47 Infantry Brigade specified that it was to fly out to Sri Lanka from two airfields, half the unit from Hyderabad and the other half from Dindigul. It was the first unit to begin landing at Palaly airfield, and the first complete unit to land in Sri Lanka, concentrating there by 10.30 a.m. on 30 July 1987, under its C.O., Col. O.K. Verma.

54 Infantry Division's concentration was completed by 4 August 1987. The division spent the next few weeks in trying to turn itself into a properly deployed and organized peace-keeping force, deployed for impartial policing duties. Its role was intended to be limited to accepting the surrender of arms by the militant groups and the supervision of the cease-fire between the militants and the SLAF. The IPKF was initially thus structured as just 54 Infantry Division minus its heavy equipment, its armour and its artillery.

*Tasks Allotted to IPKF*

Headquarters 54 Infantry Division merely received the wording of the Indo-Sri Lanka Agreement* in the afternoon before the first troops were embarked. In addition, they received an Order of the Day from the Chief of Army Staff, which was to be read out to all troops prior to their departure from Secunderabad airport. This clearly indicated that 54 Infantry Division was being sent into Sri Lanka for policing duties, and that its role was to maintain peace. The tasks allotted to the IPKF *after* its arrival in Sri Lanka, and therefore to 54 Infantry Division, were as under:

1. Separate the two warring groups, i.e., SLAF and LTTE, and ensure observance of the ceasefire.
2. Take over weapons and munitions being handed over by LTTE and other Tamil militant groups. *(This was part of the Indo-Sri Lanka Agreement, tacitly underwritten by India, and meant to be put into effect by the IPKF).*
3. Ensure dismantling of all SLAF camps established after May 1987.
4. Help the local population to return to their homes so that they could live in peace. (Soon after induction, when inter-militant clashes took place, another task was added).
5. To maintain law and order *(No directions were given as to actually how the troops were to prevent inter-militant clashes, which were taking place at locations far from any Indian Army presence).*

54 Infantry Division on induction deployed as under:

| | |
|---|---|
| Divisional Headquarters | Split between Palaly and Trincomalee, with the GOC at Palaly, and the Deputy GOC, Brig. Kulwant Singh, at the other part of the HQ at Trincomalee. |
| 47 Infantry Brigade from Hyderabad (under Brig. S.K. Dhawan) comprising 11 Madras, 5 Maratha LI, and 14 Sikh LI. | Brigade HQ at Vavuniya |

*Given at Appendix 'B'.

| | |
|---|---|
| 76 Infantry Brigade from Poona (under Brig. I.M. Dhar) comprising 2 Maratha LI, 25 Rajput, and 12 Garhwal Rifles | Brigade HQ at Batticaloa |
| 91 Infantry Brigade from Secunderabad (under Brig. J.K. Ralli) comprising 5 Madras, 1 Maratha LI, and 8 Mahar | Initially located at Jaffna with its Brigade HQ at KKS, the HQ later being shifted to Valikkamam in north Jaffna. |

In Eastern Province, the IPKF's area of operational responsibility was initially limited to Batticaloa, but after a few days Amparai was also included.

### *Uneasy Peace, LTTE Intransigence, Sinhala Discontent*

The IPKF's arrival in northern and eastern Sri Lanka had been greeted with euphoria by both the Tamil inhabitants and by the SLAF personnel deployed in the Tamil areas. For these SLAF personnel, the ceasefire meant the end of an unpleasant war. To the LTTE, however, it appeared that the Indo-Sri Lanka Agreement was the beginning of the end of their rise to total power among the Tamils of Jaffna. Pirabakaran was in fact at the time under virtual house-arrest in Delhi, and had only reluctantly "agreed" to go along with the provisions of the agreement. The LTTE were unhappy to hand over their weapons, and only began doing so when Pirabakaran was returned to the island on 2 August 1987, and was formally handed-over to the LTTE by the GOC 54 Infantry Division. He arrived from Delhi with his wife at Palaly airfield, and was formally accompanied back by Maj. Gen. Harkirat Singh and C.O. 14$^{th}$ Silkh LI to Suthumalai near the LTTE HQ in the Jaffna University campus, the escort being provided by "C" Company 14$^{th}$ Sikh LI under Maj. S.C. Kochar.

The arms surrender "ceremony" on 5 August 1987 was the beginning of the arms hand-over, but the LTTE did not really comply with this part of the agreement. The major problem was that the Indian RAW continued to supply arms to the other large Tamil militant group, the EPRLF *(Eelam People's*

*Revolutionary Front)*, about which the Ministry of External Affairs knew, and the IPKF learnt much later, but which the Army was unable to prevent, as it was being orchestrated at the highest level in Delhi. Arms surrender by the LTTE came to an end by 21 August.

Of this period, M.R. Narayan Swamy, in his book, "Tigers of Lanka,*" narrates:

"Jaffna's population was receptive to the IPKF despite the LTTE's growing restiveness. On 12 August, two IPKF members, including Jaffna-born Major Dilip Singh,** died when they stepped on a land mine. The two had been clearing mines laid by Tamil militants. The Jaffna Traders Association immediately requested all shops to fly black flags to mourn their deaths. As the news spread, there was genuine grief in Jaffna. But when the traders tried to collect money for the dead soldiers' families, the LTTE intervened and quietly but firmly asked them to drop the idea."

Regarding the IPKF's problems in trying to maintain law and order by preventing Tamil-Sinhala violence and trying to resolve issues between different Tamil groups, he states: "Its officers and men were in right earnest trying to restore a semblance of civil order to the war-torn north-east. The Tamil areas and its population were witness to an intermission of peace in the immediate aftermath of the IPKF arrival. The Indians were doing their best to keep everyone happy."

Lt. Gen. Sardeshpande summarizes the initial phase: the IPKF induction and deployment in Sri Lanka: "54 Div and 340 Brigade under the former were flown to Sri Lanka in July 1987 – with the Div HQ, Artillery Brigade and one infantry brigade in

*'Tigers of Lanka: From Boys to Guerillas', published by Konark Publishers Pvt. Ltd., Delhi, 1994, 3rd edition, 2002.

**Born in Jaffna and died in Jaffna. The IPKF's first casualty, Maj. George Herbert Dalipsingh, was a Tamilian born in Jaffna, educated at the Sainik School, Amravathinagar, Dist. Coimbatore, Tamil Nadu and joined the NDA's 45th Course. He was commissioned from 55th Course IMA into the Corps of Engineers. In Jaffna he was with 8 Engineer Regiment, a regiment of the Madras Sappers and Miners.

Jaffna, a brigade each in Vavuniya, Trinco and Batticaloa. As Srilankan intransigence and LTTE obduracy continued under contrived subterfuge, the requirement of additional troops became imminent. 36 Div HQ was sent in to Trinco and took over Trinco *(area)*; another independent brigade ex Punjab was inducted between Trinco and Batticaloa."

*Interview with Pirabakaran in August 1987*

Immediately after the signing of the ISLA, and before the outbreak of hostilities with the Indian Army, Pirabakaran was interviewed in Jaffna in August 1987 by T. S. Subramanian, reporter for the newsmagazine *Frontline*. Sachi Sri Kantha has placed it on the net for all to be able to understand Pirabakaran's views at the time.

*Responses to T.S. Subramanian*

Two questions which elicited revealing responses from Pirabaharan were the following:

*Subramanian:* "What happens to the cyanide capsules that your men wear round their necks? Are they necessary when there are no arms?

*Pirabaharan:* I think the capsules are needed most. They are indispensable now. They are the only weapons for the cadres to protect themselves in the Eastern Province from hoodlums, the rival groups and the Sinhala army. Not only that; they would continue to wear them in remembrance of those comrades who fought along with them and sacrificed their lives.

*Subramanian:* What are the shaping influences on your life?

*Pirabaharan:* Ra. Su. Nallaperumal's serial Kallukkul Eeram (Its's wet inside the stone) published in *Kalki* magazine. I have read it five times. It revolves round the Indian freedom struggle. Mr. Nallaperumal balances the ahimsaic struggle and the armed struggle. Generally, I read anything on any freedom movement. I used to read books on Joan of Arc, Napoleon and so on. I was always interested in history. Shivaji was the first guerrilla to have fought against the Mughal rule. When I was young, I always had a picture of Netaji Subhas Chandra Bose. I used to keep his picture on my table when I used to study. I had written on my table, 'I will fight till the last drop of my blood for the liberation of my mother-land.'"

Tensions between the LTTE and the IPKF slowly began, and continued to mount as anti-ISLA and anti-IPKF demonstrations were organized by the LTTE. Nevertheless, the LTTE and the IPKF had very cordial relations at the personal level at this stage. The Sinhala majority and many in the Government of Sri Lanka were unhappy that the IPKF had arrived and were protecting the Tamils.

*Thileepan's Fast unto Death, Failure of NEPC Talks, Suicide by Pulendran and Others*

Amirthalingam Thileepan *(also spelt as Dhileepan)*, the propaganda chief of the LTTE and head of its political wing in Jaffna, undertook a fast-unto-death at the Nallur Kandaswamy Temple in Jaffna in protest at the Indian Government's supposed disregard for the LTTE's demands regarding the number of its members and its demand for the right to nominate the chief administrator of the proposed new North-Eastern Province. Thileepan's fast was undertaken with the stated objective of getting the Indian Prime Minister to give the LTTE all that he had apparently promised, but the Government of India as represented by its pro-active High Commissioner, J.N. Dixit, was in no mood to concede an overwhelming authority in the Tamil areas to the LTTE. Maj. Gen. Harkirat Singh, the GOC 54 Division (and GOC IPKF) was located at Palaly near Jaffna, and was the senior Indian officer on the ground in Sri Lanka, and thus most aware of ground realities and local sentiments. Moreover, he had good rapport with the LTTE. However, the GOC 54 Division's repeated suggestions to the Indian High Commissioner to visit and talk to Thileepan were ignored. Thileepan died at about 10:50 AM on 26 September, after 11 days and 58 minutes of fasting. About a lakh of people.

primarily from the Vadamarachchi region, a LTTE stronghold, gathered at the Nallur temple. Though the LTTE cadres managed to control the crowds and prevent much violence, there was some arson, and tension was high.

Thileepan's death was the first major event, and very likely an avoidable one at that, in the breakdown of relations between the LTTE and the Government of India. It also created a tremendous impact on the local Tamil population, including the LTTE cadres, with Thileepan acquiring great status in death.

*Starvation-unto-death as a penance had always been regarded in India as an act of supreme fortitude and merit. It was greatly admired in ancient times, the classic example being that of the Chera King, Cheraman Perum Cheralatan*, at the battle of Venni, near Tanjore. He and his army were defeated by Karikala Chola, he himself being pierced by a shaft which went through his body to emerge from his back.*

*Since a wound on the back was considered to be cowardice, the Chera Raja sat facing north and fasted to death to wipe out the humiliation. This act evoked great sympathy and admiration, and even Karikala Chola felt that the brilliance of his victory was snatched away by the vanquished Chera's self-immolation. This fasting-unto-death of the Chera Raja has been glorified by the bard Kalath-thalaiyar in his verse (Puram 65), and by another bard Vennil-Kuyathiyar. Thileepan was continuing a grand tradition, and thus acquired great merit in death.*

*(Also known as Perum Tolatan, and as Adu Kodpattu Cheralattan).

*Failure of NEPC talks, and of Dixit-Pirabakaran Meeting*

The talks regarding the formation of the North-Eastern Provincial Council (NEPC) between the Government of India and the various Tamil groups on the one hand, and between the Government of India and the Sri Lanka Government on the other, broke down because the "honest broker" was unable to create a satisfactory via-media. The creation of this NEPC was perhaps the most important point of the ISLA, as it merged the two separate Tamil-majority Northern and Eastern Provinces into one province, provided for a fair amount of autonomy, and was a reasonable substitute for an independent Tamil homeland, which thanks to its own problems at the time in Punjab, Kashmir, Nagaland, and even Tamil Nadu at one time, the Indian government was not interested in supporting.

President Jayawardene was adamant in not accepting the LTTE nominee as the Chief Administrator of the North-Eastern Provincial Council, and the LTTE was very annoyed that India would not accept it as the only representative of Tamil opinion. President Jayawardene, in fact, had chosen one of the three names forwarded by the LTTE initially, but the LTTE changed their stand and began to insist on the nomination of one of its nominees, N. Pathmanathan, as the Administrator-in-Council of the Interim Administrative Council for the new North-Eastern Province.

As stated by Gen. Harkirat, the High Commissioner had urged him on the night of 14/15 September, to shoot Pirabakaran and Mahathiah in the period before the fighting with the LTTE broke out, on an occasion when they were to arrive for talks with him. This the GOC 54 Division had refused to do. This was during the period of truce, when he was charged with task of trying to get the LTTE to comply with the provisions of the ISLA. He had also told the High Commissioner that as an organized and honourable army, the Indian Army didn't function that way. Maj. Gen. Harkirat Singh was no stranger to diplomatic affairs, since he had been India's Military Adviser accredited to Italy, Romania and Yugoslavia from 1977 to 1981. In this refusal he was supported by his superior, the OFC, Lt. Gen. Depinder Singh, and also by the Director-General Military Operations (DGMO) at Army Headquarters, Lt. Gen. B.C. Joshi, but apparently the Army Chief, Gen. Sundarji had not been amused. He believes that it was probably this incident that led to the reported letter from the High Commissioner to the Government of India that the GOC 54 Infantry Division needed to be changed due to the IPKF being totally unprepared for the task at hand, because they were extensively fraternizing with the LTTE. In fact, up to the total breakdown on 5 October, the IPKF had been tasked with taking the LTTE along in its efforts to ensure implementation of the ISLA, so the fraternizing was part of its job. That the Government of India's other agencies, RAW and the MEA, were following a different agenda of trying to build up other Tamil groups and arming them, and attempting to gradually marginalize the LTTE, was never formally communicated to the IPKF.

The Indian High Commissioner added fuel to the fire at a stormy meeting with Pirabakaran on 26 September, at which Mr. Dixit attempted to bulldoze his way through. Had the career diplomat even attempted to behave diplomatically rather than as a dictator, when speaking to a battle-hardened politico-military leader, the outcome may well have been different. Dixit's arrogance put a quick and permanent end to India's fast-eroding influence with the LTTE. A clash of egos between a career diplomat and a foreign leader with whom the country is negotiating is the worst way in which to conduct negotiations. Pirabakaran, a natural leader, did not give in to Dixit's bullying. The political and diplomatic manoeuvres of the Indian Government failing, the stage was set for an armed showdown with the LTTE on the one hand, and on the other, an uphill task to force the Sri Lanka Government to actually go ahead with preparations for the creation of the NEPC, the only possible solution to Sri Lanka's Tamil problem. The IPKF's military tasks were set to begin.

By end-September the GOC IPKF had recommended to the OFC, the Army Headquarters and to the High Commissioner that the ISLA appeared to be doomed unless various political and diplomatic measures were taken. Militarily, he suggested that the IPKF should not be assigned policing duties, for which the Sri Lanka police should be activated. He also advised against adopting a hard option against the LTTE. These recommendations were outlined in his assessments of 17

September and 20 September to the OFC. At the end of September an inter-services fact-finding team of the Joint Planning Committee (JPC) came to Jaffna, headed by Brig. V.R. Raghavan, the Deputy Director Military Operations at Army Headquarters. Maj. Gen. Harkirat Singh repeated his recommendation against adopting the hard option against the LTTE. In his assessment of 5 October to the OFC, he recommended, *inter alia,* that:

"1. Hard line against hosts should be examined in order to ensure unity in the areas under reference.

2. GOC, IPKF does not recommend counter-insurgency operations because due to current political trends and unfriendly attitude of the Sri Lanka Government the possibility of its pulling out support to Indian involvement in such operations cannot be ruled out.

3. The Tigers have full support of Tamil population. Therefore, they will exploit the anti-India situation with corresponding effect in Tamil Nadu."

After Thileepan's death, tension was building up rapidly, as the anti-IPKF sentiment was spreading fast. Early on 2 October, an IPKF post near the Trincomalee town hall, which was being manned by the recently-inducted battalion, the 26$^{th}$ Punjab, was fired upon from a civilian vehicle and Sepoy Gorakh Ram was killed on the spot. Induction of 340 (Independent) Infantry Brigade into Sri Lanka commenced on 3 October. In order to maintain law and order, and also to prevent the SLA from moving out of their barracks, to which they had been confined under the terms of the ISLA, 11$^{th}$ Madras was moved from the northern province to Trincomalee by road. The Commander, 76 Infantry Brigade, Brigadier I.M. Dhar, was given the responsibility of Batticaloa and Amparai Districts till additional troops could be inducted and concentrated.

### *The Boat Tragedy*

Pulendran, the Jaffna "Area Commander" of the LTTE was wanted by the Sri Lanka Government for 34 murders, including the killing of 13 Sinhala policemen in the early stages of the

LTTE's rise to power in Jaffna. He was also implicated as having masterminded the killing of over 100 Sinhalas, including about 70 Sinhala soldiers on furlough on Good Friday, 17th April 1987. On the night of 2/3 October, Pulendran, Kumaran, the LTTE's Trincomalee 'Area Commander,' and 15 other LTTE cadres, were apprehended by the Sri Lankan Navy in a boat off Point Pedro in the Palk Strait. The LTTE had wanted that the IPKF not allow their transfer to Colombo for trial, but since they had been carrying two automatic rifles, a G3 and an M-16, supposedly for "self-defense," which was contrary to the terms of the Agreement, they were brought in to the Sri Lankan naval base. Protracted and tense negotiations involving the LTTE, the IPKF, and the Sri Lankan Government eventually led to their being left to the Sri Lankan Army to be moved to Colombo, after a piquant situation arose that would have been farcical if its consequences hadn't been so tragic: 13 dead LTTE cadres, followed by the outbreak of war with the LTTE, and the death of 1,200 Indian troops in the entire operations. The burden of the political-diplomatic failure had to borne by the troops.

The overall situation in the first week of October, 1987 in both the Northern and Eastern Provinces was becoming explosive due to violence engineered by the LTTE. The "Boat Tragedy," as it has been called, was the final straw that broke the camel's back of the fragile understanding, and is worth examining. The impounded boat was at the Sri Lankan naval base, surrounded by Sri Lankan troops. Pirabakaran sent an urgent message through the LTTE Deputy Commander, G. Mahendrarajan, known as "Ajit Mahathiah," to GOC 54 Infantry Division. Pirabakaran took strong objection to the LTTE men being taken into custody by the SLAF, as the LTTE had been granted amnesty. Mahathiah urged Gen. Harkirat Singh to prevent these LTTE cadres from being sent to Colombo, otherwise they would be tortured. Mahathiah reminded Gen. Harkirat that since the IPKF had been sent to protect the LTTE, this was imperative. Pirabakaran's message added that in case these men were allowed to be taken to Colombo, the IPKF would be responsible for the consequences: the LTTE would not observe the cessation of hostilities, and would not cooperate with the IPKF in establishing peace in the Tamil areas. Since as per the ISLA, the Sri Lanka Government had granted an amnesty to the LTTE, the IPKF "rescued" the men and transferred them to the Palaly airbase.

The contretemps became a highly-charged emotive issue. Pulendran was a prize catch for the SLAF. The Sri Lankan brigade commander in Jaffna, Brigadier Jayaratne was told by his government to get these men at any cost and fly them to Colombo. A Sri Lankan aircraft was kept ready at Palaly to move the LTTE prisoners. Brigadier Jayaratne was told by Colombo that if he couldn't send the LTTE prisoners, he should resign and come back in the aircraft himself. On the ground the situation was that at Palaly, in a cabin of the airport terminal, there were the LTTE detainees, around them were a protective ring of Indian troops, around these were Sri Lankan troops, around them were Indian troops comprising the 10 Para Commando battalion and one company of mechanized infantry under 91 Infantry Brigade, around whom were APCs (armoured personnel carriers) and about two platoons (totaling approximately 60 men) of the Sri Lankan Army. Gen. Harkirat asked for the diplomatic establishment to resolve the issue. It had the all the makings of a very messy and unpleasant fight between the Indian and the Sri Lankan troops, should the Sri Lankans attempt to take the LTTE detainees by force.

Mostly likely to get Maj. Gen. Harkirat Singh away from Jaffna, as he was being seen by the Sri Lanka Government as being too "close" to the LTTE, or possibly to put a little indirect pressure on the Sri Lanka Government, Gen. Harkirat was ordered to go to Trincomalee and immediately take over the airport, and deny its use to Sri Lankan troops for re-inforcing the area. This was carried out, causing considerable ill-feeling with the Sri Lankan Army, but in the meantime, Gen. Harkirat asked for Dixit, who was on leave in Delhi at the time, to be sent back to Colombo, to help resolve the boat problem.

Dixit and Lt. Gen. Depinder Singh, who, as Army Commander Southern Command was also "Overall Force Commander IPKF" with an ad hoc additional office in Madras, came and met Maj. Gen. Harkirat, and then went to Colombo to meet President Jayawardene. The Sinhala ministers who had been opposed to the ISLA from the beginning, Premadasa and Lalit Athulathmudali, the hawkish Minister for National Security, were adamant on the Sri Lanka Government having Pulendran in their custody to stand trial. The Indian delegation were unable to convince President Jayawardene and so on 5 October, Gen. Depinder Singh flew into Trincomalee to meet Harkirat and told him, "Hand over; let them go and do whatever they want." At 2 PM the same day while still in Trincomalee, he received a message from the Force Headquarters in Madras: "Why is the GOC IPKF interfering in the "constitutional activities of Sri Lanka?" Please lift your siege in Jaffna, and let the Sri Lankans do what they want to."

Now that he had an order in writing, an upset Gen. Harkirat spoke on the telephone to his Colonel General Staff (Colonel GS) (his senior operations staff officer at his divisional headquarters in Jaffna), Col. Hoshiar Singh, and asked him to withdraw the protection provided to the LTTE men. Around 5 PM on 5 October, the Indian troops withdrew, the Sri Lankan troops charged forward, and the LTTE men swallowed cyanide in order to commit suicide. Those who chewed the capsules died immediately. Four of them swallowed the capsules and were saved by the Indian Army medical unit which had been put on stand-by with ambulances and stomach pumps kept ready. The twelve dead included* "Lt. Colonel" Kumarappa, "Lt. Colonel" Pulendran, "Major" Abdulla and "Captain" Nalan.

The "Boat Tragedy" created a major stir and a further breakdown of cordiality between the three major parties concerned, the LTTE, the Government of India and the Government of Sri

*[Note: As per the LTTE, the dead were:
Lt. Col. Kumarappa, Lt. Col. Pulendran, Maj. Abdullah, Capt. Nalan, Capt. Ragu, 2nd Lt. Ananthakumar, Lt. Thavakumar, Lt. Anbalagan, Capt. Karan, Capt. Miresh, 2nd Lt. Reginald and Capt. Palani.]

Lanka. The LTTE were furious that the IPKF could not save their men and declared their withdrawal from the ISLA. On 5 and 6 October the LTTE began another round of their characteristic violence. They killed six Indian soldiers who were returning to their camp from Jaffna city. Since six of the deceased leaders hailed from the Valvettithurai region, the reaction in that region was immediate. The LTTE began to kill Sinhala soldiers and innocent civilians alike: Eight Sinhala soldiers captured earlier during two attacks on the police quarters and the telecommunication building at Pannai in Jaffna town were executed on 6 October, four Sinhala employees of the Sri Lanka television "Rupavahini" were abducted and killed in Palaly as they were driving home after dropping a Tamil colleague, and the Sinhala General Manager and the Deputy Manager of the KKS cement factory were shot dead. Sri Lankan Army camps in Point Pedro and Thondamannar were attacked by the LTTE on 5 October. LTTE cadres launched an attack on the Jaffna Fort camp on 6 October which continued till late in the evening. In the Northern and Eastern Provinces they massacred about 150 Sinhalese civilians including women and children. It has been reported that supporters and members of other Tamil militant groups were also killed.

The senior man on the spot for India, Gen. Harkirat Singh squarely blames the diplomats and the Army Headquarters for allowing this turn of events to happen. If India's man on the ground had his way, the LTTE detainees would have been saved, as he has gone on record saying that he had the capability to do so. He also blames Dixit, India's High Commissioner, who had the Indian Prime Minister's confidence and support, and had apparently been given a free hand in handling Sri Lanka affairs, for not being tough with President Jayawardene when it was needed.

General Sundarji arrived in Palaly (Jaffna) on 6 October on a fact-finding and inspection visit, en route to Colombo. But from 5 October onwards the spark that triggered off the LTTE-IPKF confrontation had already become a fire. The situation was rapidly deteriorating.

*Breakdown of Peace, KC Pant's and Gen. Sundarji's Visit to Colombo*

With the ISLA rapidly-disintegrating, apparently due to LTTE intransigence, but also greatly due to politico-diplomatic mishandling of the LTTE from the very beginning of the process which led to the drafting and signing of the ISLA, and by continuing the arming of the EPRLF, the Government of India made a last-ditch attempt to patch up relations with the Sri Lanka Government. President Jayawardene, who had reluctantly agreed to sign the ISLA, had to be seen by Sri Lankans as having taken the right decision, in spite of the open opposition from some of his own and influential ministers and the chauvinistically Sinhala JVP. The Sri Lanka Government had already received great respite thanks to the ISLA, due to the fact that the Sri Lanka Armed Forces, freed from the responsibility of having to continue their fight with the LTTE after the arrival of the IPKF, had gone to work on the JVP in southern Sri Lanka in full force, and battered them into quiescence. But the proof of the pudding of the ISLA, as far as most Sinhalas were concerned, was in getting the LTTE to the negotiating table AND getting them to work peacefully towards setting up the NEPC, which most Sinhalas had been opposed to, as to them it smacked of what amounted to creating a Tamil *Eelam* under Indian pressure and blackmailing. *(The IPKF was seen by most Sinhalas as an Indian force sent to create a Tamil homeland by force, which was a major part of the diplomatic problem with Sri Lanka, since its elected government had to take public perceptions into account in their dealings with India)*

The Indian Defence Minister, K.C. Pant, the Indian Army Chief, Gen. K. Sundarji, and the Overall Force Commander IPKF, Lt. Gen. Depinder Singh, arrived in Colombo on 6 October 1987, and were there that day and the next. President Jayawardene categorically told them that in case the IPKF took no action against the LTTE, he would be forced to call out the Sri Lankan Security Forces to protect the Sinhalas, thus breaking the ISLA. This left no option or reaction time for further planning and preparation. Though Lt. Gen. Depinder Singh tried to postpone the start of the IKF offensive against the LTTE, he was overruled by Gen. Sundarji, and a fresh directive was issued by the COAS on 7 October 1987, laying down the operational parameters. The breaking away of the LTTE from the ISLA and the killing of the Indian soldiers had its effect on the essentially fair-minded Indian Prime Minister. He had decided between 5 and 6 October, with his advisers, that stern action had to be taken, a message of firmness had to go out to the LTTE, and the LTTE neutralized, whatever be the scale of the operations.

In Colombo, Gen. Sundarji made the astonishing statement that the Indian Army would finish the LTTE in a week! This showed the extent of the lack of knowledge of the LTTE's fighting capabilities, meant to be provided to the Prime Minister and to the Army by the RAW, as well as the Army Chief's lack of understanding of the actual capabilities of the IPKF, as it was then deployed in Sri Lanka. Nevertheless, there is no doubt that he intended to make good on his statement, using whatever resources he could fling into the fray.

The LTTE was quite ready and very willing to go to war against the IPKF, and had been preparing for a showdown. The LTTE leadership knew that only a war would help them regain their stature, and also help it prevent the Indian Government's intention to keep Sri Lanka united. In Chennai, the LTTE's Kittu told Indian Tamil sympathizers, "The Indian army has not fought a war since 1971. We will teach it how to fight."

*Pirabakaran's Retaliatory Philosophy and Tactics: His "Go Ahead, Make My Day" Department*

Though Maj. Gen. Harkirat Singh is probably the one man in the Indian armed forces, serving or retired, who knows Pirabakaran's mind best, and believes he understood his mentality even before the ISLA broke down, it is Sachi Sri Kantha to whom we are indebted for an analysis of his retaliatory philosophy and tactics. These are based on his character and temperament, which matches those of the characters portrayed by his favourite actor, Clint Eastwood, in his various Western movies in particular. The character traits portrayed are exactly those displayed in real life by his fan – prudence, intelligent shyness, self reliance, suspicion of the intentions of strangers and dogged determination. The journalist Jared Lubarksy, (quoted by Sachi Sri Kantha), commented in 1986: "I find it a little disconcerting myself, that this particular freedom fighter learned his notions of warfare from Eastwood spaghetti Westerns. As far as I can tell, Eastwood's loftiest strategy in these movies is to shoot the shit out of anything that moves. That doesn't bode well for the future of Sri Lanka."

*The Jimmy Malone Offense:* Sachi Sri Kantha believes that Pirabakaran has perfected what he calls a "Jimmy Malone Offense." To quote him: "Jimmy Malone was the veteran Chicago cop character played by Sean Connery in the Al Capone bio-picture *The Ubntouchables.* Malone, in his professional wisdom, gives an advice to the young Eliot Ness about tackling the American icon of crime, as follows:

"You want to get Capone? Here's how you get him. He pulls a knife, you pull a gun. He sends one of yours to the hospital, you send one of his to the morgue. That's the Chicago way."

The type of retaliatory attacks perfected by LTTE, the Jimmy Malone offense, have been a trade mark for the no-nonsense image of the Israeli armed forces led by skilled warriors Moshe Dayan and Yitshak Rabin. Even before Israel was born, President Roosevelt's army avenged the 1941 Japanese attack of Pearl harbour by eliminating Admiral Yamamoto, using a Jimmy Malone manoeuvre.

One can argue whether what Pirabakaran did was ethically correct or not, but for the first time in the recent Tamil history of the island, he stood up for the aggression against Eelam Tamils, with a signature act that scared the pants out of his adversaries. Until that moment, Tamils have been passive victims of state-supported aggression for decades."

### *Additional Inductions*

As the role of the IPKF got gradually expanded, one more infantry brigade plus additional troops were inducted into the

Eastern Province. Thus by the end of September the IPKF consisted of four infantry brigades plus, under an infantry divisional HQ, the troops deployed to cover the entire area of the Jaffna peninsula and the Northern and Eastern Provinces. However, none of the units and thus none of their superior formations was at full strength due to routine courses, leave etc, still being the order of the day, and the total strength on 7 October 1987 was about 29,000 personnel. The infantry battalions were at about half or less of their authorized strengths, and including the later inducted battalions, the average inducted strength of an infantry battalion was about 350 to 400, instead of its authorized and fully-mobilized strength of over 800 combatants.

Headquarters 36 Infantry Division quickly inducted into Trincomalee, and on night 7/8 October was given command over 76 Infantry Brigade of 54 Infantry Division which was already employed in Batticaloa and Amparai districts for the maintenance of law and order. The Tactical HQ of 54 Infantry Division located at Trincomalee was moved to Palaly by road to join the rest of the divisional HQ.

Thus by 8 October 1987 the IPKF had been built up to five infantry brigades functioning under two infantry divisional HQ, with HQ 54 Infantry Division at Palaly controlling the north and HQ 36 Infantry Division at Trincomalee controlling the east.

54 Division had under command 91 Infantry Brigade for the Jaffna area and 47 Infantry Brigade for the Vavuniya area. 36 Division had 18 Infantry Brigade for the Mullaitivu area and Trincomalee, (though this brigade was later moved out to Jaffna), 340 (Independent) Infantry Brigade and 76 Infantry Brigade.

Supporting Units Available as on 8 October were:

15 Mechanized Infantry Battalion

831 Light Regiment of the artillery

One artillery battery from the 17 Parachute Field Regiment

8 Engineer Regiment

110 Engineer Regiment, less one of its field companies.

## Chapter 3

# 'Operation PAWAN' – Phase II: Start of Operations and Capture of Jaffna Peninsula

Maj. Gen. Harkirat Singh, GOC 54 Infantry Division and GOC IPKF, recounts: "On 8 October 1987, Gen. Sundarji visited IPKF Headquarters at Palaly and ordered me to adopt the hard option against the LTTE. The IPKF from being a peackeeper had to suddenly adopt an offensive stance. At this point the area in which 54 Infantry Division was operating was vast; it was deployed over some 540 km, from north to south and east to west in Sri Lanka.

As soon as he landed Gen. Sundarji [at Palaly airfield] caught me off guard by saying, "I am aware that you are not getting on with the High Commissioner who I know is doing his job and you must take action on his instructions." The OFC intervened to say that it was incorrect to say that "Harry" did not give the High Commissioner his due.

The COAS was then escorted to my headquarters. He said that he was fully aware of the operational situation and did not need any briefing. He handed me some papers and asked me to read them. After quickly glancing at the pink sheets of paper, I understood that the prime minister had accepted the recommendations of the COAS, and that I was required to adopt a course of action contrary to my own recommendations.

Before leaving for Trincomalee, the COAS told me in the presence of Lt. Gen. Depinder Singh *(the OFC)* to launch operations that night itself. I was staggered at this tall order and could not resist saying, "To attack tonight, with what? We have come to Sri Lanka in battle order to maintain peace, we lack battlefield mobility, fire support and being monsoons, it is the wrong time to launch an offensive." The OFC saw that the Chief was getting upset because his orders were being questioned. He told him that we would do something tonight against the LTTE; in short, he accepted the Chief's directive."

Maj. Gen. Harkirat Singh felt that his immediate superior, the OFC and GOC-in-C Southern Command, Lt. Gen. Depinder Singh, should have supported his stand about not going into an offensive against the LTTE at that particular time, in the same way as Gen. Maneckshaw had resisted the prime minister's wish to attack in East Pakistan in March 1971, when the Indian Army was unprepared and the monsoon was due to arrive soon. In that instance, Gen. Maneckshaw had first consulted Eastern Command Headquarters who had firmly stated their unpreparedness at that time and at such short notice. Additionally, in October 1987 the Military Operations Directorate at Army Headquarters, then under Lt. Gen. B.C. Joshi as Director-General Military Operations, was also fully aware of the GOC IPKF's recommendations, and could have advised the Chief to prepare for an offensive against the LTTE only after appropriate build-up and after the monsoon rains.

The GOC IPKF continues by saying: "The war had begun, but I as the GOC, IPKF did not have a clear-cut brief on what action to take against the LTTE. I did not have any option except to launch the unprepared IPKF, with multi-pronged thrusts, towards Jaffna town to divide the enemy, and so, make up for the inadequate infantry and supporting elements at my disposal. All available troops were employed on ground-holding tasks and were widely dispersed; there were no reserves to influence the battle."

Lt. Gen. Sardeshpande comments: "When orders finally came from the Army Chief to capture Jaffna and disarm the militants forcibly the situation was:

(a) The LTTE leaders had disappeared;

(b) There was no information of where their arms caches were;

(c) The order came as a shock to the IPKF after the four-month lavish honeymoon with the LTTE; the IPKF had a lot of apprehensions, reservations, doubts; and

(d) Nobody had thought that the LTTE would hit the IPKF squarely in the face with benumbing violence unleashed by deadly IED's and vicious small arms fire in built up areas and across lagoons."

The GOC, IPKF, may have been militarily disadvantaged due to conditions neither of his own making nor of his own choosing, but nevertheless he got on with the job as best any general could have done under the circumstances. However, as on 10 October, there were no tanks available to support the operations in the Jaffna peninsula. Inductions of additional troops were hurriedly being done on an ad hoc basis by Army Headquarters in Delhi, and because of the urgency the Order of Battle (ORBAT) of various incoming formations was completely broken up, often destroying the cohesiveness of the formation. Maj. Gen. Harkirat Singh notes that because all the infantry battalions inducted were seriously under-strength, "a task that could have been performed by one infantry battalion had to be allotted to two infantry battalions." Whatever may or may not have been the errors of omission or commission of the Indian foreign-policy, intelligence and military systems, there is no doubt that Maj. Gen. Harkirat Singh was the man left holding the baby "when the balloon went up."*

*New Directive of 7th October 1987 to the IPKF*

The salient aspects of the Army Chief's directive were:

(a) Seize/destroy the LTTE radio/TV transmission equipment in the Jaffna Peninsula;

(b) Seize or jam LTTE communication network;

*A common expression in use in English in the Indian Army in the period up to the early 1990's, referring to the outbreak of a shooting war, i.e., the opening of actual armed hostilities.

(c) Carry out raids on LTTE camps, caches and strong points;

(d) Detain LTTE personnel manning LTTE offices in the East and interrogate them to gain information. In case of resistance, force to be used;

(e) Actions to further consolidate hold of IPKF in the region.

In the meantime, thousands of mourners paid homage to the dead LTTE leaders, joined by Pirabakaran himself. Their bodies were draped in the red LTTE flag with the tiger emblem, and were laid out according to their rank in the LTTE military hierarchy with Pulendran's body placed first, followed by Kumarappa's and Abdulla's. Hundreds of mourners wept at the cremation at Valvettiturai on the evening of 8 October.

*Decision to Capture Jaffna*

The decision to disarm the LTTE by use of force had been taken on 6th October, 1987, and mobilization was ordered, though it was too late to affect the units still being inducted hastily into Sri Lanka, or those already there, who continued to remain under-strength.

*Aim:* The aim, or "mission" as it is known in American military terminology, was to capture Jaffna at the earliest. The contingency plan was ordered to be implemented. The OFC's Operation Order stipulated that the task was to be completed within four days, and that troops must gain moral ascendancy over the LTTE soonest.

In spite of the known military difficulties of fighting in a built-up area, the decision to capture Jaffna was taken because Jaffna had come to symbolize LTTE power and authority, and had withstood all the efforts made by the Sri Lanka Armed Forces (SLAF) to capture it. It had become necessary, therefore, to wrest control of this symbol, to force the LTTE back into the mainstream of the ISLA.

*Contingency Plan:* As part of contingency planning in case the IPKF had to undertake offensive operations against the LTTE, Headquarters (HQ) 54 Infantry Division had already prepared a concept which had been approved by the Overall Force

Commander (OFC) IPKF, Lt. Gen. Depinder Singh. This was:

- Capturing Jaffna town earliest using multiple thrust lines, including air and sea-borne landings.
- The opening of at least one axis of maintenance behind the advancing troops, to ensure continuous supply.
- Air supply of troops not dependent on the axis of maintenance, till supply by road could be started.
- Air, naval, and artillery fire support to be confined to confirmed targets only.
- The Navy to establish a sea blockade.

*Start of Military Operations by IPKF*

On the night of 9/10 October, 1987, operations were launched by 54 Infantry Division to capture the LTTE radio station at Tavadi and TV station at Kokkuvil, and the printing presses of two LTTE sponsored newspapers were destroyed. This led to LTTE inspired demonstrations on 10 October by civil organizations. In reprisal, the LTTE indulged in the following offensive actions against the IPKF:

(a) Automatic and mortar fire on the posts at Tellipallai held by 5$^{th}$ Madras;

(b) Ambush of the convoy of 58$^{th}$ Bn. CRPF moving from Tellipallai to Periyavalian, in which four CRPF jawans were killed and seven injured;

(c) Hijacking of a jeep of 10$^{th}$ Para Commandos and the killing of all five OR occupants.

(d) Opening fire on a routine patrol of 1$^{st}$ Maratha LI as it was returning to Jaffna Fort, and heavy mortar fire on the fort itself.

*The IPKF's Jaffna Offensive*

GOC 54 Infantry Division, Maj. Gen. Harkirat Singh's own narration of the planning for the offensive is the best way to understand the subsequent events as they unfolded. In his own words:

"I had to ensure the safety of the Divisional Maintenance Area, protect Palaly airport; defend the KKS harbour; and above all hold the Dutch fort in Jaffna town at all costs. I selected these vulnerable areas and earmarked troops for their defence. I decided to launch the offensive in five phases based on the broad concept that I had spelt out. Lt. Gen. Depinder Singh approved the manner in which the operation was to progress. The need for additional troops was driven home, but since the OFC had accepted the Chief's directive, I was given no time to wait for the build-up. The phases of the operation were as follows:

*Phase 1:* To capture Jaffna town using multiple thrust lines at the earliest and to simultaneously prevent the LTTE reinforcements from the eastern province from getting to Jaffna. To stop them from reaching Jaffna, I decided to seal off all routes of entry including the ferry sites to the Jaffna peninsula, by blocking all land routes, imposing an indefinite curfew and simultaneously establishing a naval blockade with the Sri Lankan Navy.

*Phase 2:* To clear all the outlying areas of Jaffna town; open a minimum of two road axes from Palaly to Jaffna town; ensure maintenance of the land route and clear all the outlying areas of the Jaffna subdivision.

*Phase 3:* To clear Vadmaradchchi division (east and west).

*Phase 4:* To clear Valikamam west, including Kayts and Karaitivu islands.

*Phase 5:* To clear Tenamaradchchi division and Pachchipalli subdivision.

I could not spell out the specific time-frame or earmark troops for the various phases as they were dependent on the induction plan for additional troops from the mainland. Unfortunately, the staff at Headquarters, OFC, failed to keep my General Staff informed, and as a result, no advance planning could be carried out to ensure proper grouping, regrouping, and effective employment of the units/formations that kept arriving at Palaly airport."

*LTTE Strength:* The estimated strength of the LTTE in and around Jaffna was about 1500, though this was later reinforced to about 2500. About 75-80 per cent of these were armed with rifles: the short AK-47 automatic-firing assault rifle of Russian design, mostly of Chinese manufacture, the German G-3 automatic rifle, and the American M-16; light machine guns (LMG's) and medium machine gums (MMG's), mortars and rocket launchers (mainly the Soviet RPG-7, another favourite of insurgent and terrorist forces world-wide, like the AK-47).

*LTTE Defences:* The LTTE had constructed well-sited defences and heavily fortified them, in three successive defensive tiers, to defend Jaffna from an attack by the SLAF, basically covering the major road axes converging on Jaffna town. The defences had machine-guns and automatic weapons, and snipers with telescopic sights were located on tree-tops, elevated water tanks and housetops. The roads were mined with large improvised explosive devices (IED's) in 200-litre barrels and in jerrycans, capable of blowing up large vehicles and even damaging BMP-2 infantry combat vehicles and T-72 tanks. These successive tiers were:

- *First (Outer) Tier:* Along line Sandipai—Chunnakam—Puttur.
- *Second Tier:* Along line Kotitadi—Kopai North—Urumparai—Kondavil—Manipai—Arali.
- *Third Tier:* On the outskirts of Jaffna town, along line Navatkuli—Kopai South—Kokuvil and on to the coast.
- *Fourth (Inner) Tier:* Within Jaffna town.

*Available Strength:* Thanks to continued induction of more troops after the arrival of 54 Division, the available force from about 7 to 12 October was about two infantry divisions worth (under HQ 54 and 36 Infantry Divisions) approximating a total of six infantry brigades. (The normal complement of an infantry brigade is three infantry battalions, but these brigades were not at full strength, as already brought out. In addition, the other fighting components of an infantry division, such as an artillery brigade of three artillery regiments, an integral armoured regiment, and other elements, were not present. These were

## THE LTTE'S DEFENSIVE TIERS FOR THE DEFENCE OF JAFFNA

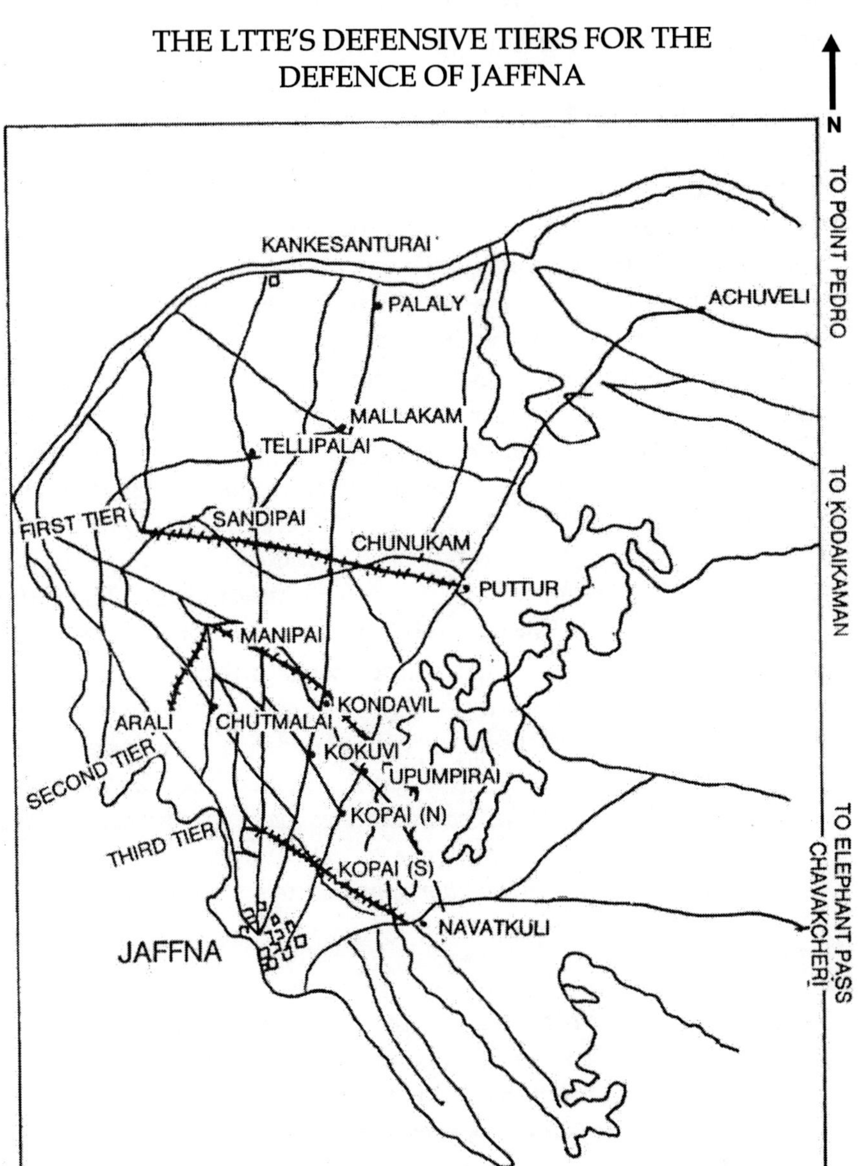

reduced-scale divisions sent in with primarily their infantry elements and signals components only). The additional combat units available were one mechanized infantry battalion, one artillery regiment, and one parachute commando battalion. Between 10 and 12 October, just three T-72 tanks from an armoured regiment also arrived by air in Il-76 aircraft at Palaly, being flown in from Meenambakam airport in Chennai (Madras). The problem with this availability of forces was that four of the six infantry brigades were located in the Trincomalee Sector, where they had been inducted by sea, including two out of the three integral brigades of 54 Division. 54 Division had in hand only one of its own brigades (91 Infantry Brigade), and another brigade (18 Infantry Brigade) of the other division.

*In the Jaffna area itself, the immediate availability of troops for the ground offensive was just two infantry battalions with a third battalion located within the old Dutch fort and not immediately available to be brought out for an operation involving movement. The attack, therefore, began with just the two available battalions.* Other battalions of the different arriving brigades commenced their tactical movement forward immediately after arrival into the sector, along the designated axes of advance for their respective brigades. Not a very neat or well-coordinated way to start a multi-pronged offensive. *(However, in this case there was no artillery fire planning to be coordinated at the division level, nor was there a necessity for leap-frogging of artillery gun positions, or of planning and coordinating artillery ammunition supply convoys).*

*The Plan*

- *Basic Plan*: The broad outline plan was to capture Jaffna town, while enforcing a naval blockade on the Jaffna lagoon and around the Peninsula, then establish full control over the "neck" of Jaffna via Elephant Pass and Chempianpatu, and finally fan outwards to other parts of the Peninsula and other north-eastern and north-western parts of Sri Lanka.

- *Area of Responsibility*: The IPKF's area of operational responsibility was divided into two; the Jaffna Sector being the area North of Elephant Pass, i.e., the Jaffna Peninsula, operationally placed under 54 Infantry Division, and the rest of north and eastern Sri Lanka under HQ 36 Infantry Division. The problem with this was that the Jaffna Sector, which needed six to seven brigades for the capture of Jaffna town and its surrounding area, initially had only two available brigades.
- *Trincomalee Sector*: With the Jaffna Sector decided upon as the sector in which the main operations were to be prosecuted, the Trincomalee sector was to maintain a low profile by conducting aggressive patrolling, but undertaking offensive operations only if a lucrative target presented itself. Ideally, great pressure should have been put on the LTTE in this sector while the attack on Jaffna was in progress, so as to prevent any LTTE reinforcements from here being sent to Jaffna. But since the bulk of the troops in the sector actually had to be withdrawn, tasked for the capture of the Jaffna Sector, a thinner IPKF presence in this sector had perforce to be accepted.
- *Timing of the Operation*: Though it might have been sensible to wait for the arrival of more troops which were in the process of being inducted, the arrival of these reinforcements could not be precisely timed and catered for in the attack plan. The available forces and their locations were known to the LTTE; had the IPKF waited for the arrival of reinforcements before starting offensive operations, the widely-dispersed units could have been isolated and come under attack during the process of concentrating them. The area around the Palaly airfield and the KKS jetty had to be secured, as the maintenance stocks of 54 Division, including its ammunition and its fuel reserves were located there. It was vital to clear the area of all LTTE and to make this area into a secure logistics base area by providing it depth. It was equally vital to threaten Jaffna at the earliest and thus put the LTTE on the

defensive. (The LTTE actually began fiercely attacking the IPKF from the 10th October 1987).

- *54 Infantry Division Plan for the Capture of Jaffna*: The outline plan for the capture of Jaffna town was as under:
- Initiate two thrusts, with 18 Infantry Brigade from the East, and 72 and 91 Infantry Brigades from the North. (72 Brigade expected to be inducted 10-12 October)
- One infantry battalion ex 91 Infantry Brigade, embarking at KKS in naval assault craft, to effect a landing from the sea west of Jaffna Fort and to link up with the garrison in it.
- Raid on the LTTE headquarters located in a building in Jaffna University to be conducted as a heliborne operation with one parachute commando company and one infantry company. Link-up to be effected by 91 Infantry Brigade and 72 Infantry Brigade within 24 hours.
- 41 and 115 Infantry Brigades, expected to be inducted after the commencement of the attack, were to either reinforce existing thrust lines or to develop new ones, or, if the operations were proceeding satisfactorily, to occupy the Point Pedro and Kodikaman areas in the north-east.

As the advance progressed, rear areas along at least one axis needed to be kept secured so as to prevent the LTTE from interposing themselves between the advancing troops and the Divisional Maintenance Area (DMA).

Though the 54 Division's plan was basically sound, it was contingent upon the timely availability of naval (landing craft) and air force (helicopters) resources, which, since there was no 'Joint Command,' could not be ensured by either the OFC *(whose title was misleading since his command, even in theory, was only over the Army elements, but even in this there were practical constraints)*, or the divisional commander. As in all the wars fought by the Indian Army since Independence, and even before, the three armed services had fought their own separate wars, merely "cooperating" with each other. The IPKF's operations in Sri Lanka were no different. The progress of the plan was also dependant upon the upon the timely arrival of the expected additional infantry brigades, which since they had to

OPERATION PAWAN
THE FIVE BRIGADE AXES OF ADVANCE OF JAFFNA

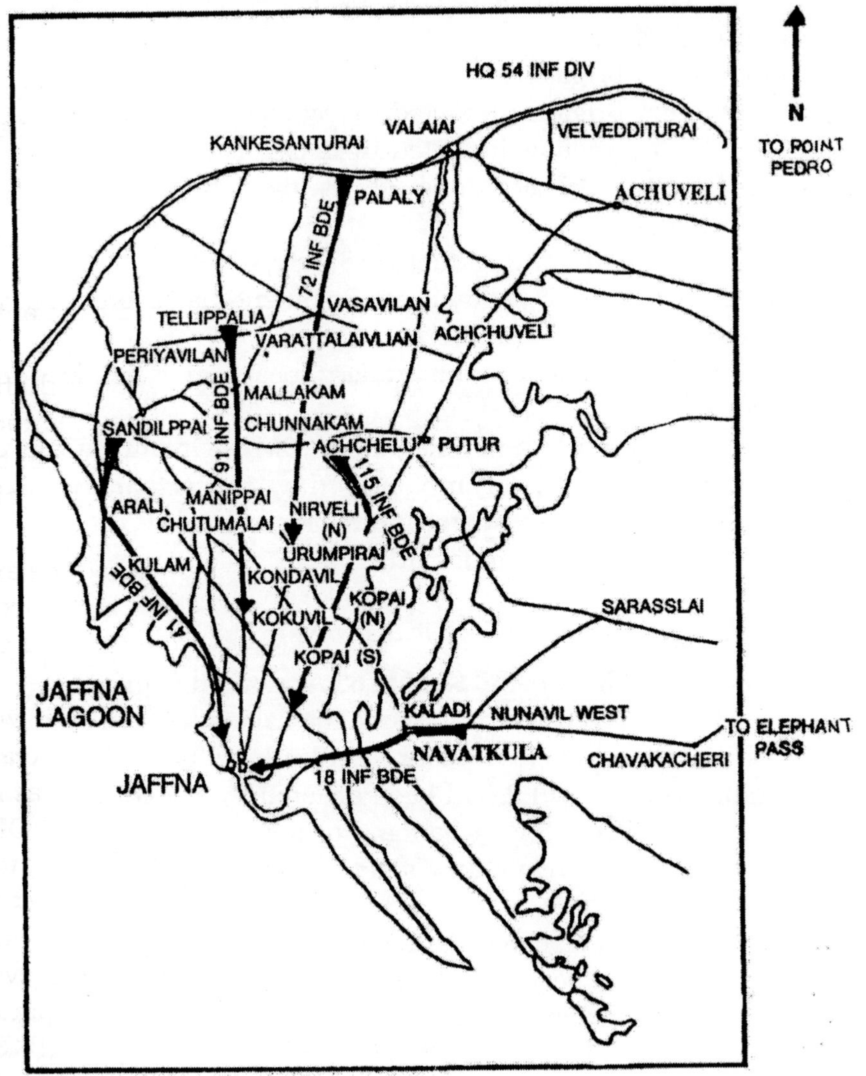

arrive from their peace-time locations by a combination of means; railways, and sea or air, could not be accurately predicted by the IPKF, since they were being moved forward by Army HQ, and not by HQ OFC, the ad hoc HQ in Madras.

*Forces Earmarked for the Jaffna Sector:* HQ 54 Infantry Division was to have the following forces under command for the capture of Jaffna:

- 18 Infantry Brigade
- 41 Infantry Brigade (inducted 15 October 1987)
- 72 Infantry Brigade (inducted 10-12 October 1987)
- 91 Infantry Brigade (one of its own brigades, initially inducted)
- 115 Infantry Brigade (inducted 18 October 1987)
- One squadron 65 Armoured Regiment (later built up to regiment less one squadron)
- 831 Light Regiment of the artillery (heavy mortars), less one battery
- 25 Mechanised Infantry Regiment (BMP-2 Infantry Combat Vehicles), less two companies, (i.e., the actual available strength was one company and the regimental HQ)
- 10 Parachute Commando Battalion

*Induction of 65 Armoured Regiment's tanks*

In the words of Major Anil Kaul of 65 Armoured Regiment*,

"... I had received orders to move the balance of 'A' Squadron tanks of my regiment into Sri Lanka by HQ Indian Peace Keeping Force (IPKF). I had been ordered by my commanding officer (CO), Col. S.P. Khanna, to move to Madras (now Chennai) and relieve a fellow squadron commander Major Ajit S. Bhinder.

Accordingly, I reached Madras on 4 October 1987, only to be told that Ajit had been inducted with four tanks into the island, specifically Trincomalee (where trouble was likely to erupt between the IPKF and the LTTE) by air. Tanks can be ferried by

*As recounted in his book, *"Better Dead than Disabled,"* Parity Paperbacks, New Delhi, 2006, reproduced with the kind permission of the publishers.

the air force in their Il-76 nicknamed *Gajraj*. I was then told to stay on in Madras and coordinate the move of the rest of the regiment from Babina, a military station near Jhansi. I moved to the dockyard area of Madras port where the entire IPKF force was being concentrated for its move across the Palk Strait to their respective destinations in Sri Lanka.

We knew that these moves had been in the offing since June of that year as we had been on stand-by mode since. The original plan, as explained to us, was to do "a Bangladesh" to the northern and eastern provinces of Sri Lanka with the help of the LTTE, using them as we had used the Mukti Bahini in 1971. The came the July 29 accord between our then Prime Minister Rajiv Gandhi and Sri Lankan president Jayawardene. There had been a 180-degree turn: the LTTE was now to be disarmed, the Sri Lankan army confined to barracks, and our IPKF to keep the peace.

A raid on the LTTE HQ then located inside Jaffna university campus on the night of October 11-12 was executed both by land and air. On the same day, a decision seems to have been taken to move in the tanks. Most of what were available were either in Trincomalee or on their way in cargo ships. The only alternative was the six tanks with me in Madras.

I moved the tanks on tracks through the streets of Madras at midnight from the dockyard to the airport. An IL-76 arrived at Meenambakam international airport in Madras, which had been closed to any civil air movement on the afternoon of 10th October. One of my tanks was loaded, and the aircraft flew into the southern sky. Next day two more Il-76's arrived and, since it was late, we were told to be ready to move the next day."

*Commencement of Main Operations*

Large-scale operations to capture and clear LTTE from the Jaffna Peninsula were launched from 11 October, 1987, in phases, so as to capture Jaffna town, clear Jaffna area, Vadamarachchi area and the remaining areas.

*Forces Available on 11 October in Jaffna Sector*

The actual availability of forces at the start of the IPKF's operations for the capture of Jaffna by 54 Infantry Division was:

- 18 Infantry Brigade commanded by Brig. J.S. Dhillon, at Elephant Pass with two infantry battalions, 4th Mahar, and 12th Grenadiers, which had been inducted into Sri Lanka on 5 October, and though a part of 115 Infantry Brigade, had been allotted to 18 Brigade, and was located in area Point Pedro-Velvettithurai-Karaveddi East. This brigade was earmarked to become part of 36 Infantry Division, and its third battalion, 18th Garhwal Rifles, had already reached Trincomalee, and then sent off to Battiacaloa, where it had been allotted to 76 Infantry Brigade, thus breaking up the brigade's original composition.
- 91 Infantry Brigade under Brig. J.K. Ralli of the Guards, in Keerimalai/ Valikkaman in north Jaffna, with 5th Madras in the Vadamaradchi-Tenmaradchi division deployed along the line Tellipalai-Periyavian, 8th Mahar in Valkamam division west, and 1st Maratha LI (*Jangi Paltan*) in Jaffna Fort with responsibilities for maintaining law and order in Jaffna town and the defence of the islands of Mandaitivu, Kayts, and Karainagar.

*Operations on 11 October 1987*

54 Infantry Division's advance to Jaffna town began on 11 October, with much less troops in terms of actual numbers of men and weaponry, than was indicated by the military task. This was partly due to the units themselves not being up to full strength, as indicated earlier, and insofar as the weaponry was concerned, due to the deliberate political policy of causing the least number of civilian casualties and the least amount of damage to buildings. A very awkward way to fight, more so when the opponents were not following any form of "Queensberry Rules" or Geneva Agreement restrictions themselves; what was described in the media as the Indian

Army "fighting with one hand tied behind its back." The question of whether politics should dictate an actual method of fighting, once the situation has deteriorated to the point of actual armed combat, does not seem to have been seriously debated, or objected to, at the higher echelons of the Army command. "Yes-men" in the higher ranks allowed such military nonsense to become operational guidelines. The soldiers and their officers on the ground had to bear the brunt of this political restriction, and eventually so did the families of those unnecessarily and stupidly killed and wounded as a result. Added to this was the effect of not having given the time to the infantry units for adequate briefing of their men: they were not psychologically conditioned to fight the LTTE the way they should have been. The "peace-keeper" mentality was bolstered by the ridiculous operating restrictions imposed on the IPKF. There had, of course, been no briefing on anticipated LTTE defences, and no specific-to-task "battle school" pre-induction training and practice.

The attack commenced as planned, but was an attack of a novel kind for the Indian Army. It was advancing upon a town which was heavily-fortified, with well-armed and motivated defenders with plenty of ammunition, the approaches mined and booby-trapped, but where there was no air-power being used, no artillery fire to soften the enemy defences, no tanks providing fire support in most situations. The enemy were the same LTTE whom the Indian Army's soldiers believed they had been protecting till a few days before, against whom no real hatred and desire to kill had as yet built up.

There were crowds of civilians, including women and children, milling about ahead of and around the advancing soldiers, shouting slogans, behind whom were armed young men and even women in civilian clothing, firing at the soldiers at opportune moments. In other cases, crowds of old men and young children would advance towards and right up to the troops, then suddenly run away into side-streets and lanes, while the "Tigers" who had been creeping forward behind this human screen took up firing positions nearby and open up with all their weapons. Inevitably in such circumstances, there were a few civilian casualties, which the effective LTTE propaganda machine then took up as the Indian Army's deliberate killing of women and children. This needs to be compared with the Sri Lankan Army's operations of May that year, using all the military means at their disposal, with utter disregard for any collateral damage to either civilians or buildings. The SLAF did manage to restrict the LTTE's hold on the peninsula, by capturing the coastline from Point Pedro to KKS, but their offensive on defended, built-up areas, by a much smaller and weaker army, would have been similar to their action at Vadamarachchi, in which they used extensive aerial bombardment, and caused heavy civilian casualties. As it was, if the IPKF were to operate in the normal manner, they would have assaulted, cleared and captured Jaffna town in 48 hours, after using airpower, artillery bombardment, and tanks in fire support. Initially, the restraint exercised by the IPKF in the use of firepower, was possibly perceived by the LTTE as a lack of will to use adequate force, thereby possibly prolonging the operations to capture the Jaffna peninsula.

*18 Infantry Brigade*

The brigade was ordered to concentrate at Navtkuli on 10 October, but even the concentration became an advance operation of war, with 12 GRENADIERS* being ambushed

*1. Hereafter the names of the infantry units of the attacking brigades have been mostly been written in the abbreviated style used in the Army's Operation Orders, Situation Reports, and signal correspondence, and will thus be familiar to military readers. Only the number of the battalion of the regiment to which it belongs and an abbreviated form of the name of the regiment is used. For example, "4 MAHAR" is formally "4th Battalion, the Mahar Regiment," "12 GRENADIERS" is "12th Battalion, The Grenadiers," while "13 SIKH LI" is "13th Battalion, the Sikh Light Infantry," and 4/5 GR (FF) is formally "4th Battalion, the 5th Gorkha Rifles (Frontier Force)." Similarly, "1 MARATHA" is 1st Battalion, The Maratha Light Infantry, "5 MADRAS" is 5th Battalion, the Madras

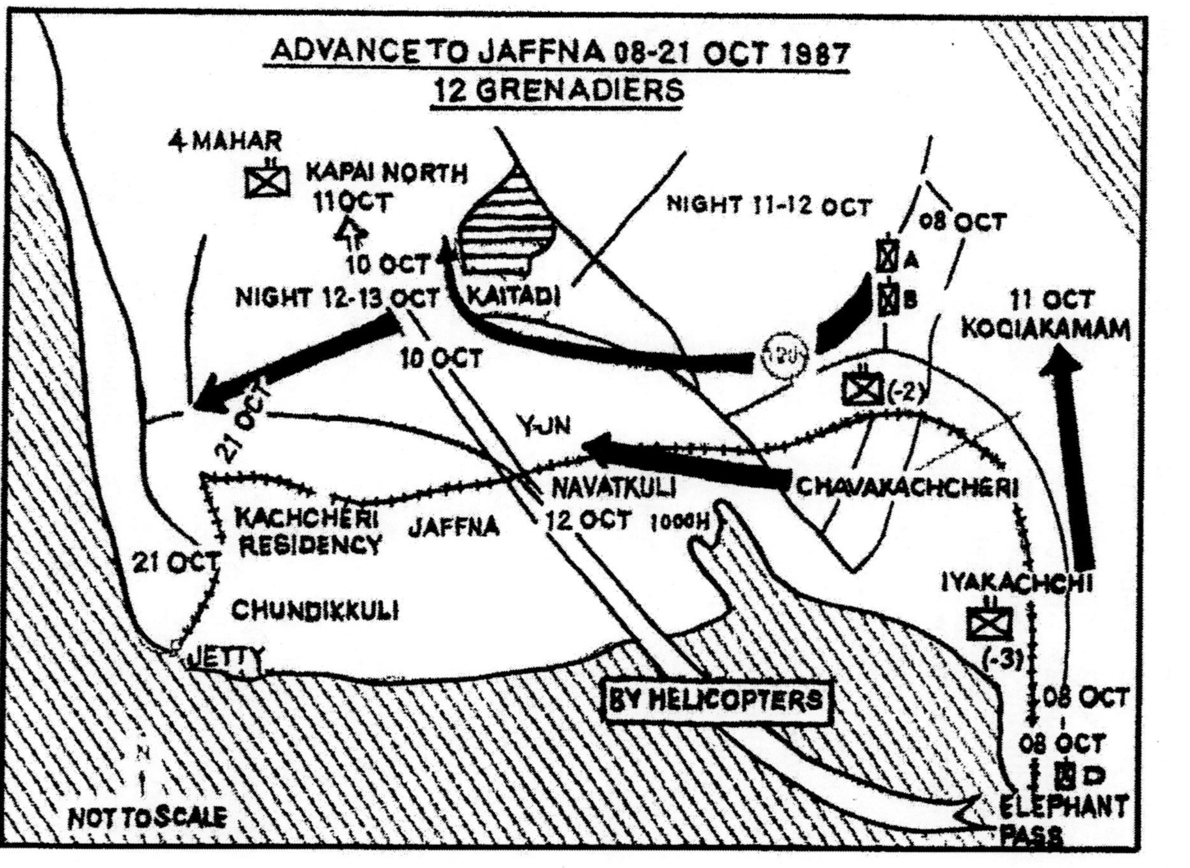
ADVANCE TO JAFFNA 08-21 OCT 1987
12 GRENADIERS
4 MAHAR
KAPAI NORTH
11OCT
10 OCT
NIGHT 12-13 OCT
KAITADI
NIGHT 11-12 OCT
08 OCT
A
B
11 OCT
KOQIAKAMAM
10 OCT
(-2)
21 OCT
Y-JN
NAVATKULI
CHAVAKACHCHERI
KACHCHERI
RESIDENCY
JAFFNA
12 OCT
1000H
21 OCT
CHUNDIKKULI
IYAKACHCHI
(-3)
JETTY
08 OCT
BY HELICOPTERS
08 OCT
D
N
ELEPHANT
PASS
NOT TO SCALE

seven times in their move forward up to Navatkuli. 12 GRENADIERS was actually able to concentrate at Kodikamam by the morning of 11 October. 4 MAHAR was diverted to North Kopai and advanced along the Putur-Kopai axis, where it established contact with Kopai North after midnight and was immediately surrounded by the LTTE. On 11 October 'D' Company 12 GRENADIERS under Major Srinivas was heli-lifted to help extricate 4 MAHAR. The brigade commenced its advance on two thrust lines on the eastern approach with 4 MAHAR on the Putur-Kopai axis, while 12 GRENADIERS advanced along the Navatkuli-Jaffna Fort axis. 'A' Company 12 GRENADIERS under Major Sukumaran advanced towards Navatkuli opening the road axis. The brigade's main body commenced its advance at 1330 hours on 11 October, with 'A' Company 4 MAHAR leading, all in commandeered civil vehicles. Col. Verma, CO 12 GRENADIERS, recounts the experience in the Grenadiers' regimental history, *Right of the Line*:

> I now had a mixed fleet of about 75 vehicles and three APC's in my Battalion column. Having discussed the further course of action with my officers, I decided to move at 0400 hours the next morning.

Regiment, and 11 RAJ RIF is 11th Battalion, The Rajputana Rifles. Only capital letters for individual units are used in this abbreviated system, and the civilian reader should be able to deduce the full names of other units named, but whose names have not been expanded in this note. The layman's English form has also been used together with this where a doubt may arise in a non-military reader's mind whether the whole unit is meant or only elements thereof.

2. Gorkha regiments had retained their pre-1947 naming system, in which ALL regiments had both a number and a name, for example, the Sikh Regiment of today was then "The 11th Sikh Regiment," and its second battalion was therefore, "2nd Battalion, the 11th Sikh Regiment," or "2nd/11 Sikhs" in short. The Gorkha regiments were numbered from 1 to 11, with gaps for the four regiments transferred to the British Army at Independence in 1947, the 2nd, the 6th, 7th, and the 10th Gurkha Rifles. India's Gorkha regiments are the 1st (1 G.R.), 3rd (3 G.R.), 4th (4G.R.), the 5th Gorkha Rifles (Frontier Force) [5 G.R. (F.F.)], 8th (8 G.R.), 9th (9 G.R.), and the 11th (11 G.R.), each with several battalions of its own.

At about 2230 hours, while thinking about the none too happy situation, and as commander of this assortment of sub-units, it occurred to me that the LTTE may not be very effective at night. I decided to march the column immediately. I placed one company on either side of the road and ordered them to carry out speculative firing whenever they were in doubt, thereby prompting the LTTE to blow off their mines prematurely. While passing through Chavakcheri, we blew off the street lights to avoid aimed fire by the LTTE. The battalion was able to make it to Navatkuli by 1000 hours on 12 October.

*Night 11/12 October: The Heli-borne Operation*

The aim was to strike at the nerve centre of the LTTE, achieve surprise and to capture the top leadership of the LTTE, which was functioning from a particular building in Kokkuvil. The plan was to heli-land a para-commando company to secure the landing zone (LZ), which was the Jaffna University football field. Thereafter a company of 13$^{th}$ Sikh LI was to land in successive waves and take over the defence of the LZ. The Para Commandos were then to conduct the raid on the LTTE HQ building, return to the helipad, and wait for the link up by 72 and 91 Infantry Brigades. The operation was launched on night 11/12 October after meticulous planning and aerial reconnaissance of the target area.

Five Mi-8 helicopters were initially made available for the mission. 'D' Company 13 SIKH LI were to land after the Para Commandos, relieve them at the LZ and take over the security of the LZ. Thereafter the Battalion HQ and 'C' Company 13 SIKH LI were to land at the secured LZ. The five helicopters were to complete the landing in fourteen sorties. 'D' Company, the first company of 13 SILH LI to go in, were allotted all the five Mi-8's. As per the Regimental History of the Sikh Light Infantry, the plan was as follows:

"The Battalion *(13 SIKH LI)* (actually two companies) was to land by helicopters at 2.30 a.m. on the 12$^{th}$ in the Jaffna

University area at the LZ secured by the Para Commando Team *(the equivalent of an infantry company)*. On landing of 'D' Company, the commandos were to be relieved of their LZ securing task. The remainder of the Battalion *(i.e, one company and Battalion HQ, plus supporting elements)* was to build up on 'D' Company by helicopters. The Commandos were to seek and destroy the LTTE HQ in the vicinity of the University campus. The Battalion (less two companies) was then to link up with the 10 Para Commando Team, mop up the area and destroy the LTTE remnants by first light 12 October 1987. 72 Infantry Brigade with the Gorkha battalion was to advance on the main axis Palali-Jaffna at 6 p.m. on the 11$^{th}$ and link up with the 13$^{th}$ (less two companies) at the Jaffna University area by 6 a.m. on 12 October. After link-up, the Brigade with one and a half battalions now under command was to flush out the LTTE from the entire area and destroy them in day operations on 12$^{th}$ October.

At 6 p.m., the Battalion, or what there was of it on the ground, viz, two weak companies, learnt from the Brigade Commander who was about to leave with the link-up force of 4/5 Gorkha Rifles (FF) that the 10 Para Commando Team was to take off at 11 p.m. that day (11$^{th}$) from the Palali airfield and secure the designated LZ. 'D' Company of the 13$^{th}$ was to follow in five Mi-8 helicopters and relieve the Commando Team which was to capture the political HQ of the LTTE. The battalion HQ and 'C' company were to land at the secured LZ. Thereafter the two-company-strong 13$^{th}$ was to capture the military HQ of the LTTE at Jaffna University by first light of the 12$^{th}$ – all in one night within hours of landing."

The first wave of the Para Commandos took off at 10.30 p.m. The main body of the Para Commando team followed at 15 minutes past midnight on night 11/12 October (00.15 hours on 12 October). At 1 a.m. on the 12$^{th}$ the first helicopter of 'D' company took off.

The Regimental History of the Sikh Light Infantry describes what happened:

"As soon as the first wave of the commandos landed at the LZ, they realized that they were under heavy but inaccurate small arms fire. They positioned themselves to protect the LZ from physical assault. The second wave could not locate the LZ and did not land. The first wave of the helicopters went back to the airfield and the first load of the 13th Sikh Light Infantry emplaned. At this stage Wg. Cdr. Sapre learnt that the second wave could not deliver the load. He asked the pilots of the second wave to wait at the airfield and himself took the second load of the platoon of the 13th which was 30-strong. The platoon carried one MMG detachment and one ton of mortar ammunition. Mortar ammunition was given priority over manpower despite the earlier decision to send maximum troops. Since ammunition took time to unload, the helicopters received many bullet hits whilst waiting. Wg. Cdr. Sapre went back and brought the remaining commandos despite the fire at the LZ."

Between 2230 hours (10:30 PM) on 11 October and 0230 hours (2.30 AM) on 12 October they landed 103 commandos of 10 PARA CDO under Major Sheonan Singh, and 30 men of 'D' Company 13 SIKH LI, comprising one JCO and 28 other ranks (OR) *(approximately an under-strength platoon's worth, but actually comprising the available men of one platoon and one MMG detachment)*, and their company commander, Maj. Birendra Singh in the first wave of the infantry company. By this time the helipad was under intermittent fire which the commandos could not silence. Three helicopters were hit by small arms fire, and the Air Force expressed their inability to fly any more sorties, and therefore the heli-landing of the rest of the Sikh LI company could not be proceeded with. The company commander was stuck on the ground at the LZ (Landing Zone) with less than one-third of his command. *(An infantry rifle company at full strength has about 130 effective men for such a situation, organized into three platoons and supporting elements plus a small HQ)* This information could not be conveyed to the Sikh LI platoon, as its radio set had been damaged. The commandos, who were in HF radio communication, could have given them the information, but by then they had moved ahead to carry out their mission.

The Sikh Light Infantry's Regimental History elaborates: "The Para Commandos, on their HF link, learnt that the helicopters were not airworthy. When orders were sought from Division HQ, there was no staff officer present to monitor the progress of the landings. There was no alternate plan either. The GOC of 54 Infantry Division, after discussion with the C.O. of the 13th (who was then held up in his move forward on the ground), ordered at 3 a.m. that the team of Para Commandos should proceed to raid the LTTE HQ as planned earlier, and the Company HQ and elements of 'D' Company should stay behind at the LZ and await link up.

Maj. Sheonan Singh, the Team Leader and officiating Second in Command of 10 Para Commandos, pointed out to the general that on daybreak, no force of any magnitude would be able to hold the open patch of ground surrounded by buildings which were occupied by the LTTE. But he was overruled."

Gen. Harkirat has said that apparently the commandos got into the nearby buildings, and asked the Sikh LI company commander to move his men into cover. He apparently said, "No, no, my commanding officer is going to come. So I must meet him here." Maj. Birendra Singh was obviously sticking to the plan of the rest of his battalion linking up with him at the LZ.

With no more helicopter lift available, the remaining troops of 13 SIKH LI ('C' Company and 'D' Company less the one platoon at the LZ) were ordered to join the link-up force and move in six 3-ton vehicles. They left Palaly at 1.30 a.m. (12th). They were to follow 4/5 G.R. (F.F.) to Jaffna which was just over 19 km away.. In the meantime, the LTTE had taken up positions and established blocks to prevent the move forward of the vehicles of 13 SIKH LI. By the time these blocks were removed and contact established with the Gorkhas, it was already 6.45 a.m. But the Gorkhas were not near Jaffna, having been held up at Urelu, north of Urumparai.

As quoted in *Rediff.com*, Gen. Harkirat Singh had this to say about the situation at the time: "I planned with nine helicopters. I needed nine helicopters to land the troops. When the hour came, when the flight had taken off to mark the landing zone (LZ), the next flight had taken off to land the people to secure the LZ, I am told, 'Sorry, helicopters are not available hereafter.'"

He asked the Air Force why the helicopters were no longer available. He says he was told, "They have gone to the east, there is some exercise going on." "But my requirement was nine helicopters, it was accepted by [*Lieutenant General*] Depinder Singh. [*Major General A S*] Kalkat had confirmed that our plans are approved. And now you are saying the helicopters are not available? It is too late!" Maj. General A. S. Kalkat was then MGGS (Major General, General Staff or MGGS for short), Southern Command, and not directly in the chain of command, but was the OFC's principal operations staff officer in Gen. Depinder's other role as Southern Army Commander) "It was too late for an operation: half on the ground, half in the air. Bad luck. But that chap of a major who landed there in the third flight.... Five flights went in, he landed in the third. Out of the five, one had a hole in it, so it never came back. But our aircraft support at the last minute was called off. In place of nine helicopters, we were given five and four in the second sorties."

With the arrival of Indian troops at his HQ, Prabhakaran sent out a message to all LTTE radio stations that the LTTE HQ was under attack, and that he might not be able to escape. In Gen. Harkirat's words, "At that time Prabhakaran said, "I have had it, I am not going to survive." We had surrounded his headquarters. All the commandos were behind the back. And we were very happy because this intercept was taken by the Sri Lankans. The Sri Lankans were our interceptors, incidentally. We had no interception set-up, everyday, every morning we used to get intercepts from the Sri Lankan Army. And we had a good rapport with the Sri Lankan people; they were ready to give us all intercepts."

The commando company under Maj. Sheonan Singh moved off at 3.45 a.m. to carry out their mission, but at this stage they allowed themselves to be misled by a local whom they had apprehended, and who "guided" them off their intended target. As daylight arrived they found themselves under observed fire, but they managed to hold off the LTTE till nightfall, when they managed to break contact. "The Para Commandos got involved in their battle in the built-up area north of Kokkuvil railway station at a distance of 600 to 800 m from the LZ as the crow flies. The radio link between the Para Commandos and Maj. Birendra Singh snapped at 6.30 a.m. of the 12th. Thereafter, the Commandos heard MMG fire from the LZ area till about 11 a.m.," notes the Sikh Light Regimental History.

After daylight on 12 October, the Sikh LI platoon put up a most gallant fight from the football ground. However, by noon on 12 October, Maj. Birendra Singh and his men of the Sikh LI had run out of ammunition and so he had ordered a bayonet charge. One man, Sepoy Gora Singh, was wounded and captured. Gen. Harkirat adds, "Prabhakaran came there and kicked one chap. 'Let him survive to tell the story, he said.' All the others were killed. 29 people lay dead." The bodies of the killed were put on public display at a temple "in tribal style," as per M.R. Narayan Swamy, and burnt after being doused with oil.

Six commandos were killed and nine were wounded. The following personnel were killed:

| *13 Sikh Light Infantry* | *10 Para Commando* |
|---|---|
| Major Birendra Singh | Naik Babu Lal |
| Subedar Sampuran Singh | Naik Ganga Ram |
| Havildar Ajit Singh | Naik Lakhmi Singh |
| Havildar Swaran Singh | Naik Umesh Pandey |
| Havildar Kashmir Singh | Naik Manohar Singh Rathore |
| Lance Havildar Sher Singh | Paratrooper Manuwa Kujur |
| Naik Surjit Singh | |
| Naik Gurmail Singh | |
| Naik Mukhtiar Singh | |

Naik Satwinder Singh
Lance-Naik Hira Singh
Lance-Naik Manjit Singh
Lance-Naik Darshan Singh
Sepoy Lal Singh
Sepoy Ranjit Singh
Sepoy Kuldip Singh
Sepoy Jarnail Singh
Sepoy Sohan Singh
Sepoy Gurdial Singh
Sepoy Gurbax Singh
Sepoy Gurnam Singh
Sepoy Satnam Singh
Sepoy Joginder Singh
Sepoy Sakinder Singh
Sepoy Bakshish Singh
Sepoy Somnath Singh
Sepoy Harjinder Singh
Sepoy Sukhwant Singh
Sepoy Sukhwinder Singh

The disastrous heli-landed operation was a very poor start to the IPKF's operations.

*72 Infantry Brigade*

72 Infantry Brigade, commanded by Brig. B.D. Mishra, with its HQ and only two infantry battalions, 4/5 GR (FF) under its CO, Lt. Col. I.B.S. Bawa, and 13 SIKH LI less two of its four companies, and part of one armoured (i.e., tank) squadron of 65 Armoured Regiment, which was scheduled to arrive at Palaly on 11th October, actually arrived piecemeal and could be said to have arrived fully by the night 11/12 October. 4/5 G.R. (F.F.) had arrived at Palaly airfield at 10.30 A.M. on 11 October, having been flown in from Gwalior. The Army Commander and OFC, Lt. Gen. Depinder Singh, and GOC 54 Infantry Division were present at the airfield to receive them. The Army

Commander, himself an officer of the 8th Gorkha Rifles, addressed them in Nepali, and informed them that they were *required to go into action the same night.* 13 SIKH LI, commanded by Lt. Col. R.S. Sethi, which was also flown in from Gwalior, was under the impression that they were being flown in for garrison duties. They had previously once, on 23 March 1987, been put on six hours' notice "to move to Colombo, as part of the contingency plan of the army—offensive operations against the Sri Lankan Army. Because of the secret nature of its role, the men were not recalled from leave nor those in the unit briefed. On 1 October, the 13th was informed that it was taken off the role to fight in Colombo.," as given in the Sikh Light Infantry Regimental History. "The battalion had never been told that heliborne operations were in the offing within hours of landing in Sri Lanka." The two missing Sikh LI companies had been diverted to Agra in northern India when the aircraft carrying them developed some technical fault. It was planned for this brigade to advance on the axis Palaly-Amparai-Urumparai-Kondavil-Jaffna. The Brigade Commander got his orders at about 4 p.m. The brigade was ordered to commence its advance just two hours later.

The *History of the 5th Gorkha Rifles (Frontier Force),* Vol. III, 1858 to 1991, tells the story of the advance by 4/5/G.R. (F.F.):

> "The task given to the Commanding Officer was to link up with a Sikh Light Infantry battalion and a platoon of the Para Commandos which were near Kondavil to the south. The link-up was to be effected by 2 a.m. the next morning.
>
> The Colonel was told that the civilians were not to be fired upon, and were to be treated with due civility. The troops soon learnt that the LTTE dressed like the civilians and were difficult to identify. Though many of them spoke English, they refused to converse in that language, or any language except Tamil, making the task of the Gorkhas difficult. Since no serious opposition was expected, all this did not matter. The battalion was issued four radio sets, one for each rifle company, just before leaving for its task.

The order of march was 'C' Company (Maj. A. Varghese), 'A' Company (Maj. A.D. Gardner), Battalion Headquarters, 'D' Company (Maj. N.J.D. Singh), and 'B' Company (Lt. Raj Sinha).

The Battalion commenced advance at 6.30 p.m. from Vasavilan school area on the main road towards the south-west. After about 4 kms., 'C' company reached Punnalaikadduvan where heavy fire came in the direction of the company from one of the houses. Maj. Varghese sent one platoon behind the house and charged it with another. He caught some LTTE men, and a search of the other houses yielded some land mines and explosives.

'A' Company of Maj. Gardner, which was closely following the leading company and nearly parallel to it, also came under fire from the village school building. This fire was so heavy that Gardner put in a request for tanks to neutralize it. He then surrounded the village, while 'D' Company of Maj. N.J.D. Singh established a road-block and acted as reserve for 'A' Company. Maj. Gardner then set about clearing the school building, and the houses in that village, one by one. It was during this operation that a land mine exploded and the 4/5$^{th}$ suffered its first casualties. Rfn Ganesh Bahadur Thapa was killed, Maj. Gardner was wounded in the leg, and so were three other ranks. Gardner had to be evacuated to Palali. Maj. Randhir Singh, the *Vazir*, took charge of 'A' Company.

The advance was resumed, this time with 'D' Company of Maj. N.J.D. Singh taking the lead. The next village on the main road was Urelu. In the meantime, Maj. A. Varghese, who talked to the men in Tamil, was fired upon as he left a group which he thought consisted of civilians. To his utter surprise, a girl had fired at him and wounded him in the shoulder. As he was evacuated, Sub. Bhaira Singh Gurung took over his company. By 4 a.m. (12 October) all the four companies had reached within one kilometre of Urelu.

Colonel Bawa once again put in a bid for tanks as the battalion had suffered a number of casualties due to unanticipated opposition."

*Operations on 12-13 October 1987*

The Sinhalese were overjoyed to have the Indian Army fighting the LTTE, since it appeared that India had taken over their fight for them. Sinhala politicians expressed snide satisfaction that the "old fox" Jayawardene had outsmarted the "cub fox" Rajiv Gandhi and got him to neutralize the Tamil separatists.

All three brigades advanced against stiff opposition, similar on each axis of advance. All cross roads were strongly held by LTTE occupying fortifications inside buildings dominating the area. The bunkers built inside the houses were very strongly constructed, and afforded excellent observation and fields of fire. The IPKF was provided totally inadequate intelligence about the LTTE's capabilities in terms of weapons, quality of training and motivation, their ability to improvise ranging from claymore mines to huge underground mines containing 100 kg of high-explosive, capable of blowing entire trucks and infantry combat vehicles into the air and killing all their occupants, detonated from a safe distance at the precise time. The IPKF was not even aware that the LTTE had designed and was producing and using its own 155 mm mortar, the "Kutty Sri." *(For comparison, the Indian Army's own mortars are of 61 mm at the infantry rifle platoon level, of 81 mm, with an approximate maximum range of 5 km, at the infantry battalion level, and of 120 mm, employed by the artillery.)*

Up to 13 October, the use of civilian crowds as a human shield continued to be used by the LTTE, slowing down the rate of advance.

*Advance of Tank Troop of 65 Armoured Regiment*

Maj. Anil Kaul of 65 Armoured Regiment continues his narration of the induction of his regiment's tanks: "Three interesting incidents took place in the next few hours. The first was an altercation between me and a staff officer from IPKF HQ. He was very upset when I showed my inability to provide planks for loading the tanks into the aircraft. They were just not part of my kit. The second involved the sudden sickness of the senior-most junior commissioned officer (JCO) of the squadron. He complained of stomach gripes and vomiting blood. I saw red. The real reason was that he seemed to have become "yellow." He also had in his custody a fair amount of imported goods to be carried back—these belonged to the actual squadron commander and therefore could not be left unattended. I just asked him to disappear and not show his face again or I would shoot him.

"The third incident clearly etched in my mind was the crowd of civilians at the gates of the airport. One initially thought they were just curious onlookers watching the 40-ton behemoths being loaded into a large bird. It turned out, however, that they were political party activists carrying banners calling us "THE INDIAN TAMIL KILLING FORCE." Some even threw stones at us. I distinctly remember a man in traditional *lungi* and shirt with dark glasses leading this crowd, exhorting them to make their sloganeering heard.

"Rather unpleasant, going to battle in a foreign country being heckled by your own compatriots. Loading over, we flew into the great blue yonder at exactly 8.30 a.m. on 12 October 1987.

"As we landed at Palali in Sri Lanka, we saw on the taxi track a couple of Sikh soldiers sitting amidst a pile of tents dumped on the side. The tanks were unloaded at the airfield amidst the din of other aircraft landing and taking off, as also definite explosions in the vicinity. The scene seemed rather surreal, and no one could have been in doubt that it was a battle zone. I was whisked away to the divisional HQ of 54 Infantry Division and ushered on straight to the GOC in the form of Maj. General Harkirat Singh of the Brigade of Guards.

"Incidentally, he had been my Senior Instructor at the Staff College, Wellington, a few years ago. He met me warmly and said to no one in particular, "Now my old student has come with his tanks, he will break the LTTE's back." I thanked him for his kind words of praise and asked him for my orders. He replied rather incoherently though the words have haunted me ever since. Rocking back and forth in his chair, he said in Punjabi, "I was sent to keep the peace. Suddenly they expect me to fight a war."

"A case of history repeating itself, that the best of plans are never executed once the first shot is fired. This is so as the enemy will not function as you presume he will. The Colonel General Staff *(Colonel GS)*, an officer called Pathania, if I remember correctly, cursorily briefed me. It was this briefing that really got me worked up. He told me that the road to Jaffna had been cleared of all opposition—however, I was to be careful of improvised explosive devices, snipers sitting on trees or high buildings along the road, and medium machine guns operating from hides. *Otherwise* the road was clear, he said, an understatement par excellence.

"I then met Lt. Col. Sushil Gupta, whom I knew from a posting in Lucknow. He offered me breakfast, my last meal for the next five days, gave me instructions that mattered, and set about arranging a map and a radio set. The map turned out to be a photocopy of a tourist map of Jaffna district—the radio set was to be provided by the brigade I was to join. Pleasantries over, I walked across to my tanks, being prepared for battle. I looked around for the third one which had been flown in the night before. To my horror, I was told that it had been ordered to move alone, against all covenants of the teaching and practice of armoured warfare.

"The last attempt made by me to get clearance from my CO was from the HQ of 54 Infantry Division at Jaffna to HQ of 36 Infantry Division in Trincomalee. I was told by the Colonel GS of 36 Division, Jagdish Chander, that the CO and the squadron commander had boarded an IAF flight from Trincomalee to Agra, as presumably the squadron commander had to proceed on casual leave and the CO was keen to revert to his command in the hinterland rather than oversee the impending operations. I had no one to look to except my own judgment. I took the plunge.

"One tank was leading the advance of an infantry brigade. I was left with two tanks. Under these circumstances, two tanks out of a structured troop of three, one without its commander (he was bringing the leftover ammunition in another aircraft), no radio set for communication directly with the controlling HQ, no possible artillery support to be banked upon and to cap it all, the CO and the original squadron commander winging their way home, operating under commanders one had neither met nor rehearsed with, in a foreign country. Just the orders: "Assist 72 Infantry Brigade for the establishment of a firm base for the capture of the LTTE HQ in Jaffna University."

"We offloaded all the extra items of baggage and other effects that a tank crew perforce has to carry even in battle, among them a 50-gallon water container, cleaned the guns and readied them for use. The T-72 carries a 125 mm main armament, a 7.62 mm secondary armament and a 12.7 mm anti-aircraft gun mounted on the turret. It has a crew of three, a commander who could be an officer, a Junior Commissioned Officer (JCO) or a non-commissioned officer (NCO), a gunner and a driver to perform the duties associated with their respective tank stations. The armoured corps follows a concept of dual trades training for all its tradesmen so that one can perform the duties of the other if the need arises. Officers and JCOs are trained in all trades and are expected to take them on if required, in addition to commanding units, sub-units, as also their own tanks simultaneously. On that day, though a squadron commander*, I was in charge of a troop of tanks.

"At 10.30 a.m. we exited base with a company of infantry riding piggyback on my tanks, loud cheers from the Sri Lankan troops then confined to barracks, and TV cameras of

*A squadron commander is appointed to command a squadron of 14 tanks, comprising four troops of three tanks each and a squadron HQ.

Doordarshan capturing on film a scene which was repeatedly flashed on TV screens back home, so as to give the impression of the advent of a large body of tanks and troops into the battle for Jaffna. We were to be guided by a military police vehicle till we reached the Palali-Jaffna road. Guidance is normally a case of leading from the front—however, in this case the personnel so detailed had decided, I would say wisely but unethically, that guidance would best be carried out from the rear of our motley column than from the front!

"We soon passed by the burnt out shells of buildings and vehicles, some still burning. Bodies of unknown persons littered the bylanes and a strong smell of decay mixed with cordite permeated the morning air. Driving down a tarmac road was easy and in about an hour we reached the infantry brigade we were to marry up with. They were at a point referred to as the Urelu temple crossing. I saw to my relief the third tank that had moved with the brigade the day before, only to learn with shock that the gunner had been shot in the neck and evacuated.

"I stopped my tank short of it and ordered all personnel riding piggyback to dismount. A quick look around, and I spotted the brigade commander and a few other officers sheltered in a depression in the road. I got out of the tank and stood on the mudguard. A Gurkha JCO came running and advised me not to expose myself as an LTTE sniper sitting on top of the temple was taking a heavy toll of our soldiers. I jumped down and walked across to the makeshift brigade headquarters, where I met the Brigade Major, a course-mate from NDA, M.K. Mandanna, the C.O. of 4/5 Gurkhas, Col. I.B.S Bawa, and Col. S.K. Sharan, the Deputy Commander of the brigade."

*Advance of 18 Infantry Brigade*

4 MAHAR cleared Kopai North and contacted Kopai South, where it encountered intense fire. 12 GRENADIERS could only manage to advance 3 km against fierce opposition.

Immediately on their arrival in Navatkuli at 1000 hours on 12 October, 12 GRENADIERS were ordered to cross the lagoon and enter Jaffna town, and to link up with the Garrison Battalion in Jaffna Fort. Under the CO were only two of his own companies and one company of 4 MAHAR. Col. Verma narrates, in the Grenadiers' regimental history: "There was only one bridge across the lagoon, and it was covered by the LTTE. It started raining heavily that night. Taking advantage of the weather and the darkness, the 12th crossed the lagoon at night and completely surprised the LTTE at daybreak."

*Advance of 91 Infantry Brigade*

5 MADRAS contacted Chunnakam. 8 MAHAR making a wide loop to the West, contacted Navanturai. The sea-borne landing was called off as the naval assault craft (LST's) were not available. 1 MARATHA in Jaffna Fort attempted to probe the area around the fort but any move outside the fort came under intense fire from the built-up areas around the fort, and the battalion was initially unable to gain any ground.

*72 Infantry Brigade*

4/5 GR (FF) continued to advance and established contact with a strong LTTE position at a location named "Pond Crossing." 13 SIKH LI (the battalion HQ and two rifle companies, less a platoon from one of the companies which had been used in the heliborne operation on night 11/12 October), started its advance along the Palaly-Vasavilan-Urumparai axis at 3 a.m. on 12 October, to link up with the rest of 72 Brigade.

The Sikh Light Infantry's Regimental History has this account: "At 8.15 a.m. Sethi received orders to turn right and take a side road to the beleagured platoon. He had received a message from Maj. Birendra Singh in the meantime to the effect that he would hold on till his arrival. "

The side route was through a thickly built up area in which the LTTE cadres had taken up positions. They fired on the small convoy, trying to hold it up. Two OR of 'C' Company sustained bullet injuries. Of these one died. With the LTTE men wearing lungis as the civilians did, it was difficult to distinguish the unarmed civilian from the armed LTTE man. By 1.30 p.m., Colonel Sethi and his men were once again heading south on a road parallel to the main road to Jaffna. They were held up at 2.15 p.m of the 12th, to use the phrase of the unit account, by "a wall of fire" "just 1000 m short of the given RV from enemy mortars, RPG's and automatic weapons. This was the RV given to the 'D' Company platoon earlier. Meanwhile there was no news of the fate of the platoon of 'D' Company with Maj. Birendra Singh"

Meanwhile, to return to Major Anil Kaul (65 Armoured Regiment)'s narration of the events that followed his link-up with the brigade: "As it transpired, further progress of the brigade towards Jaffna had been stopped effectively by a roadblock put up by the LTTE at the crossing of the two roads —the Palai-Jaffna road and the Urumparai-Mathanamadan road. Taking stock of the situation at noon on 12 October 1987, we understood the following:

(a) Troops of the 13 Sikh LI and 10 Para Commando—or what was left of them- landed by helicopter in the Jaffna university campus, were still surrounded by the LTTE.

(b) A company of 4/5 Gurkhas ordered to secure the landing zone for the helicopter landing had never reached the appointed location, and was isolated somewhere between our present location and the university.

(c) The 13 Sikh LI battalion, less two of its companies, sent to contact the heli-borne force, was marooned at a third location.

(d) One company of the battalion sent to contact the rest of the battalion was moved on arrival at the crossroads. It too soon got embroiled in sporadic fighting with the LTTE and was told to hold at a fourth location.

(e) My tank troop was at the cross roads held up by the roadblock.

(f) Most roads and tracks had been possibly mined or wired with booby-traps and these covered by fire.

"A quick meeting of all present was organized in the ditch, and the brigade commander asked me what the possible course of action should be. Interestingly, he had been one of my instructors at Wellington about three years prior, and had waxed eloquent on my poor understanding of tactical situations and problems. I could not help but tell him, "Sir, you are the instructor, and your red pen has cut across a lot of my work. For a change, why don't you tell me what to do? In fact, I have three tanks and they will be used as you order. I don't want posterity to blame me for taking poor tactical decisions."

"The Senior Instructor of my division at the Staff College had been Brig. Harkirat Singh, and one of my tutorial Directing Staff (DS) had been Col. B.D. Mishra — the same officers under whom I would fight a battle. At the Staff College they would teach us the theory of war. On the ground these, these instructors would be taught the practice of unconventional war by the militants of the LTTE.

"The first question he had was whether my tanks could move cross-country or not. I was rather surprised, as the tank is primarily meant to traverse any kind of terrain and not meant to be a Rolls or a Mercedes. Coming from a senior officer it sounded a bit absurd, but then under battle conditions thoughts do tend to get clouded. A small demonstration to show the prowess of the tank under enemy fire was given. The next complaint from the [Brigade] Commander was against the JCO commander of the tank whose gunner had been shot and wounded. Apparently, in the absence of his gunner the JCO refused to fire the guns, claiming it was not his trade. I had to position my tank close to his, fire my main armament at the temple roof from which the LTTE sniper was supposed to be firing, a distance of 600 metres. The militant did not stand a chance, as the roof of the temple was blown off. This was also an indication to the JCO to get his act together and get cracking on the gun controls lest I fire my pistol at him. Thirty seconds later, the JCO's tank belched flame, and I knew that message had gone home loud and clear.

"I suggested to the brigade commander that the only way to break the roadblock was to bypass it and hit the militants manning it from the rear—a typical armour manoeuvre. He agreed, and we moved along the Marthanamadan road. We had covered about a kilometre when I saw the KKS-Jaffna railway line in front of us. A lesson from military history—of jeeps driving on their wheel rims on a railway line in Burma during WW-II—made me turn my tank to the railway line. Fortunately the line was flush with the ground and there were no embankments as is the usual case. We made good progress as the opposition probably never expected anyone, let alone tanks, to drive on a railway line. It also helped us to avoid the explosive devices strewn over all important roads."

The 5th Gorkha's Regimental History records: "The troop of tanks arrived, and the advance to Kondavil was resumed at 3 p.m. (12 October) along a cross-country route nearer to the railway line to the east."

Major Kaul's narration continues: "I was in the leading tank, with the others following me in manner of fire and move, or keeping one foot on the ground. This implied that while my tank halted and provided covering fire, the other two would move ahead, and vice versa. The infantry followed on foot. The promised radio set materialized but was quite useless on a tank, and as a result all the communication between the tank commander and the infantry commander was carried out by means of a runner carrying verbal messages. The saving grace was a high frequency (HF) radio set of the para commandos but using it meant stopping, laying out the aerial and then communicating, hardly conducive to mechanised warfare or mobile battle. Nevertheless, so it was through the day."

Major Kaul says the main gun had to be fired twice, against the GOC's orders.: "Firstly, when were fired at by what seemed a medium machine gun from a beautiful villa flying a white flag. The effect of our fire on the villa was devastating, as I used the armour-piercing ammunition to make a hole in the wall of the house and then used a high-explosive round to blow it up. It was heart-rending to see such a pretty house and possibly its occupants go up in flames. The second time we were fired at was from a water tank next to a bombed-out railway station. Once again the main gun was used with telling effect to bring the water tank down and send its occupants to Valhalla.

"Memorably, a Gurkha soldier who suddenly spotted an LTTE cadre* threw his rifle on my tank and ran after the fleeing militant, unleashing his *khukri* (traditional sword) at the same time. As we turned the corner I saw both adversaries so close that they could possibly smell each other's sweat. The LTTE cadre had an AK-47 rifle in his hand and was a good six inches taller than the Gurkha. The Gurkha, had nothing but his *khukri* and plenty of guts. In a fraction of a second the *khukri* had done its job. The decapitated body of the militant went through its death throes as the Gurkha wiped his *khukri* with the slain militant's *lungi,* picked up his rifle and went on back to marching with the column as if nothing had happened.

"Then, an ever-alert Para Commando on my tank noticed a wire entwined in the bushes of a vineyard my tanks were crashing through. We stopped and two commandos ran the length of the wire leading to an IED and disarmed it. The firing mechanism consisted of two pencil cells of 1.5 volts each.

"As we moved ahead, suddenly Tamil villagers appeared in the middle of a cultivated field. As we looked past them, wondering what they were up to, a burst of medium machine gun fire greeted us from behind the villagers and eight Gurkha soldiers went down, never to rise again. The response was furious from our side, and I say this with no qualms. The firing

*The term "cadre" has been popularized and perhaps legitimized by the print media from the time of the Communist-KMT (now also written GMD) civil war in China which ended in 1949, and is the usual translation of the Mandarin Chinese "Can Pu," which means junior leader, and was usually applied in a political context. It was commonly applied to describe the revolutionary fighters of the Viet Cong in the Vietnam wars of 1945-1973, and is now often applied to al revolutionaries and guerilla, as well as to non-militant functionaries of political parties.

from our side only stopped whezn each militant lay stretched out. In the bargain some innocent men, women and children were unfortunately killed. The meaning of "human shields" sank in with disgust.

"Then I was to have my own hands-on experience of combat; it occurred as we were moving down the railway line and had come to a point which was behind the roadblock. Realizing what we were up to, the LTTE force at the roadblock began moving back and in the process had to cross the railway line. I had enough of being fired at and I saw a number of militants emerging from a gap in the underbrush close to the railway line and crossing it at the same point. I brought my anti-aircraft gun to bear on the gap and fired a burst at a few militants running away. This gun has an effective range of 2,000 metres. The distance I was firing at was roughly 700-800 metres. When 12.7 mm bullets meet human flesh at a velocity upwards of 4500 m/per second, the human body literally splits open like a can of cheese. I counted 16 such bodies as my tank crossed the area of the gap. We had passed two stations on the line by then: Illuvil and Kondavil. While the first was more of ruins than a station, the second seemed to be a defended locality with bunkers and slit trenches. The water tank I had destroyed was at Kondavil and probably was being used as an observation tower. Our progress had been so fast that it had precluded the LTTE from occupying the position to give us a determined fight. We were not sure, however, what other surprises were in store for us, and as a result decided to skirt the railway station.

"The route I had plotted and fed into the tank gyroscope clearly indicated that we were to move westwards along the railway line towards our destination, the campus. It was about 4.30 p.m. when I got a message from the brigade commander to turn and move 90 degrees from the designated line of march, or roughly in a north-west direction. The task assigned in the morning had also changed drastically. Instead of capturing the LTTE HQ we were to assist in the extrication of the beleagured heli-landed force. I re-checked, but was ordered to do as told. We immediately encountered built-up areas, inhabited at that.

"A moving tank seen at close quarters can horrify the bravest of the brave. Not to mention uninitiated civilians who had probably never seen one in their lives. To see not one but three of them together with their guns blazing, accompanied by soldiers armed to the teeth, is something else. The horrified looks on some such poor souls still haunts me. I remember asking some of them to take shelter lest they get hurt. On not heeding my warning, they were greeted with a fusillade of automatic fire from one of the infantry soldiers, which sent them scurrying for safety. One of them unfortunately was not fast enough and came in front of one of the tanks that could not brake in time. His mangled remains mingled with the dust of an unmarked street of the Kokkuvil suburb of Jaffna.

"Brigadier Mishra, under whom this part of the operation was being conducted, had ordered me to turn into built-up areas of Kokkuvil, resulting in restricted movement of the tank, as also reducing the 360-degree traverse of its gun to the field of view. The massive gates of the Nallur Kandaswamy temple were ahead and, unknown to us, the temple premises housed an entire LTTE training camp. I took a decision to clear out of this cul-de-sac and conveyed the same to Dalbir (Lt. Col. Dalbir Singh, CO of 10 Para Commando) and the brigade commander. An order to the driver to move, on the tank intercommunication system, drew no response. All this while, the entire street was awash with the fire of rifles, machine guns, automatic weapons and the occasional hiss of a mortar shell from both sides, while the tank's main 12-cylinder diesel engine was running. As there was no reaction from the driver, I feared the worst, and slid into the cupola to physically tell him to move.

"The fateful shot that had my name on it came soon after. On hearing his confirmation, I was coming out of the cupola when I saw the militant fire at me. The LTTE militant stood 60 metres away, aiming his rocket-propelled gun* at my tank. In a flash, he

*RPG-7, the launcher for the Soviet-design rocket propelled grenade (RPG), a world-wide terrorist and guerilla favourite, like the AK-47 assault rifle.

had fired, but probably having lost his nerve, aimed too low. The projectile hit the left mudguard of the tank, but for some inexplicable reason did not explode. It then hit the side of the main gun and exploded on top of the turret, all in a fraction of a second. I felt I had received a straight right punch, so to say, on the chin. At the same time, Lt. Col Dalbir Singh, the CO of 10 Para Commando, who was standing on the engine deck said, without looking at me, "*Yaar*, what a close shave." The he saw me, and the expression on his face told me that something was very, very, wrong. It was exactly 5.55 p.m. on the steamy evening of 12 October 1987."

13 SIKH LI's main body was not having an easy time of it either, having been held up as narrated earlier. Their Regimental History continues: "The little force suffered casualties due to LTTE fire. Its attempts to break through "the wall of fire" did not bear any fruit. The casualties were treated in a small hut. To add to the misery of the men, the rains lashed the countryside and made evacuation of casualties impossible. Communication with Brigade HQ was disrupted. Radio contact was finally established with the Brigade HQ at 5.30 p.m. and the Brigade Commander apprised of the situation." By then, the Sikh LI column had suffered casualties of 5 OR killed, and 2 JCO's and 25 OR wounded. CO 4/5 G.R. (F.F.), Lt. Col. I.B.S. Bawa, with Maj. Randhir Singh and 'A' Company of the Gorkhas, along with the troop of tanks, established contact with them at 7.30 p.m., loaded the dead and wounded on the tanks and resumed the advance.

Major Kaul continues: "We soon got out of the precarious location we were in, made contact with the 13$^{th}$ Sikh Light Infantry that we were there to rescue, and then moved to an abandoned house on the KKS-Jaffna railway line. The next few hours were spent retrieving the para commandos from Jaffna University, where they had been surrounded by the LTTE."

Major Kaul was seriously wounded on the left arm and blinded in his right eye by the exploding RPG. He remembered thereafter only the sight of the bodies of some of the Indian soldiers they had diverted to rescue hanging from lamp poles,

13 SIKH LI ADVANCE TO LINK-UP WITH
HELI-LANDED FORCE

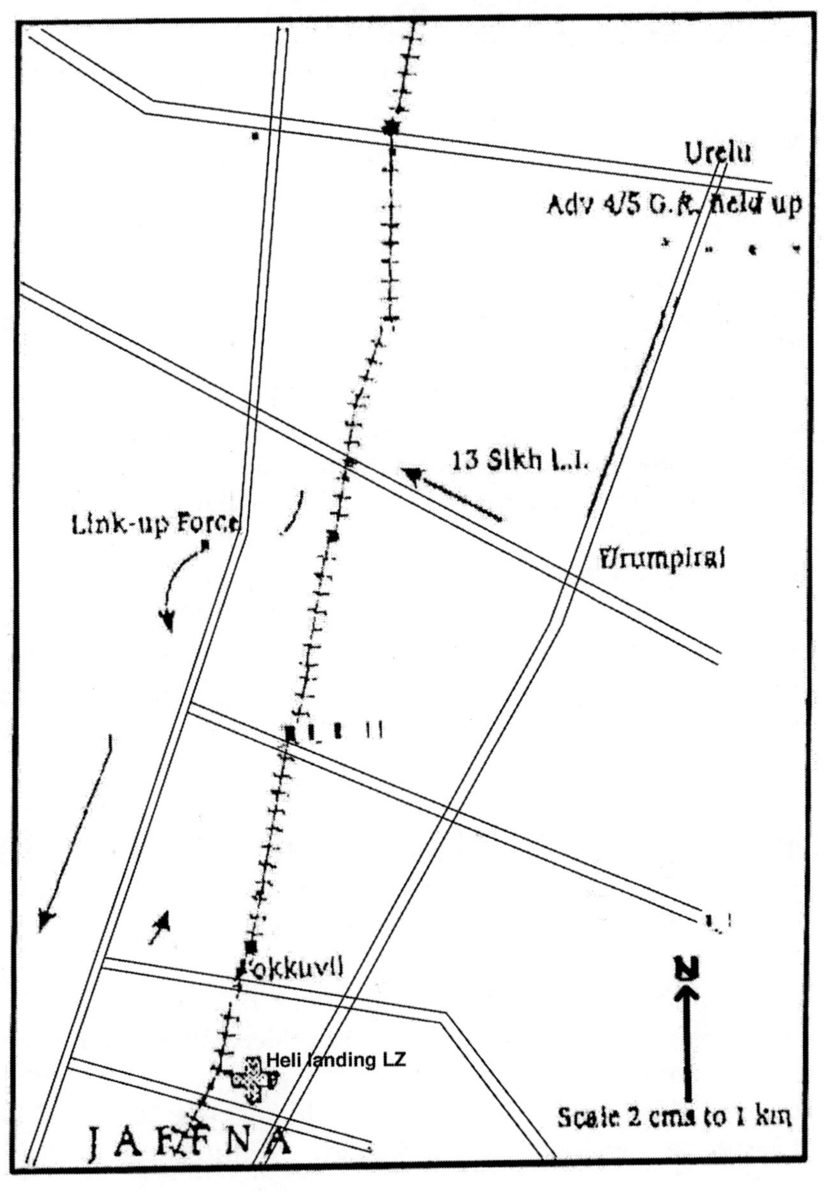

having been put under sedation by the Regimental Medical Officer (RMO) of the 10 Para Commandos.

At 11.30 p.m., the two lost companies of 13 SIKH LI rejoined the main body, and the Brigade Tactical HQ along with C.O., 10 PARA CDO. The Sikh LI Regimental History records "The dead and wounded were huddled into a few mud huts in the rain that did not seem to abate. The Battalion spent the night of 12th/13th in utter misery in the rains. The men had been without food for 48 hours."

*Night 12/13 October: Action at Kondavil*

The 5th Gorkha's Regimental History continues the story: "Lt. Col. Bawa took with him 'A' Company, now under Major Randhir Singh, and a troop of tanks. With this force, he moved towards Kondavil, neutralized the heavy fire from the LTTE men, established contact with the Sikh Light Infantry battalion and the Para Commandos, and rejoined the Battalion which was then near the railway line north of the village. The night was dark, it rained heavily throughout the time this force was out, and it was 4 a.m. of 13 October when this operation was over." The Para Commando team managed to join the link-up forces, being rescued at 4.30 a.m. on 13 October by 'A' Company 13 SIKH LI (which had by then joined the main body), two tanks and some men of 10 PARA CDO.

*13th October*

The 72 Brigade column resumed its advance towards Kokkuivl with 'A' Company 13 SIKH LI as vanguard with two tanks in support. The Para Commando team was contacted and brought into the column by 6.15 a.m.

When the wounded Major Kaul came to, after being sedated the previous evening, his tank gunner filled him in on the events after his receiving his wounds. The Major narrates: "My gunner explained that we had joined up with and relieved the 13 Sikh LI battalion, and moved with them to the university area after I got hit, and recovered most of the Para Commandos, dead, wounded or unhurt. There had, however, been no sign of the platoon of the Sikh LI till we came across their mutilated bodies. Having extricated whoever we could, we moved back to an abandoned house on the railway line only to realize that one of my three tanks had been left behind, bogged down in the clayey soil. Having offloaded the wounded, the other two tanks went back and pulled the third one out in a recovery operation even the best of specialists would have hesitated to undertake in daytime, let alone in the middle of the night and under intermittent fire from the LTTE.

"Brigadier Mishra joined me and inquired about my state. On my querying him as to the means of evacuation, he replied quite straightforwardly the situation as it obtained at the time. The air force had refused to fly their helicopters as some had been damaged during the landings in the university and the spare parts were available only in Chandigarh, which was quite a distance from the battlefield, to put it mildly. The army, ironically, did not have any ambulances to carry its wounded to forward aid posts or field hospitals. A decision was the need of the hour, and I informed the brigade commander that my tanks were leaving for the base at Palali as I had completed the task assigned to me. He was most welcome to put any number of casualties on my tanks, for their evacuation rearwards. I would also take responsibility for running the gauntlet of a 15 km distance infested with LTTE militants.

"I ordered my JCO to move accordingly. Forty-three wounded personnel including me, and 15 dead bodies were carried on my three tanks. They were those who had worn the regimental colours with pride."

The Sikh LI Regimental History notes: "The Brigade resumed its advance but soon had to make a halt as the tail end of the Gorkhas needed to be helped out. This was done by two companies of the 13$^{th}$." The 5$^{th}$ Gorkhas' Regimental History tells the story of the return journey to Palaly. "Orders were received for the whole force to return to Urumparai. The order of march for the return journey was the troop of tanks followed by the Para Commandos and the Sikh Light Infantry with the rear being brought up by the 4/5$^{th}$. The LTTE cadres which had got disorganized due to fire from the tanks and 'A' Company of the 4/5$^{th}$ picked up courage when they saw the entire force pulling back. Once the tanks were a good one and a half kilometers away at the head of the column, they opened up from all sides at the 4/5$^{th}$. They fired from within temples, houses, high ground on the flank—from every vantage point. It was here that the battalion suffered a number of casualties. Sub. Tula Ram Gurung was killed when he charged at a house from where some murderous fire was coming.

"'D' Company of Maj. N.J.D. Singh was at the end of the column. It was surrounded by the LTTE, and was being heavily fired upon. When Lt. Col. Bawa moved towards this company to arrange mortar and air support for it, he was hit in the chest. Bawa, unmindful of the loss of blood, manned the set, and gave the latest situation report to the Brigade Commander. Maj. N.J.D. Singh and his radio operator, Rfn. Ashok Kumar Thapa, too, were killed in the heavy exchange of fire though they took a heavy toll of the LTTE. This left only two officers with the battalion, Maj. Randhir Singh and Lt. Raj Sinha. The 81-mm mortars made a good job of their firepower. The bodies of Maj. N.J.D. Singh and Rfn. Ashok Kumar Thapa were recovered by Sub. Prem Bahadur Thapa at great personal risk.

"It was about 1 p.m. when a Sri Lankan Army gunship came to the rescue of the battalion. It fired rockets from the air on the temple area, and the men could see the LTTE men running away from that area. These became a target for the battalion's mortars. By then, Capt. J.K. Thapa, who was attached to the Brigade Headquarters, arrived with one tank to evacuate the wounded. This tank got bogged down in the mud. A little later two more tanks arrived, and these helped to evacuate the casualties. Lt. Col. Bawa was declared dead when he reached the Field Ambulance. The bodies of Lt. Col. Bawa, Maj. N.J.D. Singh and Sub. Tula Ram Gurung were flown to Sagar."

By approximately 2 p.m., the tanks were back at the Palaly base, from where they had set out about 36 hours before, but it was evening before most of the troops of 72 Brigade had their first meal in 72 hours.

Shekhar Gupta, the well-known and respected newsperson, who reported for *India Today* magazine as Special Correspondent, visiting the sites and interviewing many participants, from generals in Delhi to *jawans* at the battlefields, has called this operation "Commando Assault: The Lost Offensive" in his article of January 31, 1998. He quotes a para commando who said, "For those 18 hours we just prayed and fought. Everything hung by a slender thread." That night is now an inseparable part of Indian military history. Shekhar Gupta adds: "How grave the situation was is evident from the fact that directing the rescue operation was none other than Maj. Gen. Harkirat Singh himself. He was aboard a Chetak helicopter that flew so low as to have a machine-gun bullet go clean through the three-inch space between the seats to which the pilot and the general were harnessed."

Maj. Gen. Harkirat Singh, writing later, was highly critical of the manner in which this operation was handled at levels above those of his Divisional HQ: "I discussed this mission with the OFC, who approved and issued orders from my Command Post to Maj. Gen. A. S. Kalkat to project our plans to the Army Headquarters and obtain additional troops.

"Air support was entirely based on the whims of the Southern Air Command. There was no dedicated air or naval support allotted to the IPKF which I could depend on and plan operations. As such this resulted in the failure of the most talked about helicopter assault of the Para Commandos at Kokkuvil on the outskirts of Jaffna. My Colonel GS, Col. Hoshiar Singh from the Parachute Regiment, was asked to carry out the staff check and to ascertain from the MGGS at the Headquarters, OFC, about the availability of additional troops, the armed helicopters (Mi-24 Akbars), and the heli-lift for the troops assigned to assault the LTTE headquarters.

"The detailed plan for the helicopter assault by 10 Para and 13 Sikh LI at Kokkuvil was placed before the OFC and it was approved. I was informed by the MGGS that the airlift requirement was available and that the mission could go ahead. At this stage I had asked for nine helicopters to carry out the assault. But just prior to the assault, the IAF told me that only five helicopters would be made available for the airlift of troops.

"The Kokkuvil special mission was not accorded priority by the staff at Army Headquarters or Headquarters, OFC. Also they did not impress upon the Air Headquarters the necessity of the heli-lift and the IL-76 aircraft required for the airlift of infantry and tanks. They did not allot the Akbar gunships that would have provided the necessary close support to the troops. Instead the Akbars were diverted to the eastern sector. Also, the link-up combat group, i.e., 13th Sikh LI, the 4th Battalion the Fifth Gurkha Rifles (4/5/G.R.), and the squadron 65 Armoured Regiment for this mission did not get the promised airlift because the Air Maintenance Command had diverted the IL-76 aircraft for maintenance purposes. Therefore, the build-up of the link-up force could not take place and the infantry had to suffer for command failure.

"The build-up of 72 Infantry Brigade and the armoured squadron ex 65 Armoured Regiment did not take place according to the planned schedule intimated to my Headquarters because the transport support was not available. Also, very heavy LTTE firing with RPG's and MMG's prevented the forward movement of troops and thus the link-up with the beleagured 13 SIKH LI men could not be established. As a result of staff and command failure the advance to link up by first light was delayed and therefore success eluded 13 SIKH LI."

*Panic Induction: 41 Infantry Brigade*

Meanwhile 41 Infantry Brigade was told to move from Lucknow, for induction into Sri Lanka. The chaos that followed the sudden move is best described in the words of the then officiating CO of 16 SIKH, Lt. Col. M. K. Gupta Ray*:

* He was a Major at that time.

"On 16 October 1987, a Boeing 737 was flying over the Bay of Bengal at about 1500 hours along the Indian coast-line, keeping some distance away, heading towards the Palali airport east of Jaffna in northern Sri Lanka. The aircraft was carrying troops of the Indian Army, belonging to 16th Battalion, The Sikh Regiment, in short 16 SIKH. They were to form part of the Indian Peace Keeping Force (IPKF) operating in Sri Lanka. This particular aircraft was carrying the Battalion Headquarters and support troops. A similar flight had already left with some troops of the rifle companies.

A few minutes ago I had been sitting in the cockpit with the captain of the aircraft. But now I was back ..."

*Portent of things to come ...*

"Closing my eyes, resting my head on the back-rest of my seat, I tried to recollect everything that had happened in the last 48 hours. Everything happened like a high-speed, action-packed drama. I was still to reconcile to the fact that we were flying straight into the battle zone whereas less than 24 hours ago we were located in Lucknow, our peace station. Our battalion was enjoying a well-earned peace station life after grueling field duties in Kashmir for three years, from 1983 to 1986. We had moved in to Lucknow in August 1986.

"But within five months of our stay, the situation between India and Pakistan turned tense. A very high-level training exercise named "Exercise BRASS TACKS" being conducted in the winter of 1986-87 near India's western borders with Pakistan had snow-balled into a serious situation. Thus in January 1987, with just 48 hours' notice, we were moved out of Lucknow and deployed at Delhi to provide protection. We were also given an offensive task in case of the outbreak of war. Six months later matters normalized. We moved back to Lucknow in July 1987. In this process we lost one year of our peace tenure.

"Now within three months we were on active operational duty again, airborne after being given only 24 hours notice, to take active part in overseas operations in Sri Lanka. I was wondering where our higher direction of war was and what was their strategic thinking and preparation? For a split second the worried and bewildered faces of my wife, eleven-year old son and five-year old daughter flashed through my mind. Things moved too fast and beyond anybody's comprehension. The thing which disturbs one most is the uncertainty and lack of clarity. Both were present in the prevailing situation.

"Only 48 hours ago, I had been sitting in my office going through the daily mail. I was officiating as the Commanding Officer (C.O.) of 16 SIKH, though I was the battalion's Second-in-Command, since the permanent incumbent, Col. A. K. Chatterjee, had proceeded on annual leave only about a week ago, after about one year of active duty, to Kolkata, where his wife and children were staying. Suddenly at about 1215 hours on 13 October, 1987 the phone rang. Somehow, I had a premonition and a eerie feeling that the message I was going to receive would not be a normal one. Something was in the offing. When I picked up the phone, the battalion's Adjutant, Capt. *(now Colonel)* Motilal Kataria, informed me that the Brigade Major (BM) at the Brigade Headquarters, Maj. *(now Brigadier)* Rakesh Sharma was on the line. The BM is responsible for assisting the Brigade Commander in the operational planning, for preparing the Operations Order of the brigade (which routinely comprises three infantry battalions), and in coordinating the operations of the brigade. The Adjutant informed me that the BM had some urgent matter to discuss. I asked him to put me through.

After the initial telephone formalities he straight away came to the point and told me, "Sir, you are aware that the Sri Lanka accord has failed. The existing IPKF is now deeply involved in operational duties. Battles have broken out all over Northern Sri Lanka. We have some task to perform. For that reason the Brigade Commander has called for a meeting at 1600 hrs. The conference will be held in the Ops Room *(Operations Room)*.' I then called the Adjutant over to my office. I told him the situation and asked him to arrange for a conference with the company commanders and all the specialist platoon commanders.

"Our Brigade Commander, Brig. S. S. Mavi *(later Major General)*, who had been commanding our brigade, 41 Infantry Brigade, for more than two years and had been with us under all kinds of trying situations, had been posted out to undergo a long training course in the USSR and had left around 20 September. The designated new Brigade Commander was to come from Ladakh, a difficult field area, where he was waiting to be relieved. During this period Col. S. K. Singh, the Deputy Brigade Commander was officiating as the Brigade Commander.

"I reached the Brigade Headquarters at the given time and was ushered into the conference room. We knew that the "Accord" between India and Sri Lanka had failed and all was not going well. Our IPKF force at Sri Lanka at that time was having a tough time, trying to keep a balanced approach. They were being pressurized by both the Sri Lankan forces and the LTTE to protect them from the other. Apparently the surrender of arms as demonstrated during the peace accord had been a farce and the LTTE renewed attacks on the Sri Lankan forces. When the IPKF tried to restore peace, they were obliged to use force which brought retaliation from the LTTE. It appeared the LTTE had surrendered only a handful of weapons and that too of old vintage. The main bulk of its sophisticated weapons had been retained by them. The role of IPKF had changed to use of force from its initial peace-keeping act. More and more troops were being sucked into the scene.

"Our conference started as scheduled, chaired by the officiating Brigade Commander, Col. S.K. Singh. Two commanding officers were present there, viz., Lt. Col. S. Mukherjee* of 19th Rajputana Rifles (19 RAJ RIF) and I, besides

*In 1987, the Army was changing over from a system of having Lt. Cols. as COs of major units, i.e., infantry battalions and their equivalents in other arms and services, to one of having Cols. as COs. Consequently, some units had COs who were Cols, such as 16 SIKH, and some still had Lt. Cols., such as 19 RAJ RIF. Units which had Cols. as COs were authorized Lt. Cols. as Seconds-in-Command (2ICs), which was to become the case for all units when they were commanded by Cols.

the brigade staff officers, i.e., the (BM), the Deputy Assistant Quarter Master General (DAQMG), the Deputy Assistant Adjutant General (DAAG) etc. The third battalion of the Brigade, 3rd Jats (3 JAT), were to remain back at Lucknow. My premonition was of the morning was right. The conference was related to the Sri Lankan crisis situation. We were given a "brief" on the operational situation of that place which was very sketchy as things were yet to crystallize. It appeared a great deal of embarrassment had been caused to the Indian government. The Indian government was under the impression that they had a firm grip on the situation and Prabhakaran and his men would listen to their advice. The crumbling accord was also feared to have ramifications in Tamil Nadu where people were keenly watching developments and were emotionally involved. The situation was tense and uncertain. Army Headquarters had asked us to stand by and be ready to move to Madras *(now Chennai)* at short notice. We might be required to participate there in Aid to Civil Power to quell the anticipated backlash at Madras. We were asked to get ready accordingly.

"On conclusion of the conference, I left for my Headquarters as my "Orders Group" *(routinely referred to as the Battalion 'O' Group)*, i.e. the rifle company commanders and the specialist platoon commanders, who were to receive my orders, were waiting for me. From a peace station family life things were turning to be quite hot. The situation was unexpected. In case of war one gets a long time to prepare oneself emotionally and professionally. But in this case it came as a sudden knock.

"I explained the situation to my sub-unit commanders. I told them what I knew, and asked them to get themselves and their outfits ready for the task.

"Depending on the task we were to prepare ourselves. Certain preparatory actions were inherent to any task to be undertaken. Our task, Aid to Civil Power, entailed preparation in facing agitated mobs. This involved dividing the troops into various groups for Internal Security (IS) duties, which are designated as "columns", practicing special drills to encounter the mobs to achieve maximum result with minimum force, intensive knowledge about the area and if possible prior coordination with the police and local civil authority. Even for this time was too short. But I somehow had a nagging feeling that all would not end there.

"On that evening of 13 October 1987, the Adjutant handed me the latest parade state. The Parade State is a document which gives the details of people who are on and off parade, meaning available on or for duty, persons on leave, on various courses, temporary duties, participating in various sports events, on various attachments at different places. That particular day, almost three-fourth of the soldiers were out of station on various duties as mentioned above. Out of that, a major strength of two out of the four rifle companies, were away on field firing at Rewa in Madhya Pradesh. Briefly, field firing is a training exercise, where soldiers are taken to a natural type of firing range and made to practice the firing of all the various weapons of an infantry battalion. I gave orders to the Adjutant to send signals everywhere to get as many people as possible back to the unit, and as early as possible. I gave the Adjutant detailed instructions to start the battle procedure, the most important in which was to send an "Operational Immediate" signal to the CO to rejoin from leave immediately. The signals that we send in the army are allotted priorities as per their operational necessity. This one definitely deserved "Op Immediate" status. I returned to my house with the parade state in my hand. It showed me that the strength in the unit was only around two hundred against the battalion full strength of around 850. I could foresee I had a difficult time ahead.

"I had a very restless night. As a soldier I could not share my secret thoughts, the situation and its ramifications, even with my wife. The situation was very hazy. No one knew what was ahead. Why were we going to Madras? If the situation had worsened at Sri Lanka and the existing IPKF was already involved in physical battle, sending our brigade to Madras was sheer madness and a waste of available force. If at all we were to be moved we should have been asked to be prepared for Sri Lanka. I was more concerned with the preparation part. Both these roles i.e., role at Madras and at Sri Lanka, being diametrically opposite, the magnitude of preparation, both physical and psychological, were to be absolutely different. In the first case we were to meet our own brethren who were to vent their ill-feeling against the government for its controversial decision. In the second case, we were to face one of the most experienced forces to be reckoned with in both urban and jungle warfare and militancy. They had been taking on their Government forces head-on successfully for quite a few years. By then, they had developed their own tactics, logistics, administrative concepts, and most importantly, a dedicated force. I was a little disturbed due to two important reasons at our level. Firstly, we were being practically given no time to prepare ourselves for the coming battle. We in the Army generally are trained to fight a full scale war against an army who is visible, can be seen controlled in the battle field and be fought. But fighting against militancy is like fighting against an unseen ghost. This becomes more difficult if the same operation is to be conducted in a foreign country. At Lucknow we were accordingly preparing ourselves to fight our potential enemy somewhere in the western side. But in this case as mentioned before it was almost like fighting an invisible enemy in their area on their terms and conditions. We had no knowledge about who was our adversary, what was their language, what was their modus operandi. All these problems multiplied due to lack of time, training and troops. Three-fourth of our battalion's troops were away on various duties, training and courses. We were not being psychologically prepared for our task. When the army goes to battle the soldier is mentally attuned from the Day One. He, in fact, becomes more emboldened despite the imminent danger, seeing his countrymen and his family behind him, encouraging him. But in this case it was totally a different picture. The country was in a festive mood. Dussehra was round the corner.

"The morning of 14 October broke with the end of fitful, uneasy sleep. I took a fraction of a second to recollect what all had happened on the previous day. The first thing I did was to inquire from the Adjutant and the Duty Officer if there was any fresh message indicating further developments. But there was none. I got ready, had a quick breakfast and went to the office. I started inquiring about the progress of our two companies on field firing, as to how far away were they were from Lucknow. I wanted to get my men withdrawn from the local station duties and also started attending to a host of other administrative points. A few of the important points were, who all were to be left behind as Rear Party to look after our unit property, how to dispose of so many families who had came to this peace station to stay with their respective husband, father or son. Certain actions known as the Mobilization Plan are laid out when the whole army goes to battle. But we never faced such a situation at such a short notice; not even 24 hours were given for preparation.

"I also inquired from the next senior officer to me in the Battalion, who had to take over many of my duties and function as my Second-in-Command (2IC), and the Adjutant about the progress of preparations for the task we were assigned. As I mentioned before, preparation for "aid to civil power" had different connotations. There, show of force was more important than the use of force. The use of automatic weapons is normally forbidden.

"The day rolled on uneasily. We had a series of meetings at the Brigade Headquarters followed by more at our unit headquarters. In order to explain to my troops what was happening, why the situation was changing so fast and what was our task, I held a *Sainik Sammelan,* an address to the soldiers. There I explained as clearly as possible what was happening and what we might be expected to do. From the stillness one could sense how deeply worried each soldier was. They had multifarious problems on their hands. They were about to go, for an indefinite period to a far away place, for a task they were not clear and to face an adversary they did not know. At the same time they were so uncertain about their families. They did not know what to do with them. They were not sure whether their stay out would be long or short, they did not know whether, they should wind up their family from here and send them home. And most importantly: Was it going to be a bloody confrontation or a quiet stay as a part of IPKF? No body had an answer.

"The situation with regard to officers in my unit was not too bright either. An infantry battalion is authorized 19 officers. Our permanent Commanding Officer, Col. A.K. Chatterjee was on leave, as mentioned earlier. The officer functioning as my 2IC, Maj. Chowdhary, was in a 'low medical category' and had been declared unfit to go into a battle field. Many of the officers were on leave, courses, temporary duties or training. On that day a large number of officers were not available. The officers who were to accompany me were Maj. Ramchandran, Maj. N. C. Bhatt, Maj. Govind Sisodia, Capt. Padmakumar, Capt. M. L. Kataria, Lt. Nagar , and Lt. Venkatesh. The saving grace was that I found grit and determination on the face of each officer and soldier.

"At about 1.30 pm I enquired from the Adjutant if there were any further mails, or information from the brigade headquarters on the latest developments. So far we were being told that we might have to move either by rail or by air, and to be ready to move at short notice. Even a layman would realize how unprofessional the instructions were. The load tables prepared for train and air journeys are vastly different. There is no match. One would easily understand that a train would carry the entire load without any problem, whereas planes had a limited capacity. In case of air move the load table will have to be very restricted and there should always be a follow up logistic plan to move the rest of the left out load to the unit at the earliest. Under that situation with divergent instructions we did not know what to do, how to do it, what to carry and what to leave. We also did not know how much time period would be given to us to prepare. Anyhow, I was winding up my files and preparing to go home. It was about 2 pm when my phone rang. The BM was on the line. He told me that the task had been changed. We were to fly straight in to the battle zone at Jaffna in northern Sri Lanka. The mode of transportation was aircraft. We would be intimated the number of aircrafts allotted to us and the time of their arrival! My premonition came true. I had a nagging feeling as I mentioned before that our task would not end at Madras. We were going to be involved in much larger activities. I did not know it would come so fast. But this was not following the basics of planning and mobilization. I had lost precious hours of training and preparation. I was preparing for Aid to Civil Power as we were to be inducted to Madras to help quell the anticipated backlash there. How could we move into a full-fledged battle, that too most unconventional, in a foreign country, without any previous training? Such kind of battles are not conventional. They need a completely different kind of training and preparation, both physical and psychological, to fight. They need months of training whereas we did not get even a day! My soldiers were not even aware that they were going to be at the crossroads of life and death within a couple of hours without any preparation and logistic support? The unit did not even have the half of its strength present. I remembered that the Indian Army took nine months to cross swords with Pakistan after the crackdown on the Bengalis in the then East Pakistan on 25 March 1971, despite all the provocation and pressure. The Indian Army was launched into battle on 3 December, that too after India was attacked by Pakistan. Here we were moving into a totally new environment within less than 24 hrs and the soldiers were not aware even a couple of hours before being airborne as to what their task was!

"I was all the time wondering as to whether our higher echelon at all levels had lost their minds. Anyway, I had passed this fresh order to the Adjutant and also asked him to keep check on the progress of the two rifle companies who were on their way back. They were perhaps wondering as to what had happened, as we had a similar experience only a couple months back during "Exercise BRASS TACKS." That time also we were rushed back from the same field firing range at Rewa in Madhya Pradesh. That time I was with the field firing group. We drove continuously for 48 hours to reach Lucknow and another 48 hours for Delhi as if hell would befall us for any delay. The order was that the co-driver sitting beside the driver should hold a pin in order to prick the driver out of drowsiness should he feel sleepy. But there was no order if the co-driver felt sleepy! I also instructed the Adjutant to tell all the sub-unit commanders to prepare their air load-tables under the present situation and put them up to me at 1800 hours.

"Air transportation is a very difficult proposition for a standard battalion as the equipments and the organizational structure are different. Some units like parachute battalions are designed and structured for this. In case of a standard battalion like ours, a lot of re-adjustment is required. However every unit has all types of load tables prepared as a standard practice, and we also had one, but despite that, each time the load-table has to be modified as per the obtaining situation. The present situation was absolutely different, we could make no head or tail of the orders and no one could possibly know what was coming next. Besides, since the army loads are not standardized sophisticated loads, they contain all kinds of awkward-shaped loads, from arms and ammunition in cases, and vehicles, to rations in sacks, generally defence service transport aircraft are allotted.

"Immediately after my lunch I returned to my office at 1500 hrs and went through the mail. But there was nothing so important, which would need my immediate attention. Since it was an operational situation and all types of messages were being received and assessed, we started logging all kinds of incoming and out-going messages. After going through the mail I went around the unit lines and was happy to see that each individual was busy in preparing as best as he could within this shortest possible available time. I went to each group of soldiers, talked to them and tried to enthuse their spirits which was already high despite all the odds against them. Sikhs are known for their high spirit under all circumstances. This I had witnessed during 1971 Indo-Pak war also. Almost each one had the same unspoken question as to what was this all about. Where were we going and for what? After my round I again sat with my sub-unit commanders, specialist platoon commanders, the Adjutant and the Quartermaster to review the whole situation. Only a couple of hours were left to depart for an unknown destination and task. I tried to explain the situation once again, told them categorically that things were going to be tough. We would have some hard fighting ahead. I also told them to get ready as early as possible, check and recheck the details. Time was at a premium. While this was in progress a messenger came and informed us that the two companies which were on their way back from the Rewa field firing range had arrived. This was great news. I looked up and thanked God and prayed for His blessings. I told the messenger to ask the company commanders to come straight to the conference room for briefing. Within about 10 minutes Maj. Ramcharan and Maj. Govind Sisodia entered the room. I quickly explained the whole situation to them and told them about our impending task. I also told them that the time was at a premium and they should not waste any time, get cracking up and be ready as quickly as possible. It was about 7 pm. Time was running out very fast. I again contacted the BM to know about the latest. I was told that there was no further information till then. After that I left for my home asking the Adjutant to ensure the preparations continued.

"My home was not very far so I dismissed my vehicle and told the driver to also get ready, and started walking towards my home. While walking back I started evaluating the entire situation and realized what a difficult situation I was in with my troops. I could give only a few hours to my troops to get ready for an operation in a foreign country about which we had almost no clue. I knew nothing about the enemy, their tactics and terrain condition of the area we were to operate, what sort of the operation it would be and for how long. Most of us were living with our families by virtue of being in a peace station. What about their families? What about their payments at the end of the month and various other administrative problems those are associated under this condition? Most important of all was the psychological preparation of the troops. I could see their faces were blank. When we go into war preparation is always for a long period and we all know about who is our enemy. We study their tactics, their weapons, their capabilities and limitations, their past history thoroughly. There is more to fighting than just pressing triggers!

"On reaching home I told my wife about the developments. I also spoke to my children, son and daughter, who were 11 years old and five years old respectively. My daughter was obviously too young to understand the gravity of the situation. My son did realize to some extent as he already had lived separately away from me for many years at his young age. The time was about 7.30 pm. I started mentally reviewing the sequence of events and progress of preparation. I really did not know where to start and where to finish. The development of the situation was too fast for me to comprehend. It was like a fast forward movie. The scene changes before one understands what has happened. While I was "dreaming" my orderly came and asked as to what did he have to pack for me? I then realized that the battle preparation was applicable to me too! While I was giving him the necessary instructions, my wife came and told me that our TV had packed up. Smoke was being emitted from the sides of the picture tube. It needed to be repaired. I thought "My God it could not have come at a more appropriate time than this!" Anyway I thought this must be repaired or given to the shop for repair so that she has company to keep and remain abreast with the news on what was happening in Sri Lanka. I told her to get ready. Later events would show how prophetic was my thinking. After getting ready we were about to leave for the market when the telephone rang. I found the BM was at the other end. He said

"Sir, the aircraft for the fighting troops will start arriving on 16 October at 0400hrs onwards at the Lucknow Airport. Exact details of allotment would be intimated later." It meant there was no time left for further preparation and I did not know even couple of hours before departure as to what strength I would be able to take along with me. I did not notice that my wife was intently watching my expression. No sooner I replaced the telephone she asked me if it was possible for me to go to the market at that time. I got emotionally charged and replied that was the only time available. There would be none tomorrow as we were leaving at 0400 onwards for Sri Lanka by air. I immediately rang up the Adjutant, gave him the latest information, asked him to prepare the Order of March and issue it immediately. Troops were to reach the airport as per the Order of March. The head of the first column must reach the airport by 0300 am and the tail must wind up by 0330 hrs. I also told him that I was going to the market for a while and after I return from the market I shall be in the office, where he should meet me.

"Our first column reached the airport sharp at 0300 a.m. By then I learnt that we were being given Boeing 737s for troop carriage and AN 32s for carrying loads. But only one hour before take off we would know the total number. Besides that the selection of aircraft was most unprofessional. Each Boeing 737 can carry about 100 passengers. Its luggage hold is meant for sophisticated luggage like V.I.P. suitcases and handbags, not for army ordnance stores. In fact when time for loading came, airlines refused to take many of our important items of luggage. We should have got Air Force transport aircraft which were ideal for such movement. Our total strength that was present at the Lucknow airport was about 450. By normal reckoning I should have got five Boeing 737s for troops and about 16 AN 32s to carry few essential vehicles known as "F Echelon vehicles" in army parlance *(vehicles carrying essential battle loads meant to accompany the* Fighting *or 'F' Echelon)*, supporting arms, ammunition, rations, clothing, cooking utensils and so on. I asked my 2IC to divide the load as per the capacity of each AN 32.

"In the meantime the other battalion of our 41 Brigade, 19 RAJ RIF, also arrived to be air-lifted like us. So the total number of aircrafts that were needed for these two battalions, not counting the Brigade Headquarters, were 14 to 15 sorties of Boeing 737s and 35 to 37 sorties of AN 32s. Turn-around time for each air craft from Lucknow to Jaffna and back, in case of non-stop flying, would not be less than 14 to 16 hours. So it would not be possible for one aircraft to make more than one sortie a day. Which meant either we should get all the aircraft in one lot, for which Lucknow airport did not have enough infrastructure, or else our force would get divided. I wondered what would happen as I myself ruled out the first option.

"After we had grouped ourselves as per plane loads, we were awaiting for the arrival of the planes and their final distribution. I was sitting a short distance away thinking about a major development in our command and control structure that took place the previous day, i.e. 15 October, which would have a profound effect on the formation, 41 Infantry Brigade, in our forthcoming operations. As I had mentioned earlier, we were preparing for our task under the Officiating Brigade Commander, Col S. K. Singh, while the Brigade Commander-designate was on his way to assume command. The brigade was effectively preparing for the ensuing task ahead. It is very important to establish commander-to-commander relations and develop confidence with both superiors and subordinates at each level. And it takes time. In fact the personality of the commander and his fair reputation builds confidence in the subordinates and affects the result. Though we did know much about our Brigade Commander-designate, we definitely were happy to go into war with our brigade's Deputy Commander till the permanent incumbent arrived.

"The previous day at one of the conferences at the Brigade Headquarters we were told that the commander of a neighboring brigade, Brig. Manjit Singh, had been side-stepped to take over our brigade. This definitely was the most distressing of all news. He did not carry a great reputation as a conscientious commander. Firstly it violates the basic tenets of command structure. It is never desirable to superimpose somebody else who has had no affinity with the troops and formation. It is not desirable to send a formation to a battle with an absolutely new commander. Secondly, his stepping in from the neighbouring brigade was perhaps unnecessary, unless there had been a command failure in our brigade, which there had not. The later events and his ultimate fate vindicates that my premonition was right. Though given a Mahavir Chakra, the second highest gallantry award, it is believed that he was asked to resign and was sent home prematurely. However he was not seen during our induction phase when his presence and directions were very much needed to ensure that his formation was inducted in battle-worthy strength. We were told that he would join us in Sri Lanka!

"At about 0415 am, the Adjutant came to me and said that 19 RAJ RIF, the other battalion of the brigade due to move, and our battalion, 16 SIKH, were allotted merely 2 Boeing 737s and 6 AN 32s each! The allotment was abysmally low. This fleet could carry even less than one fourth of our battalion strength and hardly any heavy weapons, equipments and no vehicle. Even these two planes would not take us straight to our destination to Sri Lanka. These two would carry us only up to Delhi where we would again be shifted into an Airbus, which would take us to Madras and then again we would be transported by Boeing 737 to Palali airport at Jaffna! I did not think there could ever be more complicated and useless induction than this. With this ominous sign I looked up towards God and wondered if our top brass had lost all their sanity? Their logistic plan violated all the basic tenets of launching an operation with battle-worthy troops. I asked the Adjutant as to what about the rest of the troops, whose number was larger than the force being inducted in the first echelon, and the weapons, equipment, rations, store and the vehicle fleet that were being left behind. I was told that they would be sent by a special train which would join us in three days. Evidently it was not the ideal situation, but under the circumstances where there was no option and I had no power to alter the fateful course of action, it was acceptable. Having witnessed as to how the events unfolded in the last twenty four hours I had great doubt in my mind that this larger group of the unit with all our weapons, equipments, ammunitions, rations and vehicles would really reach us within three days as was being promised. Unfortunately my premonition proved right! In actuality it reached us after 33 days! By then many battles had been fought; many lives lost.

On hearing this, I just looked up trying to locate the Almighty seeking His blessings. How could our top brass forget the basics? Out of the strength of 850 soldiers, we were going into the battle, in a foreign country from where we would have no further connection with our base in future, without practically any strength! To give an example a platoon is the very basic sub-unit which can launch itself into an operation. Its strength is one platoon commander and thirty five solders. As per the book if the strength goes down to less than twenty two then that platoon is considered unfit to take part in any operation till their strength is reinforced. Under the present circumstances we were going to participate in military operations with around 10 soldiers per platoon!

"With the fresh allotment of aircraft, I called the 2IC, Adjutant and the company commanders for a hurried conference to discuss what to take with us and what would follow. In fact none of us had any clue nor any time to discuss what to do. After the conference I decided that all the headquarters of the companies should move with whatever numbers of soldiers that could be accommodated, and the rest of the troops, specialist platoons with supporting weapons, ammunition, equipments, rations and cooking utensils (in short the *langars*), motor transport, etc, to follow by train. I told the 2IC, who being low medical category was being left behind, to ensure that all essentials are sent. I instructed him to look after the unit Rear to include peacetime assets, the entire accommodation which was being left behind empty, and most importantly, the families. I knew at least of the case of Maj. Ramcharan who could not bid good-bye to his wife as she was lying almost unconscious for last three days with a severe attack of migraine. She was still unconscious when he left at the wee hours on 16th Oct. There would be many such cases. Children might be sick; someone's wife might have gone to her parental home, someone might have some other unfinished personal work which needed attention. I told the 2IC to look into these matters and personally visit all families to explain to them the situation and assure them that all would turn out well. I always consider it better to know the truth and know what to do than remaining in the dark and being constantly worried. With this we dispersed and went to our respective aircraft to board. There was limitless confusion and commotion in loading the civil aircraft. The items which were very essential for us to carry were not allowed to be carried by the aircraft staff as they were termed not as per their specifications, like ammunition, explosives, cook-house items, essential quantity of fuel and so on. We were going into the battle-field with practically no troops and their equipments! In an infantry battalion there are approximately thirty nine vehicles of all types for carrying loads and troops. I could take only one jeep in one of the AN 32 aircrafts. There was not much time to be wasted at the airfield as it was getting congested. Beside our troops' aircraft their scheduled aircraft were to operate.

"Besides that we had an urgency to reach our destiny as early as possible to get to know our task and area. I was interested to set up our camp at the new location before last light to be effective. Reaching an absolutely new location in the dark would add to the problems we were already facing. While occupying my seat in the aircraft I prayed that while I was prepared for various types of reports about all the difficulties which were being faced, but nevertheless things should be within acceptable limits and should not badly affect our operational capability."

*The Battle for Jaffna: 14-15 October*

Slow but steady progress against stiff opposition was made along the three axes by each of the three brigades (18, 72, and 91).

- *72 Infantry Brigade:* 13 SIKH LI was re-organized into three companies on 14 October, and their administrative base was moved forward, further south and closer to the battalion's main body. The battalion captured Urelu during night $14^{th}/15^{th}$.
- LTTE snipers on palmyrah palm trees, on chairs nailed to the trunks, and other high spots, picked out and killed IPKF officers. So many were shot that most officers stopped wearing the field epaulettes with their badges of rank.
- In a number of instances, troops ran out of ammunition because they were not carrying enough, and the fighting carried on longer than expected, while LTTE road-blocks prevented re-supply columns from reaching them in time.
- There were cases of casualties being incurred when houses were being searched for wounded or dead LTTE after an engagement. Soldiers and in cases Tamil-speaking infantry officers, were shot as they turned and were leaving, by women who had been had been left alone, but had been hiding an AK-47 under their clothes.
- A particular problem encountered was that areas which had been cleared, and then left un-held in the rear as the advance progressed, would immediately get re-occupied by the LTTE, thus necessitating the launching of another attack to clear the freshly-established road-block. One of the important reasons for the slow progress was that all the possible supporting fire, from air to artillery to tanks, was not being used, and even the fire of the infantry's own rocket launchers was placed under restriction. Casualties were incurred, including officer casualties. At times successful was the LTTE's tactic of surrounding a sub-unit (i.e., a company, or a platoon, or a section) and inducing it to expend all its ammunition, at times even by a combination of real small-

arms fire and simulated fire by using fire-crackers. These were cases of poor fire discipline and thus a clear lack of professionalism. *But the major reason for the slow progress was the paucity of infantrymen; there were not enough brigades or battalions available for rotating the forward advancing battalions.* The available brigades were short of one, or even two, of the three infantry battalions each should have had. All of the few units (battalions) involved were at about half-strength, greatly reducing the effectiveness of sub-units, when a company meant to function with 130 men on the ground had to function with only 65-70, and thus correspondingly fewer weapons. Platoons went into action with just about 15 men, and sections were of just four to six men, little more than an LMG team and a couple of riflemen. Lack of sufficient bayonet strength on the ground, and the psychological under-preparation of the men, many recently arrived with their units into a peace-station after years of tough border duties, and just re-united with their families, also caused a further loss of professionalism in many cases. With heavy opposing fire, under-strength sub-units sought strength in numbers, and tended to clump into larger groups, for example, the platoon tended to move too close together, while the company was often handled together like a large platoon. "Fire and movement, the quintessence of tactics, was conspicuous by its absence," as per the Overall Force Commander, Lt. Gen. Depinder Singh, himself an infantryman.

- Advancing in a heavily-fortified built-area, with mines and booby-traps, meant the clearing of one house at a time to maintain the advance. This made for slow progress.
- Another constraint, in the peculiar mixture of counter-insurgency and fighting in a built-up area that was forced upon the IPKF, inadequately termed 'urban guerilla warfare,' was the language problem. In most battalions there were very few, or even no one, who could speak Tamil. (Except, of course in battalions of the Madras Regiment, in which a high

proportion of the soldiers are Tamils, and where the regimental language itself is Tamil. In fact, the officers of the SLAF were amazed that the Indian army was employing battalions of the Madras Regiment in operations against the LTTE, in which task they performed well, which speaks volumes about the general level of professionalism)

- Another serious and inexcusable constraint was the lack of maps, which further compounded the general lack of intelligence, one of the traditional Indian areas of weakness.
- The security of the Palaly DMA, including the security of the transport aircraft landing and taking-off in easily recognizable "funnels" had to be taken care of. This was achieved by aggressive infantry patrolling around the area, in conjunction with an armed helicopter kept in the air whenever transport aircraft were moving in or out. Initially no such Indian Air Force (IAF) helicopter was available. The SLAF were requested to provide this armed helicopter cover, which they did during this initial period. Later, four Army Air OP *(Observation Post, for directing and controlling artillery fire from the air)* helicopters were hurriedly modified by HAL in Bangalore to mount a machine gun and sent to Sri Lanka. Finally, much later, the IAF provided Mi-24 "Akbar" helicopter gunships, the appropriate aircraft for the task.

*15–17 October*

*18 Infantry Brigade:* On the night 15/16 October, 12 GRENADIERS cleared the important rail and road crossings and entered the built-up area, thus opening the route to Jaffna from the east. It was the first success of the Indian Army. 4 MAHAR, after being held up for over 72 hours, captured North and South Kopai by 19 October despite stiff LTTE resistance. Maj. Gen. Harkirat Singh comments: "When the advance of 4 MAHAR was held up and casualties were heavy, Lt. Gen. Depinder Singh asked me if he should recommend a change in command to hasten the advance of 4 MAHAR, I stood by my Brigade Commander and apprised the OFC about the ground situation. In hindsight, I feel I should have agreed with Lt. Gen. Depinder Singh since I was fed with incorrect situation reports/information by Brig. J.S. Dhillon's formation."

*91 Infantry Brigade:* The brigade first took action to destroy the LTTE's radio and TV transmitters and their printing presses at Elamarasu and Murasoli. The brigade then advanced along the KKS-Mallakam-Chunakam-Maruthamadam-Jaffna axis. The Brigade Commander, Brig. Ralli, moving quite forward in his APC sustained back injuries due to a mine blast, but continued to command his brigade. He explained to the GOC 54 Division that, "General, it is easy to fight a war against militants, but it is difficult to forward explanations to the Headquarters OFC." The brigade secured the line Uduvil-Maruthamadam-Kopai North by the night 16/17 October. Tellipallai, Mallakam, Chunakam, and Manipai were secured by first light on 18 October.

Anai-kottai had been a problem. 8 MAHAR less one company was located near Uduvil. On 15 October the battalion was ordered to send one company to capture and hold Anai-kottai, an important village to the west of Jaffna, in order to provide a firm base for 41 Infantry Brigade's advance along the coastal road. The operation had been conceived in the Operations Room of M.O. Directorate in Army Headquarters, and planned in detail at HQ OFC. 'D' Company 8 MAHAR, commanded by Maj. P.S. Ganapathy, was given the task. It was relieved at 0015 hours on 16 October from the defences it was holding at Maruthanamadam by 5 MADRAS, and briefed by the C.O. 8 MAHAR at 0210 hours on 16 October. The link-up was scheduled to take place at 1600 hours on 16 October. The company was ordered to carry only pouch ammunition and rations for 48 hours. The weak company (of total strength 65-70), started at 0330 hours and moving cross-country reached close to Anai-kottai by about 0645 hours, whereupon it was engaged by the LTTE. The company occupied an all-round defence, and was eventually encircled during the day by about 150-200 of the enemy.

It remained under accurate and observed enemy fire from snipers in trees and heavy automatic fire from nearby positions, taking casualties, as well as inflicting casualties on the LTTE whenever it pressed forward. Three of its flanks were supported by mortar fire of both its own battalion, and those of 1 MARATHA LI in Jaffna Fort. Artillery fire support was limited by range only to some areas outside the company's perimeter. By the evening of 16 October its limited ammunition ran low, and the battalion had to send in a patrol the next night (night 16/17 October) under Capt. Sunil Chandra, which had to fight its way in with ammunition. There were no arrangements for casualty evacuation, and no secure helipad could be provided by the company. The company remained deployed in that tactically unsuitable location, hemmed in and under fire from the enemy, for the next day and night (night 17/18 October) as well. More ammunition had to be dropped by a Chetak helicopter on 18 October. The link-up took place only on 19 October at 1300 hours, after the company had been through a 72-hour ordeal for three nights and two days, from the night of 15/16 October, to the afternoon of 19 October, with insufficient food and barely enough ammunition, taking casualties of 11 dead (one officer and 10 OR) and 28 wounded (one officer and 27 OR) lying in their midst un-evacuated among them.

The link-up by 41 Infantry Brigade was 36 hours behind schedule, and even then they could not relieve the 8 MAHAR company. The link-up force, in fact, could not be launched on 16 October and thus were delayed by 24 hours to start with. It got further delayed by another 48 hours due to the link-up column encountering the enemy north of Uduvil, and being unable to fix them and to by-pass their positions at night.

*41 Infantry Brigade:16 SIKH Induction* Lt. Col. Gupta Ray's account continues:

"At approximately 5.30 am on 16 October we took off from Lucknow. The journey was uneventful and we reached the Delhi air port at about 6.30 a.m. We had been briefed that on landing at Delhi we would be received by a liaison officer from the Military Operations Directorate of the Army Headquarters. He would guide us for our further onward journey. But we found none. We did not find any Airbus waiting for us either. We started contacting the ATC (Air Traffic Control) and also the airlines manager on duty. After about three hours we could locate the Airbus at the other end of the airfield. Troops took whatever breakfast they had managed to bring in their haversacks. Due to such a short notice we could not carry even a packed lunch and I was now certain that there would be no arrangements at Madras too for any refreshments or meals. Anyway the troops started lugging the stores from one end of the airfield to the other. There was no transport available. Again we had a loading problem. We had to fit in the luggage of two aircraft into one. Though that was bigger in size, but obviously that could not give double the space of a Boeing 737. There was again commotion in loading the Airbus. There were argument and counter argument between the Airbus crew and our jawans. Both were right in their own way. One was going to participate in a military operation involving life and death so needs his essential items to survive which might look awkward to the air crews, other was going by their technical specification which was equally important. Nobody can take risk whine flying in the air. Result was shedding more stores. When the situation came to an agreeable proposition, we started boarding the Airbus.

"Initially the crew of the aircraft were nervous and detached. Not at all friendly. I called one air-hostess and talked to her briefly. She went back to her group and had a couple of minutes with them. And then all the crew came with their usual charm and broad smiles on their faces. They started serving us with more zeal then ever before. The rest of the journey was quite pleasant. All of them went repeatedly to each soldier to see if he needed anything more to eat or drink. As a good gesture before landing at Madras they handed over to us all the foodstuff they had, which was more than welcome and helped us for the time being. I would always be thankful to them for their most cordial and affectionate gesture.

"By the time we reached Madras air port it was about 1.30 p.m. Again the situation there was the same: no one to receive and brief us. After some time I saw 19 RAJ RIF, also in a similar plight, waiting for instructions and allotment of aircraft. I also noticed after some time that another battalion of our Sikh Regiment, 22 SIKH, was already there. As per their briefing they were to be inducted on 22 October but were hurried up due to operational exigencies. I met the C.O. of the battalion, Col. Baluram, six feet two inches tall, a tough and upright officer. We had served together for many years before in the same unit, 9 SIKH, in which I was commissioned in January 1969. That was an indelible bond very difficult to understand by the persons who have not served in the army especially in an infantry unit. I found we were all in the same boat, with very little difference. We all were keen to reach the destination before nightfall. I was not too sure as to what type of reception we would get there. My soldiers had nothing to eat since the morning other than the refreshment we had in the aircraft, courtesy Indian Airlines. I was not expecting much at the place of our landing, and we had been forced to shed many crucial administrative items as the civil aircraft were unable to carry them. A few very important things like cooking oil, and cooking utensils which were very big in size, had to be left behind. We were therefore eager to reach there well in time so that we could secure the area where we were to stay at night and also set ourselves up administratively. If supply depots were open and something was available there we could place indents for those. We would be almost blind-folded if we reached after darkness as we knew nothing about the area.

"The waiting was agonizing. We were maintaining close contact with the airport authority. Nobody seemed to know anything for sure. Precious time was clicking by when all of a sudden we saw a cavalcade of three to four cars heading towards us. The leading car had a flag and three stars on it. When they came closer I could make out that the Southern Army Commander, Lt. Gen. Depinder Singh was coming, most probably to meet us. After a while the cavalcade screeched to a halt near us and a young officer leaped out of the car and came towards us quickly. Lt. Col. S. Mukherjee, C.O. of 19 RAJ RIF, and I instinctively started walking in his direction. On meeting him he said "Lt. Gen. Depinder Singh, Army Commander, Southern Army, has arrived to meet you." In the meantime the general also got down from his car. We exchanged greetings and shook hands. Though we exchanged very few words but lots were spoken through unspoken words and body language. Both understood each other's message. Basically he wanted to convey "My friend there is tough work ahead." We reciprocated by saying that there was nothing to worry about; we would carry out our task as would be given to us but we wanted our force together as early as possible. We, i.e., each of our battalions, should be deployed as one unit in full strength. Presently we were split. Ironically only a few days before our induction, I had been reading a book "A Bridge Too Far." It was a story of the Second World War. A division comprising almost 15,000 soldiers was para-dropped by the Allied Army behind the retreating German Army to capture a vital bridge and occupy certain important positions, to stop them and cut them off. The move was very bold but it failed on two counts: one, while being para-dropped the troops had got scattered; and two, the link-up by the ground troops which was to be effected within 24 hours could not be done due to bad weather. The division was badly mauled. After the brief talk the General climbed into his car and the cavalcade left. We again resumed our waiting for our planes.

"Around 1430 hours the first plane was made available to us. The first lot of the troops boarded the plane. We started our third and last phase of our journey. While I was going through my flash-back sitting in the plane, suddenly I felt a tap on my shoulder. On opening my eyes I saw an air-hostess standing in front of me. The captain of the aircraft was inviting me into the cockpit of the aircraft. I went there. We exchanged compliments and he started showing me the Indian shoreline and also northern Sri Lanka which was our destination.

"With this my flash back of the past 48 hours came to an end and I came back to reality. I was told that within a couple of minutes we would land at Palali airport, our destination. Our induction was going to be over and our real job would start. Thoughts about the soldiers I had left behind flashed through my mind. The question in my mind was: could they have started their journey, if so, when would they meet us?"

*17th-19th October*

*41 Infantry Brigade:* The brigade had arrived pell-mell at Palaly on 15th October with just two very under-strength and disorganized battalions, 19 RAJ RIF and 16 SIKH, and was tasked with executing a hook along the coast road to contact Jaffna from the West, a manoeuvre which had originally been intended by sea using 8 MAHAR of 91 Brigade. 19 RAJ RIF and 16 SIKH, both severely under-strength and having been suddenly air-lifted overnight from Lucknow with no notice whatsoever, and consisting of only some 220 men each, a quarter of each battalion's strength, with the four rifle companies at strengths of about 30-35 men each, not even a full-strength platoon. The two battalions were under their Officiating Brigade Commander, the brigade's Deputy Commander, Col. S.K. Singh, who had come with them from Lucknow, 19 RAJ RIF being commanded by its C.O., Lt. Col. S. Mukherji, and 16 SIKH being commanded by its Second-in-Command, Maj. M.K. Gupta-Ray. The brigade moved out from Palaly in considerable confusion on 17 October, advancing along the Uduvil-Manipai-Kulam-Mile 1.5 axis, on the coastal road to Jaffna fort. The brigade's "Recce Group" ('R' Group), consisting of the new Brigade Commander, Brig. Manjit Singh (who had just assumed command on 16 October, taking over from the original Deputy Commander of the brigade), and the two CO's of 19 RAJ RIF and 16 SIKH, which had gone up in a helicopter to look at the route of advance and the approaches to Jaffna were unable to get back to their "Fighting Group" ('F' Group) before dark. In the meantime, the

'F' Group itself had been ordered forward and got engaged with the enemy, losing some men and one officer, before the CO's could return and physically command the advance. Maj. Gen. Harkirat Singh adds, "Formation commanders were superimposed without the knowledge of the troops and the staff officers comprising it. Brig. Manjit Singh was made Commander of the 41 Infantry Brigade during an important stage of the battle. This act virtually broke up the cohesiveness of this formation." He goes on to say: "Brig. Manjit Singh, an outspoken officer, stated on arrival that he had walked into the Army Chief's office and sought an opportunity to command a formation in Sri Lanka. Brig. Manjit Singh terrorized his staff and unit commanders and tension prevailed in this formation."

41 Brigade, on the coast road, fought its way through opposition, losing two BMP's *(infantry combat vehicles, or ICV's),* one to a mine, and the other bogged down in a soft field. The brigade made slow but steady progress. On 18 October afternoon, the Commander 41 Brigade, Brig. Manjit Singh, taking two companies of 5 RAJ RIF, a battalion which had been added to the brigade, set out from Manipai. The brigade linked up with the beleagured 8 MAHAR company at Anai-kottai at 1300 hours on 19 October. Contact with the Jaffna Fort garrison was established by Brig. Manjit Singh on 19 October.

*115 Infantry Brigade:* 115 Infantry Brigade arrived at Palaly on 17 and 18 October with two battalions and was launched into the operations on 19 October, tasked to reinforce the advance on axis Palaly-Vasavilan-Urumparai-Jaffna. The Regimental History of First Gorkha Rifles records about 5/1 Gorkha Rifles: "At Gwalior the Battalion strength came to 480 all ranks *(when they were suddenly ordered on 16 October 1987 to move to Sri Lanka).* It was ordered to take two jeep-mounted MMGs, two RCLs, first-line ammunition, seven days' rations, arrangement for independent platoon actions and logistics for the same. WE* tentage and minimum office requirements were to be

*War Establishment.

carried. Instructions were for leave parties to join via Madras-Trincomalee, through the embarkation authorities. The Battalion less heavy equipment and vehicles were flown in one IL-76, two An-32's and five Boeings from Gwalior to Palali airfield, Jaffna, on 18 October. That very night they were assigned their task of advancing astride the axis from Palali to Jaffna via Urumparai, to link up with 4 MAHAR then considered under pressure at Kopai North. They had been given a section of engineers to clear mines or make divisions, a battery of field artillery and a mixed mechanized column of five tanks and seven Infantry Combat Vehicles (ICV's) assisted them. The Fifth *(5/1 G.R.)* was the advanced guard of the brigade. It was decided to advance with two companies up, upto Urumparai; subsequently the mechanized column was to be fixing the axis along the road with the infantry companies moving cross-country but parallel to the road axis. The advance commenced at 11.30 a.m. on 19 October." The brigade was moved through Urumparai towards Kopai North and Kopai South, where 18 Infantry Brigade was facing very determined resistance to their advance towards Jaffna, linking-up on night 19/20 October, after an action at Temple by 5/1 G.R. became a three-hour plus battle to clear the route up to Road Junction, with the brigade taking casualties of ten killed and seven wounded (mostly the tank crews), while the enemy had six killed and nine wounded.

### *41 Infantry Brigade*

#### *Advance on Jaffna*

Meanwhile, 16 SIKH began its advance on Jaffna as per their orders. The CO's account of those fateful two days is given in the paragraph that follow:

"17 October morning at 8 o'clock, 16 SIKH started its advance towards Jaffna Fort. At that time the fort was held by 1st Maratha Light Infantry (1 MLI) which had been inducted as part of 54 Division, the initial IPKF. This 20-ha fort was surrounded by the city on all three sides except the west where lay the Palk Strait, the narrow strip of sea connecting the Bay of Bengal and the Arabian Sea, and was presently besieged by the LTTE. Jaffna Fort, built by the Dutch after 1658 on the site of earlier fortifications built by the Portuguese in the 16th century to control the trade route to India, had always been considered a symbol of strength and authority. Jaffna had seen many battles since 1500 B.C. including invasions from East India, South India, Portugal, Holland, and Britain. The Dutch captured Jaffna from the Portuguese after a bitter three-month siege in 1658, losing it to the British in 1796. The IPKF took over the fort when it entered as a peace-keeping force and had not got into this messy situation it got into later. In olden days it provided domination on all sides of the fort. It was secure from the land forces as it was located on dominating ground and on the west was the sea. In due course of time there were many high-rise buildings which came up all around the fort, except in the west which was facing the sea. Later on these high rise buildings provided excellent positions to bring down observed fire on 1MLI. Any small movement by the troops of 1 MLI resulted in harassing fire from the LTTE.

"16 SIKH's advance started from near Palali airport to the north-east of Jaffna, where the battalion landed in the evening of 15 October 1987. The newly-posted Brigade Commander of our 41 Infantry Brigade, Brig. Manjit Singh, had just taken over the brigade the previous day, 16 October 1987. The plan given by the new Commander, at the HQ 54 Division very near Palali Airport, was to link up and relieve 1 MLI in Jaffna Fort. Brig. Manjit Singh did not give any formal orders. Instead, he gave us a briefing. He asked us to undertake something like a speed march, with our first major "bound"* in the area where the Battalion Headquarters of 8 MAHAR was located Thereafter to continue to move and to link up with a company of 8 MAHAR,

* A "bound" is a military tactical term for a specific point on the route of an advance where the force halts very briefly, as a tactical halt, re-groups if necessary, and continues the advance.

# 16 SIKH / 19 RAJ RIF (41 INFANTRY BRIGADE)
## 18 OCT - 21 OCT

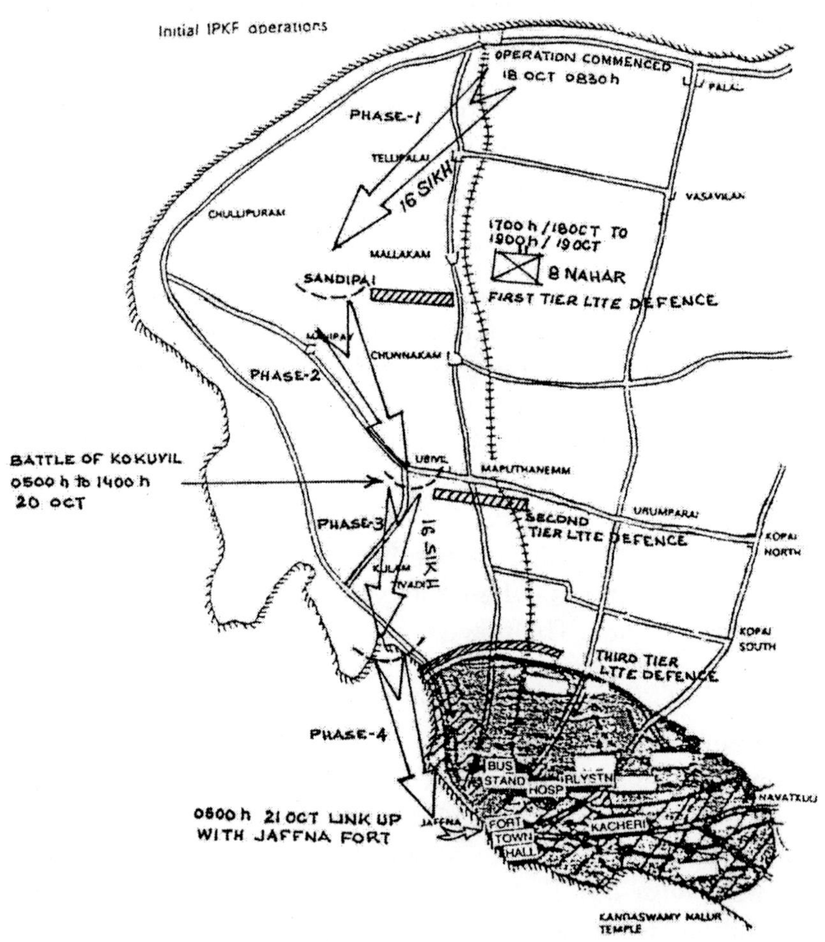

short of Jaffna Fort on the coastal road. This company was kept pinned down by LTTE from all sides and was very low in ammunitions and rations. It was continuously suffering casualties. The area it was holding was not ideal for defence, being cultivated open land with very little cover. The whole distance from Palali to Jaffna Fort was about 27 km. The roads were supposed to be heavily mined or charged with Improvised Explosive Device (IED). Ideally all metal roads were to be avoided. There was no mention of fire support by supporting arms or any plan for replenishment or for evacuation of casualties. In fact there was no Administrative Order which always follows an Operational Order.

"Having been told our task we consulted the map which was given to us. We were given only four photo-copies of a tourist map. These maps did not give many details of physical features of the area which are essential for planning military operations. We needed to very carefully study all the available details of converging and lateral roads and tracks and also various physical features important to plan operations. Details of roads and tracks give information about the axis of advance and our capability to switch troops from one axis to the other in case of stiff resistance. This also gives us enough idea of enemy capability of moving his troops. Beside roads, maps give us informations on various aspects like existence of rivers, nullahs, vegetation, forests, high and low areas and a host of other details related to terrain conditions which help to formulate plan for move, suggest places of likely engagements and formulate plans for own operations. From the given map we found there were two distinct axial roads leading to the Jaffna Fort from Palali Airport where we were located. We were to assess relative advantages and disadvantages of both these roads. There were two basic points to consider and arrive at a plan. These were the availability of time and enemy interference. We were to relieve one company of 8 MAHAR, en route to Jaffna, which was kept constantly engaged by the LTTE and was continuously suffering casualties. They were to be relieved as soon as possible. After this was done we were to link up with 1 MLI who were equally being kept under heavy engagement by the LTTE. All these tasks were to be carried out in one night! We were told that all the villages and the built-up areas were heavily fortified. Each house would have a bunker in its backyard from where stiff resistance was expected. As regards enemy interference was concerned it was bound to be there. Anybody occupying the bunker would be deemed to be an LTTE cadre.

"I wondered how all this could be achieved in one night. Even if you calculate the speed of an uninterrupted night march as two and a half kms an hour, it would take about 14 hours just for the marching, plus extra time for rest, not counting any enemy operations. Our main consideration was speed to avoid longer exposure. We should give the enemy the least time for them to react. After all they were being engaged in other sectors also. In such a situation, ideally we should have divided ourselves in two to three company groups with a minimum of one company as a reserve to be launched depending on the degree of enemy interference. But we could not dare do that. We had only one-fourth of our authorized strength present. The total strength present in the battalion, including non-combatants, who were meant to provide only administrative support e.g. cooks, carpenters, armourers etc, was only 220, against our authorization of approximately 850. The authorized strength of each rifle company consists of approximately 120 whereas we, even having distributed all our non-combatants to the rifle companies to increase their bayonet strength, could not raise it to more than 45 per rifle company* at the start of the operation. Besides that we did not have the most essential equipments needed for battles, particularly where troops are spread out, like vital signal equipment and maps.

"We had two obvious choices. One was to take the longer, that is, the coastal route, or to take the other route which was going almost straight reaching the outskirts of Jaffna Fort

*The strength came down to below 40 by the time we reached the outskirts of Jaffna town due to casualties and administrative requirements.

cutting through the countryside which had a number of inhabited localities as well as open areas with patches of trees and wild growth. Both these routes had a some advantages as well as disadvantages. As regards the coastal road, the advantages were that: our right flank would have been protected by the lagoon which was touching the road, the area was sparsely populated therefore the LTTE would have difficulty in mingling with the locals, and we could engage the enemy from a distance as the area was relatively more open with less vegetation and growth. There was more space to manoeuvre. The coastal route definitely was a longer route. This would obviously take longer time to traverse thereby having longer exposure to LTTE interference. The existence of the lagoon would restrict our manoeuvring space. The LTTE could create choke points for us at ground of his own choosing. Since we did not have the required map with the physical details we would not be able to do a proper map study of the ground, therefore we would not be able to make anticipatory movements to counter possible enemy plans. We did not have any logistic plan to cater for any kind of upset in our time-schedule which was very likely under such a situation. And we were to go far away from the support base.

"The LTTE, over the years, had almost perfected the art of hit-and-run operations. Their strong points were: excellent intelligence network, ingenuity in handling explosives and complete knowledge and mastery of the ground. The best way to fight such operations is by out-manoeuvering them, by moving in a number of groups and keeping the enemy guessing. In this way they would get outflanked or encircled rather than us. But this was not possible because of lack of troops, resources and training. Such training is not part of the regular training curriculum of the Indian Army, because the needs of each formation are not uniform. Such training is based on the operational needs of each formation, and is therefore done under the arrangements of each formation commander.

"Having considered all the pros and cons, we decided to take the shorter route. On this route we had the advantage of getting assistance from the headquarters of 8 MAHAR, and a company of the same battalion, both located en route on the shorter route. Though the isolated company itself was locked in a battle of attrition but once linked up it would get revitalized, and also could be extricated if needed. It would be of great help to us too. It was decided to remain off the metalled road but to keep it in sight as an aid to keeping direction. Moving cross-country instead of on the road would definitely reduce speed but would help to save precious lives. 16 SIKH was to be followed by 19 RAJ RIF. The time gap between the two was to be four hours. The brigade commander also told us during his briefing that while the battalions were advancing, the two Commanding Officers of the battalions would fly with him into the Jaffna Fort to have an aerial reconnaissance of the route being taken and the targets around the Jaffna Fort, which were to be our next phase of operations. I objected to this plan of aerial reconnaissance by the battalion commanders with the brigade commander on two grounds:

(i) I was myself the Officiating Battalion Commander; therefore, I was not in favour of handing down the operational responsibility during the advance to another officer, since there was no functional 2IC for this tactical role of that appointment, with my now officiating as the C.O. The next senior officer was a rifle company commander who did not have enough experience to command a battalion even under peace-time conditions, what to talk about battle conditions. He himself was under tremendous pressure due to the types of operational problems he would face with his own company. It would neither be fair to him nor to the battalion where the situation was live and threat was imminent. This suggestion by Brigadier Manjit Singh, who himself was absolutely new in his command of our brigade, was thus not at all acceptable to me.

(ii) There was no point in taking me for an aerial reconnaissance without my own sub-unit commanders, who in army parlance are known as 'O' Group *(short for Orders Group).* It was they who were to physically fight and remove the LTTE from their entrenched locations and reduce the pressure on both the Mahar Company as well as 1 MLI inside the Jaffna Fort. There was no point in my seeing these targets alone, especially when my troops were going for their first-ever encounter with an enemy who were not fighting a conventional battle, and where we had no experience in fighting them ever before. Beside everything else we were to start our fight in a foreign country in a totally alien environment. Everything was against us. Under these circumstances to be away from the troops of my command who were already struggling against all odds was not at all acceptable to me. But Brig. Manjit Singh would not see the logic of my points. He was adamant that I accompany him for the air recce.

"This was a grave tactical blunder committed at the brigade commander's level. At about 0730 hours on 18 October I set out for the helipad. Before starting I again briefed Maj. Ramcharan and the other company commanders on their tasks. Those, in brief, were:

(a) Start the approach march at 0800 hours. Our unit would be followed after four hours by 19 RAJ RIF.

(b) The advance, as per the brigade commander, Brig. Manjit Singh's briefing, would be non-tactical, a kind of forced march. But I warned my commanders repeatedly not to make that mistake. I warned them not to be in a hurry. We neither knew anything about the LTTE tactics nor about the terrain. We had no useful intelligence. So we must move as tactical doctrine dictates.

(c) Not to move on metalled road. Move off the road but use it as an aid to keep direction.

(d) Avoid all built-up areas and by-pass them.

(e) Since ammunition was very short, strictly follow fire discipline.

(f) Remain reasonably dispersed to avoid casualty from LTTE fire but be able to take them on as an unit in case the situation so arises.

(g) Not to approach any civilian for guidance; he might mislead us. As it was, there was an un-breachable communication gap between our Punjabi-speaking Sikhs and the local Tamils.

(h) After reaching 8 MAHAR Headquarters try to replenish ammunition and rations.

(j) I instructed the battalion's Quartermaster, the officer in charge logistics, Capt. Padmakumar, to get hold of his very limited resources and organize replenishment of all types of administrative necessities. He would have a Herculean task ahead to replenish the logistic requirements as the troops advanced. I expected need for air drops also as there was no plan, or at least not one told to us, for replenishment by surface transport.

"Having briefed the officers, I started moving towards the helipad. Thankfully, Maj. Chowdhry, who had to be left behind at Lucknow, had managed to put one jeep into one of the AN 32 transport aircrafts of the Indian Air Force. That became very handy both for me and also to get limited stores. While going towards the helipad I was feeling uneasy at being taken away from my troops who were being launched into the battle within 72 hours of being on routine peace time duties. There were plenty of major shortcomings in the overall conduct of the battle by the top-most Army brass. These were:

(a) Our strength was abysmally or unbelievably low. A battalion consists of 850 soldiers whereas we were inducted with only 220 soldiers, exactly one-fourth of the strength.

(b) We had hardly any of our supporting weapons with us. The limited number of aircraft that were allotted to us could not take our complete troops; even those who were present at the airport nor our supporting weapons. We were not issued with worthwhile maps. Only four photo-copied maps of the Jaffna area were issued to us.

(c) We were short of even basic pouch ammunition. There was no established chain of replenishment or administrative back-up worth naming till then.

(d) The troops were hungry. They could not get a proper meal for the last 48 hours. The initial 24 hours we were involved in the journey and at Pallali in Jaffna there were no arrangements to receive and provide administrative back-up to the troops being inducted.

(e) There was no Intelligence Report given to us and there was no proper Operation Order.

(f) The battalion was not provided with any person with the local knowledge to communicate with or interrogate local people in case they were needed to be apprehended.

(g) Absolutely no preparation or training time was given to us.

(h) The troops were yet to be mentally in the battle and needed to psychologically prepare themselves. I had no time to talk to them even once after we were ordered to mobilize.

(i) The troops were not trained in such kind of operations. These special operations need special training, equipments and mental conditioning.

(j) The plans were sketchy.

(k) Command and control and the chain of command were totally ad-hoc. Within 48 hours our formation and the formation commander were changed, even as we were going into battle.

"With all these playing on my mind as I reached at the helipad. I saw the helicopter parked at the helipad where Lt. Col. Mukherjee, the CO of 19 RAJ RIF, who was also to accompany us, was talking to the pilots. We were expecting the brigade commander, Brig. Manjit Singh to arrive. After his arrival we took off for Jaffna Fort at about 0845 hours. Jaffna looked serene and beautiful from the air. No one could ever imagine that in actuality it was in such a volatile condition. Death was stalking there silently and anyone could fall prey to it any time. The town was picturesque: full of greenery, small hamlets surrounded by trees. Houses mainly were single unit, bungalow type. There were a couple of tarmac roads running north to south connected by many lateral lanes and by-lanes. One could see the coastline around Jaffna. The landward part of this was a shallow lagoon for a couple of miles before the start of the open sea. This side was frequented by the LTTE by their ships and boats. The area did not look formidable but the enemy was. They knew the entire area like the back of their hands. They were in complete control of the area. Their writ used to run in Jaffna because the Sri Lankan Army and police were non-effective there for some years. The entire population of Jaffna were either LTTE supporters or mute spectators. No one was against them or could dare to oppose them. They were either willfully supporting them or were being forced to support them. All other opposition were either eliminated or made non-effective by the LTTE.

"The time taken to reach the Jaffna Fort would not have been more than 20-25 minutes. The fort was laid out like any other fort of that time. It had a high wall all around with an entry from the west side. It had number of rooms spread into different parts of the fort. What was once a formidable place of authority was now in an almost dilapidated state. The fort was surrounded by the high-rise buildings from all sides except on the side towards the sea. These buildings had made it easy to bring down observed fire upon the fort. This made life of 1 MLI, staying inside the fort at that time, very difficult. They could hardly make any kind of movement during the day. 1 MLI tried to clear the surrounding area a number of times, but that did not make much difference. Each time they cleared a portion of the area, it was re- occupied once 1 MLI vacated the area. Due to the paucity of troops they could not hold areas outside to provide depth to the fort.

"We, i.e., the CO 19 RAJ RIF and I, were given our objectives to clear after we had linked up with the fort. Basically the entire area was divided into two. After drawing a line from the middle of the area the western portion was given to 16 SIKH and the eastern portion was given to 19 RAJ RIF. The objectives for us were Ashoka Hotel, Road Junction, Bus Stand, and then we were to keep expanding outwards till the entire Jaffna town was cleared. Each of the objectives and the roads leading to them were expected to be heavily mined or laid out with very strong IED's. Since I did not have my 'O' Group or my 'R' Group *(Reconnaissance Group)* with me, I tried to get as much of a mental picture as possible of what I could see so that I could give maximum information of the area where we were to operate after a couple of hours. We had a couple of rounds of discussion with the CO of 1 MLI, Col. T. P. S. Brar, on more details of the enemy, their modus operandi, habits, strength, types of weapons used, how long they would operate at any given time and degree of resistance once contacted, strength that they would commit at one time and specially type of explosives they had been using. We discussed the methods of operation so that we could keep our casualties to the minimum. We also wanted to know what support would be available from him in terms of operations and logistics. What supporting weapons he had and up to what extent he could provide supporting fire to us? More important was availability of mortar fire which would be more effective than direct fire weapons like machine-guns. From all talks and discussions that we had, one most important piece of information that emerged was the enemy's deadly use of IED's. With this application they could inflict larger number of deadly casualties than any other weapons they had. The second most important matter at the basic fighting level was that all LTTE cadres were equipped with automatic rifles like AK 47 and G3, whereas we were equipped with 7.62 mm semi-automatic rifles. Under such type of battle no one takes aimed fire, other than sniping, which has a different purpose. Here the volume of fire is most effective, which would inflict necessary casualties or at least neutralize the area.

"While such discussions were going on I was very worried about the progress of my battalion. Since I did not have with me my signal detachment and my battalion Intelligence Officer, who always accompanies the C.O. whenever he is out on reconnaissance, I was personally trying to keep contact with the battalion headquarters through the brigade signal link. I got to know periodically that the progress was satisfactory. Other than a few minor actions and sporadic firing there was no major problem and the morale of the battalion was high. They were keeping off the road with two companies on either side of the road. At doubtful areas they resorted to speculative fire in order to draw enemy fire. Villages and the roads were empty. People had vacated their homes and fled to the jungles or to a safer area. About 1330 hrs I came to know that the battalion had linked up with the HQ 8 Mahar. I felt very happy. Beside reaching safely and being close to the point of operation, they would have for the first time some hot food worth naming. Though I did know that 8 MAHAR was in an equally desperate condition; still having been there for a longer time and being logistically better organized, my troops would be provided something better than what they had been having so far. Incidentally, 8 MAHAR and our battalion had served together in the same brigade in Kashmir in 1983-84. Therefore, many of us in all ranks were known to each other. It was again confirmed that after the meal and some rest they would set out for the 8 MAHAR company locality which was under enemy dominance for more than 48 hours. I was to be dropped by the helicopter at that place once the battalion reached there. I was anxiously waiting to be able to rejoin the battalion. Time was passing very slowly. At about 2.30 p.m., I learnt that the battalion had set out for the next bound, the 8 MAHAR company location. I was having a nagging feeling in my mind that the nearer the battalion got to the objective there was more likelihood of confrontation with the enemy. Only I was praying and hoping to rejoin the battalion before they got involved in any kind of major action. I was disturbed by the fact that I did not have any direct communication with the battalion. I had to go through the I MLI radio net to the 8 MAHAR net and from there I was just getting information in terms of a feed-back. I had no means to advice or influence the operations of my own battalion directly.

"At about 1700 hours when I was getting restless to know what was happening I got a bomb-shell! I was told that after the battalion moved out from the Mahar HQ location on their way to the link position of the 8 MAHAR company, my battalion had got into an engagement with the LTTE. One officer and three jawans had been killed, and a few were wounded. It came as a big shock to me. The name of the place was identified as Uduvil, an obscure place. The biggest problem now was how to reach the battalion. Under the circumstances, a helicopter would not be able to take me there, and they would not be able to drop me in the wilderness as a single person. Nobody had any clue of the area as we were in a foreign country where we had just landed some hours ago. After a lot of deliberation it was decided that we all would land at the HQ 8 MAHAR location. From there a small patrol would escort me to my battalion. The CO 19 RAJ RIF would wait for his battalion to arrive there. They were to start four hours after the departure of 16 SIKH. By the time we landed at the 8 MAHAR location it was about 1730 hours. Daylight was fading out, and darkness was engulfing us. Without wasting much time a small escort was provided by 8 MAHAR consisting of two officers and five jawans. We did not have any map. HQ 8 MAHAR was located near a built-up area. We had to pass through it. A curfew had already been imposed. The lanes and the by-lanes were empty. If at all any moving thing was spotted it was warned by a volley of fire as only the LTTE were expected to be on the move at that place and time. Our movement had to be very cautious. We were in the open in full view of the LTTE's look-out persons. We could be engaged from any of the houses or tree-tops around. It was a dangerous game considering the situation and the location. It was obvious that the LTTE would try to cut off all the reinforcement routes and would specially keep watch on the 8 MAHAR location as the most likely area from where reinforcements could be sent. The party escorting me were very professional and brave. They took all the precautions which were needed to be taken. Our movement was slow and cautious. We tried to project ourselves as small a group as possible. My means of communication with my battalion improved as the patrol was carrying a radio set and we could establish one-to-one communication with them. By the time we could move out of the built-up area it was totally dark. Visibility was hardly a couple of meters. We were constantly asking my battalion their location. They were mentioning some grove or the other where they had taken position. But it was very difficult to locate exactly in which grove they were in. The engagement was still on. It was not possible to distinguish firings between friend and foe. Another point that arose was that without proper identification we could become victims to our own firing. I asked the Adjutant to send a small patrol in my direction so that I could go back with them. The Adjutant acknowledged that and was trying to organize a small patrol which could do the job. I told him that one person at least should be from the Intelligence Section that was trained specially to be proficient in map reading and in keeping direction. I also knew his difficulty in providing a patrol right then. It was difficult to pick up people who were in the first line of engagement, directly involved in the battle especially when our strength was so grossly insufficient. Anyway, from both sides we were trying hard to establish contact. In the darkness all groves, clumps of trees or buildings looked alike. When the Adjutant was trying to describe to me which grove they were in we could not make any head or tail of it. We were not aware about any landmarks of that area which we could use as an aid to locate the position. At the same time our movement was noticed by the LTTE and drew their fire. We got involved in a fire fight. This went on for some time. We started feeling that we were getting surrounded and getting caught in the crossfire of the LTTE as well as our own troops. Seeing the situation I instructed the Adjutant on the radio-set to withdraw the patrol he had sent to avoid any further unnecessary loss of soldiers. We, just the few of us, tried all options to effect a link-up with 16 SIKH. But things were getting tougher and tougher without any map, adequate strength, navigational aids and last but not the least, I was not certain to what extent I should risk my 8 MAHAR friends in the patrol for my sake. By 2200 hrs 18h Oct, when we could not locate my battalion, I began to feel from the directions of fire that we were being surrounded from all sides and that the circle was becoming smaller. I decided to pull back the patrol to our 8 MAHAR base and look for other alternatives. The situation was very tense. We did not know as to whether we would succeed in pulling back to our base. We could be captured or killed any moment. At every corner we turned we had an eerie feeling of direct confrontation. We had every chance of being out-numbered and out-gunned. On the other side since the battalion had a good deal of fighting and had taken casualties, it was not possible to restart the advance the same night. There was an urgent need of reorganization and replenishment. I informed the battalion that for the time being I was going back to 8 MAHAR and would try to link-up again with suitable preparation. I told them to dig down properly, send patrols out to avoid being surprised, collect the dead bodies, and administer first-aid as best possible. Sending back wounded to the 8 MAHAR Headquarters may not be very prudent as they might bump into lurking LTTE cadres. Besides, since there was no established chain of evacuation of casualties we had to send fighting soldiers thereby depleting the strength further. Though evacuation of casualties gets priority but at that moment we had no option but to hold them there. Sporadic firing was going on. I could understand that the aim of the LTTE was to not give us any respite. I instructed the battalion to hold fire as much as possible. Ammunition could become a problem. As it was, we had started with very little ammunition; the engagement might have depleted it further. I told them that I would try and get some ammunition when I got back and would be back as fast as possible.

"We made a fighting withdrawal to HQ 8 MAHAR. There I met Brig. Manjit Singh who wore a glum face. He obviously did not like my return nor perhaps the way he handled the whole operation. I felt he was more up to showmanship than making realistic operational plans with objectivity. Such a helicopter reccc in this operation was unnecessary. The helicopter could have been better utilized by using it to track the LTTE and providing aerial reconnaissance to the advancing 16 SIKH. This could easily have forewarned us regarding the movement pattern of the LTTE. It was about night 2230 hours. The head of the 19 RAJ RIF column started arriving at 8 MAHAR location. Within about 20 minutes the battalion closed in. They were also vastly under-strength like us, with around the same strength of approximately 220. Their CO, Lt. Col. S. K. Mukherjee, received them. While the battalion was having rest and dinner we had a conference to review the situation and decide on the next course of action. My battalion by then had a number of casualties including one officer and four jawans killed. The name of the officer was Lieutenant Nagar.

"Lt. Nagar was the eldest son of the previous CO, Col. C. S. Nagar. After leaving the 8 MAHAR location the battalion had been advancing with "Alfa" and "Bravo" Companies leading the battalion. These two companies were moving astride the road. After a couple of miles near Uduvil, the battalion came under intense fire from machine-guns from all around. The LTTE had hit on a novel idea of operation. They had made small platforms in a number of tall trees which were held by a pair of the LTTE. This method had given them the advantage of long distance observation and fire. They could see the army column approaching. Consequently they would adjust their position depending on the direction of approach and open fire. Machine-guns could easily open effective fire at a range of 500 to 800 meters. Four to five such machine-guns properly sited all around could easily engage the entire column with effective fire. These machine-gun nests were miniscule targets and were next to impossible to locate. On top of that they constantly changed their position to avoid detection. Under normal battle conditions the two major factors which help detection of weapons are sound, and the dust that is kicked up by the

# 41 INFANTRY BRIGADE
# BATTLE OF SANDIPAI
# 1700 H 18 OCT - 1900 H 19 OCT

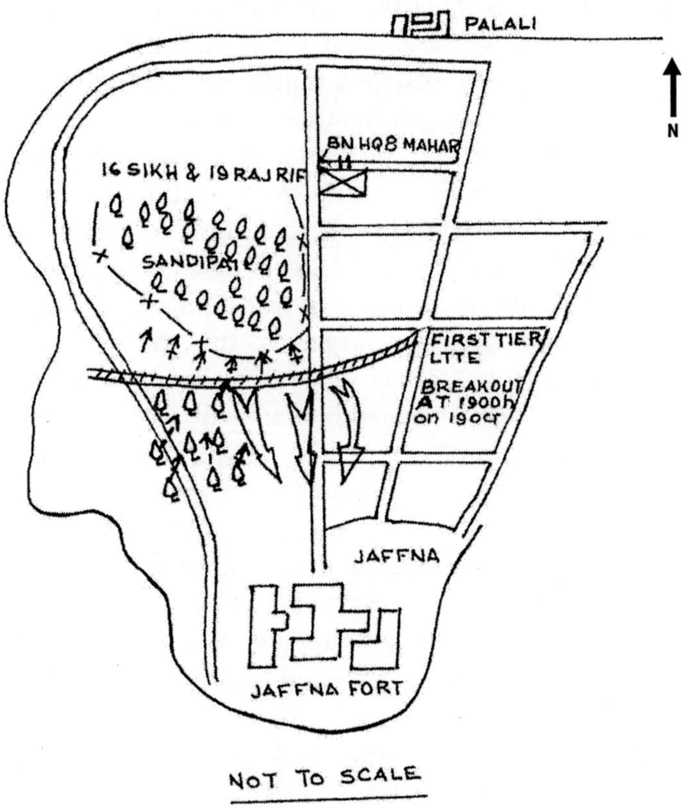


1. First engagement with LTTE.
2. LTTE surrounded 16 SIKH and later 19 RAJ RIF.
3. LTTE had prepared Firing positions in numbers of high trees in successive echelons.
4. 19 RAJ RIF Joined at around 0100 19 Oct.
5. 16 SIKH and 19 RAJ RIF group broke out on 19 Oct. 1900 h.

weapon during day, or the muzzle-flash at night. Since these guns were sited on tree-tops and well camouflaged there was no trace of flash and no dust. A number of such machine-guns being fired from various directions produced confusing echoes. Such tactics which the LTTE employed were totally unconventional and ingenious. Our troops took some time to understand the whole thing. Initially they had taken positions to reorient themselves and to make a plan of action. After some time it became very obvious that normal digging down as in a defence, or of holding a position to operate from, as taught in conventional training, would merely invite more casualties. The moment the LTTE found the target stationary they tended to close onto the target from all directions to take more effective shots. Fighting against such targets or enemy required constant change of positions and not giving them any stationary target. In fact, to make them the targets so that they also could not get respite to be more effective and close onto us. Under such circumstances creating a smoke screen to blind the enemy and prevent him from seeing the troops' movement was very important. But we did not have the means.

"Lt. Nagar was a young, energetic and efficient young officer who had recently joined the battalion which his father commanded till some months before. I had seen him growing up in front of me. Along with his outdoor activities he had a good academic career. He passed M.A. in geography in the first class. In fact, I always used to advise him to pick up a civil job. But in reply he always used to flash a smile and reply "Why Uncle, what is wrong with the army. You all are also serving in the army." I really did not have any answer to that. Since he had grown up in the battalion it was more than his home. Actually that is the type of bond we develop in the army. He was loved by each one of the battalion as a child of the unit. He was leading the forward platoon of "Alpha" Company. He was in the forefront and making minor manoeuvres as he successfully cleared a few enemy positions en route.

"As our unit was getting closer to its objective the engagements were getting stiffer and more intense. As mentioned before, the enemy was trying to surround the battalion. The enemy would reoccupy the same position after it was cleared and the unit went ahead. Then he would bring down fire from behind. Unlike conventional war there was no uniform for the enemy. They were not required to hold any ground. They could always fight for space. At that point in time and place, we were the only unit which was operating on that route. We were on the move, and so had neither the time nor the task of holding and consolidating our position. Our flanks and rear was not protected. If we had had our full battle strength we would have been able to get well dispersed and to change the centre of gravity. In this situation it would have been ideal to send 19 RAJ RIF along with us to operate as one brigade group. There was no point of sending the battalion on the same route but with a gap of about four hours. In this way the brigade's low strength got further dissipated.

"As the opposition got stiffer, the progress was getting slowed down. Under such conditions, at one point, the progress of the unit got totally stalled. Some movement became imperative in order to thwart the enemy effort to encircle the battalion. Lt. Nagar took charge of the situation. He was commanding a platoon of only ten soldiers as opposed to the authorized strength of thirty six, thus in effect he was leading what was the point section of a non-existent platoon, rather than the leading platoon, and under normal conditions his platoon would have been considered ineffective. He took his "platoon" and tried to outflank the enemy position from where a heavy volume of fire was holding up our advance. He successfully got close to the objective. While he was charging he got a burst of fire on his chest and fell down to never get up again: the sad end of a brave soldier. He laid down his life for the folly of higher ups who did not know themselves what cause they were fighting for, and how it was to be organized. Two attempts were made against a heavy volume of enemy power to extricate the body. It proved impossible. It was then decided to get the body at night under cover of darkness.

"Having considered all aspects of the situation, it was decided that 16 SIKH would be reinforced by 19 RAJ RIF. I was to go with them. By then, 16 SIKH had been without their CO for more than 18 hours at that crucial juncture!

"We started a little after midnight. Again the problem was the same: how to identify the location and reach there without any exchange of fire amongst own troops. 16 SIKH was already emotionally highly charged, and at the same time 19 RAJ RIF was getting launched into an active fight for the first time. I could very well visualize their state of mind. They had and were facing the same problems that we had faced and were facing. By then the intensity of LTTE firing had reduced. Probably they were running short of ammunition or else restricted themselves against a bigger strength. After constant radio communication and corrections of course we could ultimately link up with each other. It was a great relief for me as well as for my battalion.

"By the time I reached the battalion it was about 0300 hours on 19 October. On reaching there after so many hours I could get a full account of what had happened so far. The battalion was tired and hungry but there was no time to think about that. The first thing was to redistribute the ammunition which I had been able to get. I decided to evacuate the casualties immediately after daybreak. The escort could then get more ammunition which we needed en route. Only two hours were left for first light. I could understand that another long and tough day lay ahead. I passed instructions to intensify patrolling to avoid being surprised at night and to keep the intruding enemy at bay. CO 19 RAJ RIF was also briefed by our Adjutant, Captain Motilal Kataria, about the situation and the extent of the area we were holding. 19 RAJ RIF was also assisted in occupying a suitable defensive position so that we could take up an all-round defence. We tried to divide the area into two zones, east and west of the road. Lt. Col. Mukherjee and I decided to meet sometime later after taking stock of the situation, to discuss the further course of action.

"After a little rest for about an hour, after daybreak the first thing I did was to go to all the company locations and to talk to the men. I wanted to raise their morale and get them going. It was by no means an easy task. Everyone was hungry and tired and down to their last ounce of energy. We had been moving for three days without any rest, and practically without any food. I could not really search for the right words to communicate but for "*Shabash jawan*, you are doing an excellent job." The words sounded hollow to my own ears, as they were fighting with both hands tied at their back. However I could not leave things to that. I told them that we were to complete our given task. It was a matter of pride and honour for us, for our battalion in particular and for the army in general that we got this opportunity to help our neighbouring country and help them out of their own imbroglio. The entire nation was looking towards us. We must carry out the given task and show to the world that with all the adversities we were facing, we would take on the hard and seasoned LTTE even-handedly and carry out the task with utmost professional approach. But at the same time I also knew at the core of my heart what was going across the mind of my soldiers, who had just been blooded in battle, and who were hungry, tired and equipped much below their operational requirement.

"I was very worried about the replenishment of arms and ammunition, reinforcement of the troops, evacuation of casualties and many other problems. Under normal circumstances the administration part is given as much attention as the tactical operation itself. A chain of logistics is planned, located and executed at each level from army level down to the battalion level through Corps, division, brigade and so on. Perhaps these had been planned on paper, but were not effective on the ground as far as the soldiers were concerned. Under the circumstances, no vehicle could be used to move forward and reach us with our necessities and carry the casualties back. We had to fend for ourselves. I organized a small party who were tough and had an indomitable spirit. I put a JCO in charge and asked them to take the wounded soldiers back to the 8 MAHAR location where they could be given proper first-aid and later evacuated if necessary. By then we had four casualties who needed evacuation. They were to be carried as they were not in a condition to walk. For this I had to send one JCO and 19 O.R. which included the fighting porters who would carry the casualties, and if required also fight the LTTE if they encountered any en route. They were also instructed to bring back ammunition and some cooked food. The Adjutant forewarned the Mahar HQ what they were expected to handle and provide for us. After this I studied the map to reorient myself as I did not have a clue about our location, having been away from the battalion for the whole of the previous day. By that time sporadic firing had started with the same LTTE tactics of trying to surround us from all sides. I gave strict orders not to waste ammunition by firing for the sake of firing. I insisted that troops must be dispersed as much as the tactical siting would permit. There should be no unnecessary exposure, but the perimeter patrolling and link patrolling with 19 RAJ RIF were to continue. All these things took some time. We had one of the most important tasks at hand which was to dispose of the dead soldiers. It was the most painful task under the circumstances. In normal circumstances bodies are sent back to the unit Rear or to their respective families if possible for performing the last rites. But at that time we the fighting soldiers had to perform the task. We had to dig graves and bury them as consignment to fire was not possible at that moment. When all these things were going on at our end, the brigade and divisional headquarters, unaware of all this, were pressurizing us to start our move. No one had any time to ask or find out about our situation, our requirements, and how these were to be met, and to plan the operation.

"When two battalions of a brigade, which generally consists of three battalions under normal circumstances, are operating the tactical headquarters of the brigade consisting of the Brigade Commander and his tactical headquarters should have moved with them to direct the battle. At that time our 41 Brigade had only these two battalions under command; all the more reason for him to have been with us. Instead he tried to control the operation from the 8 MAHAR location where he was ensconced, away from the battlefield and from the realities. Having taken over the command, in actuality, only the previous day, neither the brigade commander nor the troops had the necessary cohesion and understanding so critical at this stage. Ideally he should have led from the front. There was no one to give orders and coordinate the operations of 16 SIKH and 19 RAJ RIF. We were fighting our own battle and planning our own operation.

"I had a detailed discussion with the company commanders and decided to again break out not as a single column but in company groups as our numbers were too low. But the biggest problems remained: lack of signal sets, their batteries and maps. These three things are essential for conduct of such battles which are to be fought at sub-unit level, well dispersed to be able to converge at the right time and right place to influence the outcome. It was very difficult to conduct such operation without the required wherewithal. However we decided to operate in separate groups but with some adjustments so that we would remain within mutual visual contact. Thankfully Lt. Col. Mukherjee and I had become good friends during our peace tenure at Lucknow. We had no problem in interacting with each other. We always remained in contact with each other on the radio set. I tried to coordinate our operation by dividing the area of operation so as not to be fired upon by our own troops. Under such circumstances even any small movement may cause firing. Having decided that we were ready to start, we formed ourselves into four groups. We reorganized among ourselves to ensure that each company, more or less, had almost the same number of fighting troops.

Time by then was about 1100 and I asked the adjutant, Captain Motilal Kataria, who used to be affectionately called 'Moti' (*pearl*), to inform the brigade headquarters about our plan and also to say that we were waiting for the return of those 20 soldiers who had successfully evacuated the wounded soldiers. We were expecting food and replenishment of ammunition which had become dangerously low. The troops had been existing on very scanty food for the last couple of days. We had nothing to eat in the morning and nothing was expected till we reached Jaffna Fort. As we were getting closer to Jaffna Fort the battle was expected to get tougher; holding of Jaffna as a whole was the symbol of authority and control for either side.

"It is pertinent to mention here that before 41 Brigade was launched on 18 October, 54 Division had launched its operation to capture Jaffna on 11 October, on three thrust lines with three brigades, viz. 18, 72 and 91 Infantry Brigades. While 91 and 72 were to advance from north, 18 Infantry Brigade was advancing from the east from the direction of Elephant Pass located in the east of Jaffna and which was the only road link available between Jaffna and the rest of the Sri Lanka. These brigades were facing stiff resistance from the LTTE along each of their thrust lines. Their progress had been very slow. The Army Commander, Lt. Gen. Depinder Singh had given in his Operational Directive a time period of four days to clear Jaffna town. By 17 October they could at most clear only up to half-way to Jaffna Fort from Palali in the north and Elephant Pass in the east. The advance lost momentum on all these thrust lines due to stiff enemy resistance. By 16$^{th}$ afternoon our 41 Infantry Brigade less a battalion, with merely twenty percent troops, had landed in Jaffna and with an under-strength 16 SIKH and 19 RAJ RIF were launched on 18 October on the north-west axis and 115 Infantry Brigade was launched from the north-east axis on the same day. So on 18 October a total of five brigade thrust lines were trying to converge towards Jaffna town. Three infantry brigades were operating from 11 October and two more from 18th October. That was the scenario on the morning of 19 October when we were fighting at Uduvil near Sandipai.

"The question arises as to how could the LTTE fight the mighty Indian Army on five axes and put up a reasonably stiff fight, not allowing the Indian Army easy progress. The LTTE had the advantage of fighting the battle on interior lines. They were fighting from their own land. Their rear was secured. They had the superiority of intelligence network, signal system and fire-power at the cutting-edge level. The entire population was with them whether voluntarily or coerced. Moreover, they did not have the responsibility of holding any ground. They could withdraw and reoccupy any ground held or lost at their will. And there was no need for them to put up any pitched battle. Another most difficult factor in this case was, there was no distinguishing uniform worn by them. They could always operate by mingling amongst the civilian crowd. This made firing at the LTTE a very difficult task lest there was any civilian casualty. They were completely dominating there own area and could use any lane, by-lane, tree-top, or house-top to bring down fire, and shift their place the moment their place was threatened. Their constant movement was possible as they were operating in small detachments and their battle procedure was refined after almost a decade of operational experience. They operated in small groups and moving constantly by way of walking, riding cycles or under special circumstances traveling in vehicles. Their lateral movements were excellently planned taking all the advantages of existing roads and tracks. The forest and vegetation provided them excellent cover and since they were mostly in civil clothes identification initially was extremely difficult. Their lack of strength was offset by the types of weapons they were using. Seventy five percent of them were using either AK-47 or G-3 rifles. Both these were automatic. The rest had light machine-guns (LMG's) or medium machine-guns (MMG's), mortars and explosives. Their explosives were lethal and caused maximum damage on various targets. Within every group they used to have unarmed followers who would pick up the guns from the dead or wounded compatriots. So their number of cadres would never go down. We should always remember that we were fighting against one of the most successful militant groups of our time who had unsettled their own government troops by taking them head on. They were fully trained in their own game.

"Now, to go back to the battlefield. Except for getting frequent calls from the brigade commander urging us to move there was no tactical, logistical or directional help. Between Lt. Col. Mukherjee and I, we decided that after we dispose of our dead, get some replenishment of ammunition and receive some food to eat, we shall try to break out separately by out flanking moves and shall rendezvous at the coastal road where we were to link up with the isolated company of 8 MAHAR. Lt. Col. Mukherjee and I were quite apprehensive of again starting a mid-day battle with all the advantages on the enemy's side, lest the previous day's situation was repeated. We tried to explain that to Brig. Manjit Singh but he would not listen to our joint recommendation. As he was far away from the site of happening, and did not yet have first hand experience of fighting against LTTE, and also was never a part of the brigade till one day before, he could not comprehend the battle situation. He could only ask us to hurry as the pressure was building up from the top. Under this situation it would have been ideal to hold on for the day and start operations after night fall. It would have deprived the LTTE fighters of their superior observation and fire power. It would have given us a level ground to act as opposed to LTTE domination. But our commander would not take the simple logic. We kept the timing at about 12 noon. The fire-fight with the LTTE was going on.

"We started our movement as planned. One company group was commanded by Maj. Ramcharan and the other by Maj. N. C. Bhatt. Maj. Ramcharan was to make an out-flanking move from the western direction. He was given a bound after about four kilometers. Similar was the case with Major N. C. Bhatt. He was to take the eastern flank. By reaching the given bound, we expected to circumvent the enemy positions and split their firepower. We had created a fire base to provide supporting fire to these company groups by leap-frogging, advancing by constantly changing the position as found suitable. The biggest problem confronting this move was the absence of basic needs like maps, compasses, binoculars etc. These are the essential instruments for any ground battle from section level right up to an army level operation. 19 RAJ RIF also made similar plans.

"No sooner had we started our move than there was a tremendous amount of fire that was brought to bear upon us from all directions. It appeared that the LTTE, during this pause, had reinforced its positions.

For the protection of Jaffna town the LTTE had planned four tiers of defense as follows:

(a) Puttur - Chunakam - Sandipai
(b) Urumparai - Kondavil - Manipai
(c) Navatkuli - Kopai - Coastal Road
(d) Jaffna town.

From studying the map I could make out that we had hit the second line of defence. We tried to manoeuvre out of the present situation by making out-flanking moves as planned. The advance obviously was very slow. Our weapons were out-matched by more advanced and automatic weapons of LTTE. Our support base tried to neutralize enemy fire by bringing down heavy volume of fire. But with all our efforts we could not negate the advantages that the LTTE had gained. The most important factor amongst all these was that they could see us but we could not see them resulting in a very accurate fire from them whereas our fire was speculative. At the same time we were projecting a much larger and conspicuous force than they were. As a result our casualties started mounting. Maj. Ramcharan had hit a very thick jungle which was not marked in the photocopy of tourist map that we got. Visibility inside the jungle even at noon was couple just a couple of yards. At one point Maj. Ramcharan found himself crawling over a snake! The forest was so thick with undergrowth that he could not move forward. Maj. N. C. Bhatt's route was more open, but he was facing very heavy fire. Ramcharan had already reported one dead and three wounded. Maj. Bhatt also reported casualties.

"The situation on 19 RAJ RIF's line of advance was similar. They were also facing stiff resistance. It was gradually getting clearer that any further attempt to advance would be suicidal. Fighting a battle is not being a gladiator. Discretion is the better part of valour. It was not that there was any problem with our capability of taking the LTTE head on. But as their commander, I was directly responsible to ensure that the task given to me was carried out without wanton destruction of my troops. Each life was valuable to me. They had to live for the next day to carry out the next task. We had no information about the battalion's main column which was said to be coming by train and were to join us within three days. *(Actually, this main column reached us after 33 days via Elephant Pass!)*. By about 1 p.m. casualties mounted to three dead and five wounded including our Jemadar Adjutant, who was assisting the Adjutant. He was hit in his stomach. In one case an LMG detachment commander Naik Sujan Singh had done an extremely good job before he laid down his life. When he found that Maj. Ramcharan's group, of which he was a part, got stuck, he with his detachment took the initiative and made a small hook to catch by surprise the LTTE party that was holding up Maj. Ramcharan's advance. That detachment showed a classical example of field-craft and beat the enemy at his own game. He silenced that position so effectively that Maj. Ramcharan could rearrange his positions. But unfortunately his luck did not match his valour. While changing his position, which he did a number of times, he took a bullet in his head and crumpled over his own weapon. What could be a better end to a soldier but for what? These were avoidable casualties....

"From the pattern of the casualties and enemy firing I could make out that the LTTE had sited their weapons in such a way that all open areas between the jungle or groves were covered by his machine guns. He knew that firing into the groves was less effective as his enemy was unseen. This could only help in pinning us down but actual effect could be derived once we came out in the open. To move we had to come out in the open and each effort resulted in casualties. To counter this we needed to lay a smoke screen by our 81 mm mortars which are the battalion's own integral weapons, or by artillery. Unfortunately both were missing. Our own weapons were in the train and as regards an artillery fire plan, Brig. Manjit Singh had no such plan to assist his fighting troops.

"On the other hand, there was constant pressure from the brigade and divisional headquarters asking for progress every half an hour as if we had gone out on some kind of a speed march competition! There were a couple of funny radio communications I had with Brig. Manjit Singh, and later with the officiating Divisional Commander. In one of such innumerable conversations with the brigade commander he asked me the progress and I narrated what was going on in the battlefield, and I asked him to have patience as we had to apply at least basic tactics as we were engaged in a live battle and not taking part in mock training. We had to assess the ground situation and also consider the enemy reaction. We would have to change or make amendments to our plan accordingly. But he would only insist on our breaking out and was neither prepared to the change of plan nor provide us covering fire with high explosive, or more effective under that situation, a smoke screen. I was trying to explain him the advantages that would have accrued by undertaking the same operation at night. Night operation would have made all these well-sited weapons and well planned tactics of the enemy non-effective, and we could take that advantage and proceed on our planned move. But our brigade commander was in no mood to listen to this logic. He said "Whatever the situation is you will have to move." I asked him what was so urgent; the security of our country was not in jeopardy, that I should have to sacrifice my own troops for nothing? As a commander in the field and being on the spot did I not have my own discretion to apply within the overall plan? I got one of the weirdest replies one can ever hear in a battlefield from his superior commander. He said, "The Chief has given his word to the Prime Minister, who is now visiting U.S.A., that the whole thing would be cleared in seven days. So we will have to hurry." I was flabbergasted with such an unprofessional reply. After a pause, after collecting my wits I told him "Sir, both your battalions are fighting here but there is no command element to coordinate the operation and give orders at the site. Why don't you come down here and take the lead?" In reply I heard the sound of a click and the radio set went off the air. The net result was that we found our Deputy Brigade Commander, Col. S.K. Singh, arriving and taking over command. Brig. Manjit Singh stayed put at the HQ 8 MAHAR location.

"Another interesting conversation was with the Officiating Divisional Commander. He was from the armoured corps: therefore during most of his career he had dealt with tanks. Urging us to "break out" despite my reasoning against it, he said "You have five companies to operate you must go out in five directions." Again I called for God Almighty to enlighten me and show the right direction! The basic structure of an infantry battalion is to have four rifle companies who are the cutting edge and one Headquarters Company which undertakes support work which includes transport, quartermaster element and supporting arms elements etc; which are not supposed to get involved in tactical manoeuvres independently. However due to the extreme conditions prevailing then, I already had distributed many of these elements, who are to provide administrative support, to the rifle companies in order to augment their bayonet strength. But considering them purely as a fighting element would be unrealistic.

"On arrival of the Deputy Brigade Commander, both of us briefed him and he also saw the conditions for himself. We had a short discussion. On seeing and listening to everything he also chose prudence and decided to start the link-up operation after nightfall. It was also decided that both 19 RAJ RIF and our battalion would move as a brigade group and not separately. Up to the coastal road junction and the link-up with the 8 MAHAR company, 19 RAJ RIF would lead, and after that till the link-up with Jaffna Fort 16 SIKH would again take the lead. I called the Adjutant. I gave him necessary orders for the night operation, check weapons and ammunition, make night-march-charts, and, as the intensity of the firing had reduced, to take as much rest as possible. I did not see any possibility of having food for dinner and also for the following day till link-up; I told the troops to save something for the following day from whatever little we had.

"We started our march at about 1900 after nightfall and it became completely dark. We decided to move out in small groups to avoid detection. We formed a team which would evacuate the wounded to the 8 MAHAR HQ location. This would further deplete our strength but it had to be done: there was no alternative. As much as possible we decided to move alongside the tree line to avoid giving a silhouette view of our movement. Movement was slow but steady. There was enemy fire but from a distance and not effective. I repeatedly passed orders not to fire in panic, and not to give away our position or intention under any circumstances. We had to conserve our fire now and use it at appropriate time while linking up with the Jaffna Fort. The resistance was likely to be stiffest at that time. We had informed the brigade headquarters about our plan and the start time. I instructed that no one was to lose contact or get lost. Speed was to be maintained accordingly. Our advance gradually gained momentum. It was the dark phase of the moon. We took the advantage of the total darkness which was intensified operating in jungle area. Our constant recommendation that operation at night under the circumstances will bring the desired result was vindicated. Though there had been pockets of LTTE resistance and firing but we could easily bypass them without getting involved in a fire-fight. It appeared that we had broken through the second tier of defence of the LTTE

**41 INFANTRY BRIGADE**
**ADVANCE TO KOKUVIL**
**NIGHT 19/20 OCT**

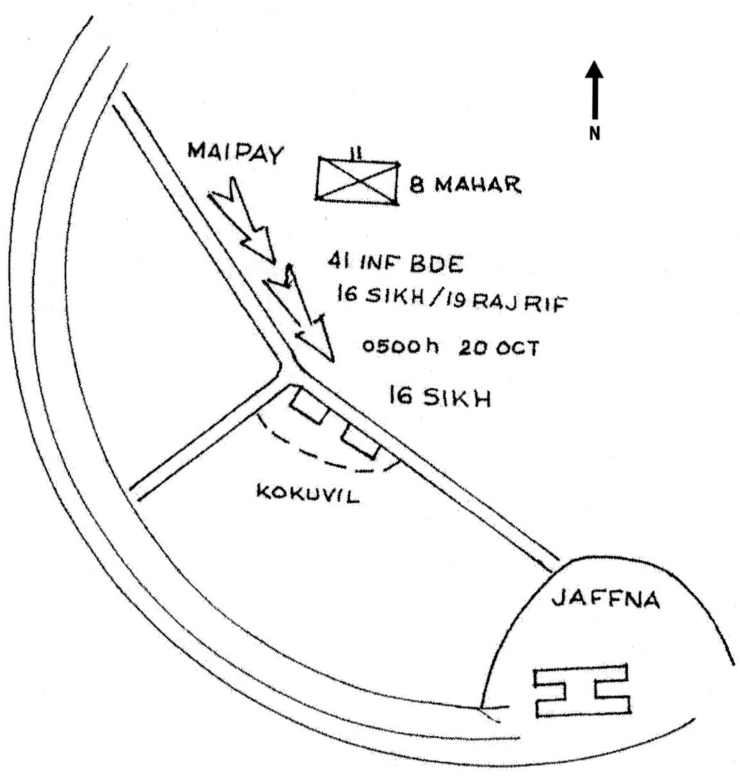

and were heading for the third tier. By then we had got a certain idea of the LTTE pattern of battle. Since they did not have adequate strength they would not come out for open battle. Their operations, at that time, were jungle-based where they could move undetected and they had prepared certain positions well in advance.

"All these I was considering in my mind while we were moving. Our battalion despite all we had gone through in the last 48 hours and being hungry, tired and fatigued, was doing an excellent job. Within one day they seemed to have adapted themselves and looked like seasoned fighters in jungle as well as semi-urban areas. Their movement, battle craft, navigation, fire discipline etc., all became perfect. For the first time I was more easy in my mind as we were doing the correct thing that should have been done from the beginning. Things were going very smoothly like a well-oiled machine. The transformation was complete. We were deftly handling the situation, fighting where needed, avoiding where possible. The best thing was that the LTTE seemed to be unable to keep pace with us as we were making unpredictable moves by changing our direction frequently though keeping our general line of direction intact. Since the LTTE did not have wide fixed defenses on the ground it was possible for us. They had to change positions every time we changed our direction of advance. Before they could do that we would be out of that area.

"It was a real hide-and-seek game but with live bullets. Our night advance went on well. We achieved total surprise. By daybreak we could reach near the third tier of defence touching the coastal road. From there our last thrust would take us to the much-coveted objective, Jaffna town, citadel of the LTTE and much cherished dream prize of both the Sri Lankan and the Indian Army which so far had eluded both. We were getting excited about it. By getting success after our initial set-backs, our morale and confidence both soared sky high. We cleared all the LTTE opposition en route and by daybreak we came very close to our second rendezvous. Col. S. K. Singh, Deputy

Commander 41 Infantry Brigade, Lt. Col. S. K. Mukherjee, CO 19 RAJ RIF, and I had a quick conference at our last halt before the day broke and discussed our future mode of action. A few things were getting obvious. These were:

(a) The battle at the third tier would be bloody. The enemy would obviously put up a very stiff fight to thwart our successful advance. Once we cleared the third tier, the road to Jaffna would be wide open.

(b) Before this all-important operation began, the troops needed rest, food and replenishment. While food and replenishment were not certain as there was no administrative plan of the brigade or division, we ought to give them some rest even if only for a few hours.

(c) In order to provide them uninterrupted rest we decided to capture and occupy a built-up area that would be adequate to hold the weakest brigade that any operation ever saw. Though there were possibilities of a stiff hand-to-hand fight, but once taken, which we became confident of taking by then, it would provide uninterrupted rest to our troops as the LTTE was not known to have artillery, and small arms fire would not be able to penetrate as in the case of a jungle.

(d) We were to keep very strict vigil IEDs planted by the LTTE on our route as our options were getting narrower.

(e) Linking up initially with the 8 MAHAR company.

(f) Fighting in the built-up area.

(g) Very important, we had the LTTE on the run. Beat them in time and space before they could reorganize. I was sure that to fight against the Indian Army they would not dare to use raw cadres. They would have to shift their veterans and that was not easy as they were engaged simultaneously at a number of locations. We had a fine moment to choose. Hopefully God and time was with us.

(h) The place should be so located that linking-up with the 8 MAHAR Company and getting on to the route to Jaffna should be easy to accomplish.

"On studying the map (photo copy of a tourist map), we decided on a built-up area, reasonably large enough to house the weak brigade, and with adequate dispersal area. This was larger than what the LTTE could hold and defend with their expected small strength. We planned to halt about 2 km. short of this newly-selected intermediate objective and send out strong patrols to get as much information as possible about the enemy location, strength, disposition if possible and entry and exit routes of the objective. But the patrols were strictly told that they were to come back at least one hour before first light and under no condition to give away their position. Less information was acceptable rather than losing surprise which was very vital. We had to surprise the enemy this time. This was our biggest weapon at that moment to achieve success with the least number of casualties.

"About 2 km. short of our selected objective we took a halt. We still had two options; one, to invest and enter the target straightaway without any preliminary reconnaissance and take the objective by sheer weight of the troops, or go step by step as we had discussed. I was all for going methodically step by step.

We had just witnessed what happens when something is done in haste. The objective was divided in two sub-sectors based on available land marks on the map for the two battalions. The sub-sectors were again divided into company objectives. Brigade tactical headquarters, as represented only by the Deputy Commander, Col. S. K. Singh, who for us was the *de facto* brigade commander with no staff officer or other staff to accompany him, and the two battalion headquarters were to be suitably lodged. Two strong reconnaissance patrols were formed, one from each battalion. Each battalion patrol would again comprise of elements from each rifle company. Each rifle company's detachments were to reconnoiter their respective allotted areas. They should locate the entry and exit routes very carefully. But it was also made clear that under no circumstances were they to get physically too close and disclose their presence. Each patrol was to be led by a company commander. In our case it was led by Maj. Govind Sisodia, a fine soldier, full of initiative and with a good tactical mind. We saw the launching of the patrols and started waiting excitedly for their safe and successful return. Operational success and saving of many lives depended on their success.

"After seeing them off, my other officers, company senior J.C.O.'s and I had a mini- conference to decide on the method of tackling the built-up area. Fighting in a built-up area is one of the most difficult as it is casualty-prone and slow. On top of that, in case the LTTE got prior warning of our intension, or this particular built up area was in their plan for preparing IEDs or booby traps as part of their defensive plan, then we were again in for trouble. We were also briefed on the radio by Brig. Manjit Singh that at the backyard of each house there would be a bunker occupied by the LTTE, or which would be occupied when the need arose. They would put up a fight from there. I personally, though, was not very convinced with that theory, but I was neither competent not interested to conduct any further research on it. We, therefore, decided against using the front or the rear entrance/exits to avoid explosives or direct firing weapons, as the entrance would definitely be covered by an automatic weapon. We planned to enter through an unexpected entry point by making a hole in the compound wall and rushing into the house thereby not giving them any chance to recover. The entire plan was discussed again and again with the officers and the J.C.O's and they were told to drill this into each soldier. I categorically told them that I want complete victory with minimum, and if possible, no casualties. It was possible as I could sense at least in our sector they were at least for the time being off balance and we must take complete advantage of it. I was myself feeling great and confident seeing the enthusiasm and confidence of my troops.

"We eagerly awaited the return of the patrol. We maintained complete signal silence only to be broken on S.O.S. Time ticked on. There was complete silence all over. I had an eerie feeling about this. I was not sure whether we were under observation of the LTTE or whether we could really hoodwink them. But the battle indications suggested that we were not under observation. Otherwise our activities would definitely have drawn their fire.

"At about 4 a.m. the Adjutant, Capt. Motilal Kataria, informed me that the patrol was back. I asked him to immediately arrange for a debriefing. The patrol did not see much of activities there. I found out that the patrol could not observe any movement enroute or near the village we were aiming to harbour in. As per the patrol leader Maj. Govind Sisodia things were calm and we should be able to get into the village without much difficulty though total avoidance of a fire-fight was unlikely. Anyhow we, as a brigade group decided to start immediately so that we could occupy the village before first light and site our defenses.

"Without wasting any more time we resumed our march. We reached the entrance of the village without much opposition, but at the entrance of the village we were fired upon. As was planned we divided our force into four company groups and made a four-pronged attack to confuse and divide the enemy force. We did not use the normal entry and exit points of the houses. That completely surprised the enemy. Breaking through the walls we systematically started clearing the houses starting from the backyards. There we found hiding LTTE fighters. Dividing our troops into a number of company groups totally surprised the enemy. They were overwhelmed. After we cleared a couple of bunkers we found for the first time that the LTTE were withdrawing. We started chasing them. There started a typical street fight. Here I experienced the problem of the paucity of radio sets. It became difficult to control and coordinate the operation. I did not want that in our over-enthusiasm we were drawn outside the built-up area and take unnecessary casualties. Even the built-up area required proper search and clearance of IED's or any booby traps. It took about one and half hours of stiff fighting before the area could be cleared. We had five enemy dead and by God's grace no casualty on our side. Our soldiers were getting seasoned overnight.

## 16 SIKH
## (41 INFANTRY BRIGADE)
## FIGHTING IN BUILT UP AREA
## BATTLE AT KOKUVIL 20 OCT

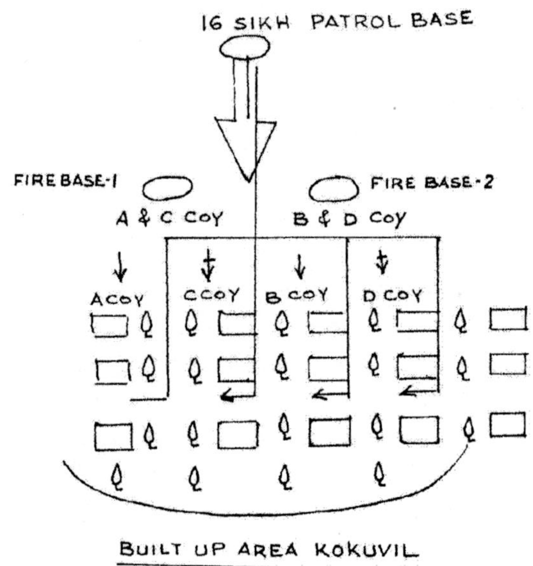


**Not to Scale**

NOTE :-

1. Operation was launched simultaneously by dividing the objective to avoid concentration of LTTE fire.
2. Obvious entrances like front and Rear entries were avoided.
3. Unorthodox entries like making holes through walls were used.
4. Two fire boses were created one for each column.

**LEGEND:**

⟶ (crossed) MMG

⟶ LMG

"It was 19 October. We had four days of continuous operations and movement with very little sleep and practically no food. I passed orders to establish a perimeter defense, to post sentries, and to take as much rest as possible till 12 noon. During this time weapons were to be maintained and ammunition redistributed. Unfortunately, I could not provide them any food. But the soldiers managed some raw vegetables from the kitchen gardens and nearby fields which they managed to boil and eat. We had the last but most important battle of this phase ahead. That was the link up with Jaffna Fort. We were also to locate the isolated Mahar company. We were not sure of its location and we did not have any radio communication with them.

"As was expected, within an hour or so LTTE fighters started engaging us with light and medium machine-guns. Our decision to take cover in a built-up area was vindicated as the firing did not have any direct effect upon us. I only asked the company commanders to ensure against any unnecessary exposure to enemy fire and to conserve ammunition which was again running low, and to keep strict vigil on any movement be it enemy or civilian as we had no way to distinguish between them. After we settled down we coordinated with 19 RAJ RIF. I met the de facto brigade commander, Col. S. K. Singh, discussed the next phase and set out to inspect the village. The impression that I gathered was that the occupants had vacated the village in a hurry. At many houses there was half-cooked foods, fridges wide open, doors of the houses wide open, clothes and other household items strewn around. The occupants had left but their presence was felt. I could understand that they were being caught between the LTTE and the Indian Army. They were only trying to save their lives.

"Though rest was essential we wanted to out-manoeuvre the LTTE both in time, space and pace. To beat them at their own game. We, therefore, decided to resume our advance at 2 p.m. which would give us adequate daylight to look for the isolated company, and also later on allow the use of darkness to start beginning of clearing the fourth tier of the LTTE defence. This was expected to be the stiffest as it would be the classical operation of clearing of a built-up area which is considered the most difficult operation in terms of casualties, destruction, and time. Jaffna, had been till then the symbol of power, authority and representation of defiance. Whosoever held it had a psychological advantage. Besides that by then each inch of Jaffna would have been well-prepared to put up a solid defence by employing explosives in various forms, siting of automatic weapons at all the vantage points, and preparing a number of defensive positions. All roads were expected to be covered by the dreaded IED's in which they had achieved great dexterity.

"We had sent out a couple of strong patrols from both the battalions to locate the Mahar company. For some reason we were not being opposed to the extent we were expecting. There could be two possibilities; one, we had out-paced them, and they were unable to bring in as much reinforcement as was required, two, they had given up on this third tier of defence and were trying to consolidate their fourth and critical tier that was Jaffna town itself. The second one was more probable.

"Our patrols were able to locate the Mahar company. It was definitely field-craft of a very high order. To locate a company in the wilderness without any kind of assistance, not even a proper map, was no mean task. The Mahar company was overjoyed; since we had relieved the pressure on them by driving out the LTTE from that area, they could easily bring in their reinforcements, administrative requirements and evacuate casualties. However we did not have much time to spend there. We were heading for the coastal road junction which would take us to Jaffna Fort. While moving in that direction we found a company of 5 RAJ RIF which was held up. We took them along with us. There we got to know that Brig. Manjit Singh while staying back and not joining his brigade, had managed two BMPs *(armoured infantry combat vehicles)*. He sat in one of them. At that time our brigade had been allotted another battalion, 5 RAJ RIF. He took troops of that battalion with him.

One BMP got blown up by the LTTE. He could manage to reach inside the Jaffna Fort before us using the other BMP. In the process that company of 5 RAJ RIF, while providing protection to Brig. Manjit Singh, had got left back.

"By about 10 p.m. of 20 October we reached the outskirts of Jaffna town. The Jaffna Fort was approximately five km away from the place where we halted. From there on we had to take the coastal road to reach the Jaffna Fort. We had to take a halt there for a couple of reasons. Firstly, some rest had become very essential before the final push. The troops had been on the march in an opposed advance for the last 48 hours without practically any food and rest. Secondly, from there on 16 SIKH was to take the lead again, therefore, a change in the order of march was necessary. Thirdly, there was a need to formulate a plan to undertake the operation. The area in front was covered by jungle. Where the jungle would recede, the built-up area would start; initially with scattered houses, followed gradually by a more thickly populated area.

"We decided that we must aim to reach the fort before dawn. Stiff resistance was expected. We were about to break the backbone of the enemy. It was a battle of guts and nerves. I had a mini-conference with my 'O' Group, and then went around to all the company groups where the men were resting, to explain the importance of this phase of the operation. "The whole nation must be waiting for this moment" I told them, and continued, "Though the enemy will try their best to stop us but presently we are making them to react to our moves. We should not get unduly cautious or be inhibited by them. The time has come to take bold action. Since it is night, therefore, the fire of the enemy will not be effective, so speed is the most essential requirement. We may not go for clearing each enemy firing position unless it is effective and hindering our advance. We must avoid *pucca* road, specially the culverts, to avoid IED's. When we get closer to the built-area we must fan out to confuse the enemy and not let him bring down concentrated fire on us." We were not fighting against a regular army. Militants are always short of troops unlike the army and they generally do not generally offer a pitched battle. They are not tasked to hold ground as in the case of an army. Therefore, we have to outflank them, get to their rear and make them vacate their positions. The only thing of importance was to avoid losing direction in the labyrinth of Jaffna. The paucity of radio sets was again going to be a problem. I asked the soldiers to follow their sixth sense and instinct. We then uttered our battle cry *"Jo Bole so nihal, Sat Sri Akal, Jai Gurujika ka Khalsa, Jai Guruji ki Fateh"* in a very subdued voice. We yet did not know whether the enemy was tracking us. But we could leave nothing to chance.

"We decided on our H Hour, i.e. our starting time, for this phase, which would be 2 a.m. 20 October 1987. We wanted to fight and cover the jungle portion during the night, have the advantage and cover of the darkness and have some daylight to fight in the built-up area, as we had no clue as to how Jaffna looked like and what its layout was.

"H Hour arrived. We started. All faces wore a very serious but determined look. My gut feeling was telling me that the tables had been turned and that we would be successful. We were having a kind of speed march off the road. The two company groups were on either side of the road well dispersed but within hearing distance in case we needed to pass any instructions. 'Alfa' and "Bravo" Companies were on the left of the road and would take care anything happening on the left, and "Charlie" and "Delta" were on the right of the road to take care anything happening on that side. Within about a kilometer we started being fired upon. But somehow I felt that effectiveness, intensity and determination were lacking in the firing by the enemy. They seemed to be firing from a distance and not from close by, unlike the LTTE. I sensed their weakness. Though the speed was reduced but we did not bother to divert our attention and clear those areas. As it was our rear was being protected by 19 RAJ RIF which was following close behind unlike in the initial stage. That might be another reason

**16 SIKH**

**(41 INFANTRY BRIGADE)**

**LINK UP WITH JAFFNA FOR**

**0500h - 2100**

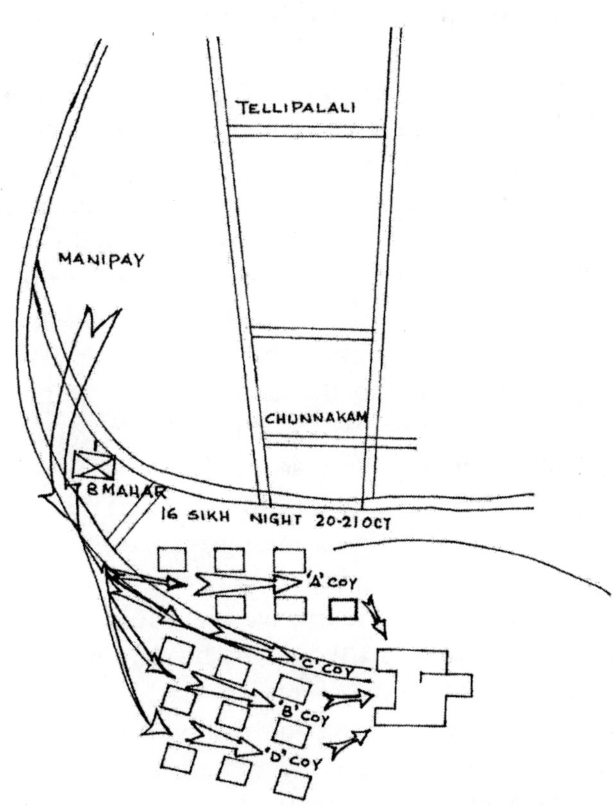


NOTE:-

1. About 3km short of the objective two task forces were created with two companies each.
2. Certain built up areas were cleared to have elbow Room before establishing link up.
3. one fire base for each task force.
4. Number of Company Columns split LTTE fire power and resistance

that they were not coming closer as this time they could not encircle us. We so far had no casualty. We were scrupulously avoiding the road. That did slow down the speed to a great extent as at many places we had to take small detours and halt for troops to maintain contact with each other. Under no circumstances did we want to lose contact.

"Around 4 p.m. we reached the outskirts of Jaffna. We could see the *pucca* houses in ones and twos. I released the companies from the column of march to get dispersed and take as many entry points as possible. We also had the advantage of 19 RAJ RIF providing further momentum. By pooling a few automatic weapons of whatever were with us, we created a fire base so that the assault group, who were busy in physically clearing the enemy positions did not lose their momentum. By then Jaffna town was only two and a half kilometers away. After some distance we started drawing enemy fire. The fire base was returning the fire and the assault troops went on to neutralize the positions. After two or three of such small operations the intensity of the resistance seemed to be waning. I felt the enemy was perhaps retreating and wanted to go inside Jaffna town and put up a last-ditch fight, having realized the futility of fighting in the outskirts and open areas where we could out-manouevre him. In our initial briefing we were told that the built-up area leading to Jaffna Fort would be heavily mined. That remained our area of caution before we could go full throttle. I was simultaneously checking the progress of the combined "Alfa" and "Bravo" Companies group and their progress was reported to be satisfactory. They were also effectively clearing the enemy opposition they were encountering. Our progress continued unhindered, and since the enemy did not put up a pitched battle anywhere we did not suffer any casualty till then. When we came almost within one kilometer of our final objective, nothing could restrain the troops, and the entire battalion and also the other troops of the brigade reached the gates of the fort with double speed: happy and victorious. The time was about 6 a.m. on 20 October 1987.

"When we entered the fort we expected some reception with a cup of hot tea and some food. Instead I was told by a brigade HQ staff officer that Brig. Manjit Singh was not happy with our performance, and so as some kind of penalty we were to stay put in the sun outside, away from the main fort, and be prepared for a night operation! There was a great resentment against this treatment being given to us by Brig. Manjit Singh, who was out to take all the credit himself and to subdue others' contribution. This is what that happens when a commander, who has no loyalty towards his troops and is basically a self-seeker, is thrust upon a formation, in such an important position of responsibility, compassion as well as professionalism."

*72 Infantry Brigade:* 13 SIKH LI secured Urumpirai in conjunction with 5 PARA, the third battalion of the brigade, on 18th October.

*91 Infantry Brigade:* On 19 October, 1 MARATHA LI, under its CO, Col. T.P.S "Tippy" Brar, in spite of heavy LTTE opposition, came out of Jaffna Fort while leaving elements to continue holding it, and established a link-up with the Commander 41 Infantry Brigade's party and the forward elements of 5 RAJ RIF, which had got held up for 48 hours at Mile 1.5 on the coastal road, with the 41 Brigade Commander (Brig. Manjit Singh) himself having got detached from his command for that entire period. The battalion thereafter was relieved from the fort to carry out operations to clear the islands south and south-east of the Jaffna peninsula.

Chapter 4

# 'Operation PAWAN' – Phase II: Capture of Jaffna Town

*20-26 October*

All five brigades continued to push forwards towards and contacted Jaffna town between 20 and 22 October.

*Operations by 16 SIKH (41 Infantry Brigade)*

Lt. Col. M. K. Gupta-Ray gives a detailed account, "On 20 October after fighting non-stop for more than 96 hours, practically without any food and sleep, we reached Jaffna Fort. We badly needed some rest, hot food, replenishment of ammunition and equipment, reinforcement, and evacuation of casualties. Having accomplished the task the troops felt very happy despite having suffered casualties and various other deprivations. We expected Brig. Manjit Singh, who was in the fort, to come and meet the troops and say a few words of appreciation. But he did not do so. He, on the other hand, made no arrangements and did not even try to make the troops comfortable. We were made to sit under the hot sun at the rear part of the Fort and the same was the case with 19 RAJ RIF. In case he had any about the conduct of the operation, he could have discussed that with me separately.

"Our troops were very brave and understanding. They understood the undercurrents. They also understood that this sudden change of command at brigade level was not a very good sign. They took it very bravely. They did not show any emotional disturbance and asked me no questions. This made my task more difficult. Anyway, I passed orders for each one to take adequate rest, maintain their weapons and do whatever maintenance was possible. There was an immediate requirement for each of the soldiers to look after his personal cleanliness. For four days we had no chance to wash. But as the LTTE was active and we were resting in the open and there was no arrangement for taking any kind of wash, it was a real problem. We made small groups of 15 to 20 soldiers, spread out and rested under the shade of available small bushes. I sent my J.C.O. Quartermaster, to liaise with the Brigade Deputy Quartermaster General and arrange for food, replenishment of ammunition, first aid to the soldiers, evacuation of wounded and a host of other requirements, as the QM Capt. Padma Kumar had been kept at Pallali to set up our administrative echelon, known as the 'B' Echelon.

"With this done I had whatever little wash I could manage and started walking towards the brigade HQ to meet the brigade commander. The distance to the brigade HQ from where we were resting was about 500 mtrs. I found him sitting with Col. T. P. S. Brar, CO, 1 MLI. We exchanged our customary compliments. I did not find him in a pleasant mood. While I was trying to give him my account, he abruptly told me that the higher HQ was not happy with our performance and our delay in linking-up was construed as dragging our feet. I laughed in my mind having seen the naked desire in his eyes to hog the credit by trying to undermine us. He seemed to have forgotten that he had avoided his command and in actuality abdicated his command to his deputy, Col. S. K. Singh. Despite being ordered a number of times by the Deputy Divisional Commander, Brig. Kulwant Singh, in the absence of the G.O.C., Maj. Gen. Harkirat Singh, Brig. Manjit Singh did not move out from the safety of HQ 8 MAHAR for the whole of the 18$^{th}$ and the greater part of 19 October till he was almost physically pushed out from there. For his own safety he was given two BMP's and an infantry battalion, 5 RAJ RIF. In spite of that he got totally bogged down by LTTE fire. At one point of time we heard him screaming on the radio set, mouthing abuses that the

LTTE fire was so accurate and intense that he could not lift his head. He was too keen to scramble to the safety of the 1 MLI location inside Jaffna Fort. He lost one BMP. His escort got scattered. He did not bother to move as a tactical formation. 5 RAJ RIF, acting as his escort, got scattered. One of the companies came with us. He was ultimately rescued by 1 MLI. He seemed to want to bully me into submission. I just told him that the troops were waiting to see their brigade commander. A couple of good words would do immense good to their morale. I also told him about our need for food, ammunition, and clothing—the soldiers were only in a single uniform—the one they were wearing needed immediate replacement due to extensive damage, first-aid and evacuation of the wounded soldiers, who, despite tremendous agony did not lag behind. I also told him that many who did die could have been still alive in case there had been arrangements for the evacuation of casualties. The case in point was of our Signal Havildar, Iqbal Singh who, though he was to retire on 31 November 1987, accompanied the unit in Sri Lanka and got a volley of bullets in his stomach. His buddy wanted to evacuate him from the lagoon but he refused to be evacuated having realized his own bad condition, he said, "You go, don't risk your life for me since I am going to die in any case." However, later on it was learnt that Iqbal Singh reached 8 MAHAR MI Room about 4-5 km away on his own at night in that bad condition. Unfortunately, life deceived him and he died the next morning. Like that we lost seven soldiers and an officer, Lt. Nagar. I told Brig. Manjit Singh that there was nothing worth naming that could be termed as a planned operation. And I also told him, bluntly, "We expected you with the brigade in the operation." I could see his red face but obviously he had nothing to say. After my conversation with Brig. Manjit Singh was over, I met his three staff officers, the BM, in charge of operations, the Deputy Assistant Adjutant and Quartermaster General (DAQMG, or "DQ" for short), and the Deputy Assistant Adjutant General (DAAG), and informed them about the state we were in and what our immediate requirements were. I also enquired about the remainder portion of the battalion which incidentally was larger than the one we had now. But I was told that there was no information about them. With this I returned to my unit.

"After about half an hour our Adjutant, Capt. Moti came and told me that the brigade commander would be visiting our battalion. I told him to inform the companies and also told him that it should not be a centralized fall-in. He should be taken to all the company locations as they were resting and the company commanders should brief him about their respective companies if and when asked. They should speak facts and openly without any reservation. The troops should not be disturbed from their well-deserved rest. I repeatedly warned him against a formal fall-in lest the LTTE got a target to fire at.

"The time was about 1100 hrs 20 October. The brigade commander, Brig. Manjit Singh came to the battalion area. I met him with my Adjutant, Capt. Moti. We took him around. He tried to speak something but that did not evoke much enthusiasm. He just had taken over the brigade only a couple of days ago at Jaffna. The troops did not know him nor did he know them. No bond was established in spite of his being from the same ethnic community as our soldiers. He left the battalion without creating any impact.

"About an hour later, around mid-day, I got a message from the brigade headquarters that I was required there. I took along my Intelligence Officer 2/Lt. Venkatesh and the intelligence section commander with me and reached the brigade headquarters by about 1 p.m. I found Lt. Col. S. Mukherjee had also been summoned and was heading for brigade headquarters. We exchanged compliments. We enquired about each other's condition. Obviously his morale was not very high either. It was not because of the sudden change of the situation but for the change of command. None of us could accept Brig. Manjit Singh as our Commander. He seemed to be fighting the battle as a stepping stone for his personal career advancement and not as a professional soldier. The word was going around that he was very close to our COAS and he had requested him to get himself side-stepped in place of the brigadier who was under posting and was on his way to take over. In fact in his very first conference with us at Palali he mentioned that he had direct access to the COAS and he would take us to task if we did not behave as he desired. Though such hollow threat did not have any impact on me but I was feeling sad for the troops who had to take orders from such a self-seeking person, and for the organization for producing this kind of commander. The word also was going around that he was not having a good equation with his own personal staff like the BM, the Brigade Signal Officer and a few others.

"The brigade headquarters had moved into one portion of the fort. I liked the mixed feel of the medieval age, the modern and the smell of gunpowder which was always bringing me back to the reality of the day. We went to Maj. Rakesh Sharma's office as we always did. (For operational briefings we go to the staff officer of the General Staff branch and to the Quartermaster's branch in case of a logistics conference)

"We were received by the ever-smiling and affable B.M. But these grueling five days seemed to have taken its toll on him too. To work and adjust under a totally new commander with all his idiosyncrasies and foul mouth under such a difficult situation was no mean task. He had been our B.M. for some time and he had become a part and parcel of us. Our sufferings and wanton casualties were his too. This was a very trying situation for him. After all he was the main agency to pass on all the operational instructions of the brigade commander to the units like ours. However after we were ushered in he told us there would be an operational briefing by the brigade commander and we would be tasked accordingly for further operations. I acknowledged what he said and started waiting for the brigade commander. We had all became super human beings by then. We felt no hunger, we needed no sleep and rest, were devoid of any emotions, were only to be ready for the supreme sacrifice apparently for no reason but just to fulfill the whims and fancies of a few politicians and the army top brass.

"While waiting for the brigade commander, I was trying to take a look at the neighbourhood of the fort. Jaffna Fort was encircled by a number of high-rise buildings, adorning it as a necklace. For scenic beauty it was looking nice but for us it was deadly. The last bullet could have come at me from any of those buildings to put me or any one of us for that matter to sleep. I could visualize that some of those would be our objectives but I till then did not know exactly which one or how many of those. Like any other growing city it was densely populated both by inhabitants and concrete buildings. Operating in a built-up area is the most difficult task for any army. It primarily is an infantry task. Even if you try to demolish each building you need to clear it one by one, room by room, floor by floor. There is no shortcut. In case of conventional battle one could by-pass an entire city and advance ahead for a deeper objective, to be choked and cleared by the follow up formations. In case of conventional battle the moment you by-pass the enemy and go for a deeper objective the holding formation feels threatened. His supply routes are cut off. His reinforcements are stopped and he is isolated. But under such conditions when you are fighting an insurgency in the enemy's own country you have no front or rear. They are amongst their own people, difficult to distinguish. There is all likelihood of unintended civilian casualties. While I was sure that most of the civilians would have fled to the jungles or any other safe area, I was definitely not certain. This town had been the citadel and seat of power for the LTTE and also the fourth and last tier of their defence as far as this sector was concerned. They knew each nook and corner of the city and they would have prepared the defences well. One more consideration was playing in my mind was the likely strength that we might face. We knew that four more brigades were advancing from the north and east. If we give a push from the south they would have no escape route towards north and east, while the south was being blocked by us. It could be possible to our great advantage that the major force of the LTTE would have escaped by now, before we broke into

Jaffna, by the southern sea route. But at our level we had to fight and clear each house, each road and each corner of Jaffna. Besides this we had to contend with dreadful IED of theirs. One well-placed and well-executed IED would do the job of a number of machine guns.

"In the case of both jungle and built-up area, a smaller enemy force could always effectively engage a larger opposition. The best way to operate in these areas is to operate in a number of columns. The enemy should be encircled and unhinged. His escape route should be sealed. However the problems in this kind of operation are: identification, as they can easily get mixed up with the civilians and escape; making them run out of supplies, this is also difficult as their need is very little. Besides that they could always take help from the sympathizers for their supplies.

"When all these thoughts were on my mind, I found Maj. Sharma walking up to me and informing me that the Commander was waiting for us. I found Lt. Col. Mukherjee was already there. I found Col. T.P.S. Brar was also standing there. The reason was obvious. He had up-to-date knowledge of the ground situation. He exactly knew the likely enemy positions, strength, habits and weapons. He also briefed us on their pattern of use of explosives. He repeated what he had told us before, that when he had cleared a couple of those positions, no sooner had the troops returned back to the Fort, the LTTE reoccupied them. This is, of course, has always been the pattern in such kind of operations.

"After the briefing by Col T. P. S. Brar, Brig. Manjit Singh gave out tasks to both my battalion and 19 RAJ RIF. Initial tasks were basically to clear the high-rise buildings around the Jaffna Fort and thereafter to expand. The town was divided in two parts, Eastern and Western. The eastern part was given to 19 RAJ RIF and the western part was given to us. The immediate objectives that came our way were Ashoka Hotel, a high-rise building, Cross Road and Post Office. The attack was to be launched that night itself. The operational need of putting on the

16 SIKH (41 INFANTRY BRIGADE)
CAPTURE OF JAFFNA TOWN

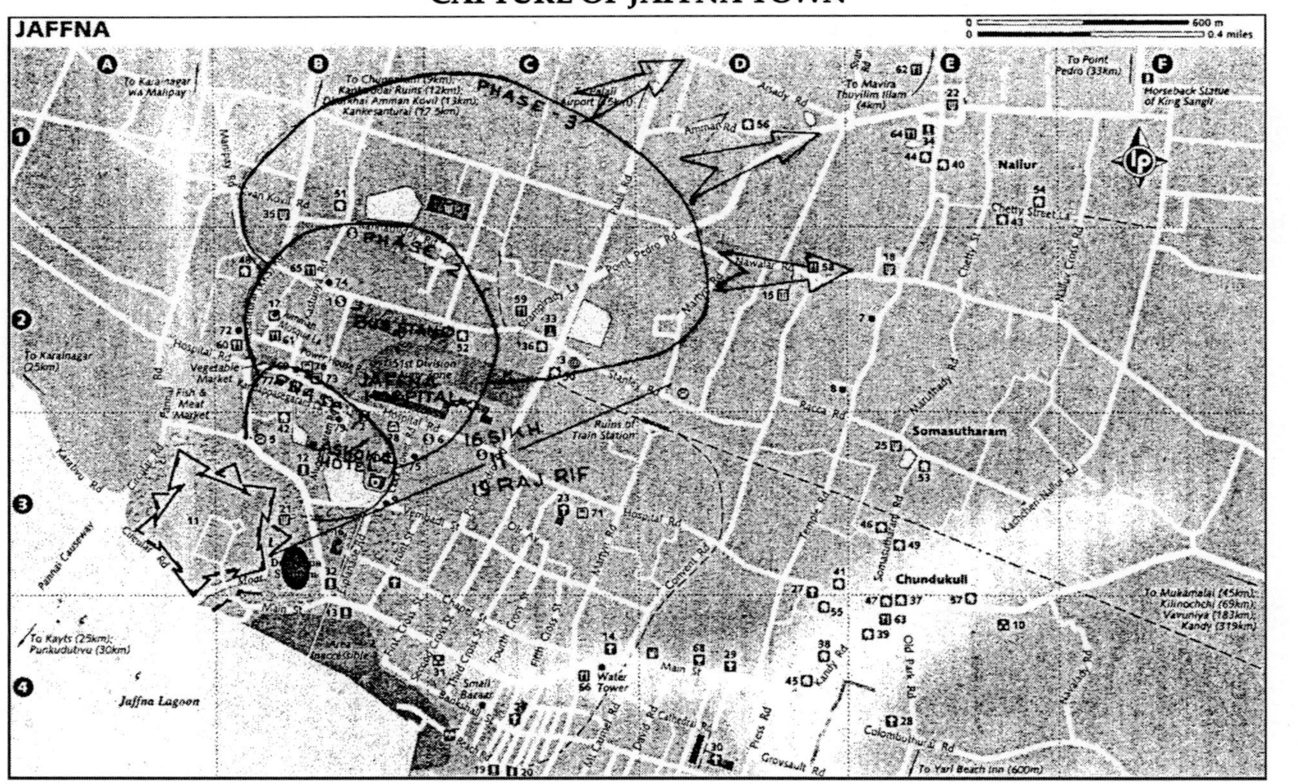

pressure and continuing the operation was beyond doubt. The LTTE was evidently on the run. There was no question of giving them any respite. Each day passing without any action would strengthen their defence potential. But the problem was the task was given to us. The strength of my battalion, by then, was reduced to about 160 persons with all the casualties, dead and wounded, including the persons used to evacuate them. If you had divided equally the existing strength among the companies it came to about 35 soldiers per company excluding Battalion HQ, Quartermaster's staff etc. It was a platoon strength, less than one-third of a company's strength. We had no supporting weapons worth mentioning. Most of our strength and equipments were somewhere en route, but no one could give correct information about its location. After operations for four days and nights the troops badly needed a rest. There were two options open: one, 1 MLI which had been operating in this area for some time and was conversant with the area and the targets, could be employed to clear the initial targets, and our troops could hold the Fort. This way our troops could get some rest for one night or, two, have a pause for one night. I was in favour of the first one and suggested this to Brig. Manjit Singh. Though 1 MLI was not under command of 41 Infantry Brigade, but such adjustment under the situation was possible if higher HQ were approached and the situation was properly explained. This would have served both the purposes. But my suggestion was overruled. We were tasked to carry out the operation on night 20/21 October. Once I got my task I called my 'O' Group. My immediate objectives were Ashoka Hotel and Road Junction. Ashoka Hotel was a high-rise building dominating the area. It was believed to be booby-trapped. Once this was held we could dominate a large area by fire and observation. The next objective Road Junction was also a very important target. A number of roads emanated from here towards the north and the east including Point Pedro. Once this was held one could effectively stop LTTE movement by road.

For these tasks I chose "Charlie" Company commanded by Maj. Ramcharan and "Bravo" Company commanded by Maj. Govind Singh Sisodia. I kept the other two companies as reserve. These were companies in name only. In reality they were of platoon strength. One could easily call these actions platoon operations and the whole strength of the battalion was that of a strong rifle company. The entire operation was in effect a company operation. Our main aim was as far as possible to avoid using the roads. It was essential for the company commanders and also their respective 'O' Groups to see as much of the area as possible during daytime. For a better view we went out of the fort and climbed a tall building. While we were trying to have a good look at our objectives we were fired upon. Our escort returned the fire. Luckily it did not last long. But it became clear that we were being watched. The enemy was expected to take counter measures. Our main concern was how to accomplish the given task with minimum casualties to our already depleted troops. The question was how to draw the LTTE out of the built-up area, and force them to give a fight in the open. One of our JCO's gave a brilliant idea. He suggested that instead of using the road, we should use a rocket launcher to create a hole in the wall of the residences and move parallel to the road but through the houses. This would give protection, save casualties, and would be likely to draw the LTTE out from their hiding places. We talked about the availability of supporting fire and the use of engineer resources to defuse explosives which was one of our major worries.

"My main worry was the conduct of the battle. Fighting in a built-up area is a different technique. Proper conduct of it needs intensive training, rehearsals, grouping of troops, perfecting the drills etc. I had nothing of these. I did not have proper troops, whatever I had in numbers were not at all fit to undertake such operation against one of the most well-trained and successful militants of the era. My troops were not even grouped in proper formation. In such kind of battles it is the rifle sections of each platoon, its LMG group, rifle group, Number One, Number Two riflemen and so on in that order that play a very important role. A section consists of ten soldiers. This is divided into two groups, an LMG group and a rifle group. Each one is numbered with a specific role to play and a position to take. Each covers the other while operating. Even an Army Group comprising perhaps 12 to 18 infantry divisions will not succeed unless this basic section-level formation is worthy of itself. The successful conduct of this operation, to a large extent, depends upon proper use of field signals and synchronization. Each person of a rifle section has a particular task to perform. This training for the operation of a rifle section in a built-up area are normally not part of the daily training sessions which are run in peacetime training programmes. These are specially conducted as per the requirement before undertaking an operation of this nature, and it is an intensive one. In this kind of battle one needs to perfect his shooting capability from different positions meant for close quarter battle. Here, reaction time is very little. It is face to face. Either kill or get killed. Use of grenade, smoke, handling of explosives, knowing karate or judo and skillful use of small arms are the essence of this type of battle. My troops had nothing of this sort of training. Any slight mistake may mean death. In this type of battle one is directly exposed to the enemy fire .. Any mistiming or slow reaction may prove fatal. There is no second chance! Under such a situation I hardly had three people per section and they were also not as per group. Some of them were raw who had just joined after basic recruit training from the training centre. They did not have opportunity to be trained in such operation. They were far below the required standard of shooting skill, handling explosives, battle drill etc. I was to perform this highly technical task with raw and under-strength troops; against the most well-trained troops of the world. I was wondering whether our senior officers, at the helm of affairs, either had such operational experience before or had forgotten their days or given up their conscience for their personal advancement. As I remember the Chief of the Army Staff, General Sundarji made the same mistake while conducting

'Operation Blue Star' where a large number of our troops were maimed. I now had to depend on my brave soldiers, on their individual bravery, on their grit, determination, and last but not the least on their regimental spirit. I saluted them. The Indian Army has achieved whatever reputation it has because of these brave and selfless soldiers like Havildar Iqbal Singh who laid down his life only one month before his retirement! They are the backbone of the Army. My only solace was that my present lot of troops had been trained by shedding blood and sweat, and therefore, learned much faster than expected. May God bless them!

"Having carried out whatever reconnaissance we could, I asked the company commanders to go back to their respective companies and brief the troops. I also told them to try and show the objectives down to the section commander level so that they could also have a fair idea of their respective targets, but in small groups, taking as much precaution as possible against loss of lives and surprise. Our no-move-before (NMB) for the ensuing operation was fixed for 9 p.m. I, therefore, instructed the company commanders to reorganize their sub-units, give them adequate rest and prepare themselves for the coming battle. I also repeatedly told them to brief the soldiers in as much detail as possible. They should form the buddy system and give cover to each other. I knew things were not going to be easy.

"By 9 p.m. we reached our Assembly Area cum Forming-Up Place (F.U.P.) from where we were supposed to launch the assault. The situation was tense. The Officiating Divisional Commander Brigadier Kulwant Singh also had arrived at Jaffna to watch the progress. Despite all the tribulations we faced it was our battalion 16 SIKH in conjunction with 19 RAJRIF who were going to free the historic town from the clutches of the LTTE. It was a great moment indeed for the IPKF. Everybody wanted to share the glory but not necessarily the responsibility. The entire responsibility lay on the shoulders of those few soldiers who did not know that they were going to make history. On that night the soldiers were almost alone, lonely, without most of their team mates, but ready to be launched into a crucial battle in the most unprofessional manner.

"We left the F.U.P. at 10 p.m. on 20 October. Unlike in a conventional attack where the attacking troops might have to cover a great distance before the actual assault, here the targets were so near but so far. We knew that we would have to fight for each inch of the built-up area to gain control and it was going to be bloody. As planned, "Charlie" and "Bravo" Companies were moving towards their respective objectives. We were all tense. Gaining an initial foot-hold is always the most difficult task. I was on the set directly communicating with Maj. Ramcharan and Maj. Sisodia. My pulse was racing. I was repeatedly reminding them to keep away from the road. The battle progressed for about half an hour into the night which seemed an eternity. A couple of initial houses were cleared with stiff fighting. It was obviously all dark. There was not a speck of light anywhere. One could not distinguish between friend and foe. There was every possibility of mishaps occurring when the teams went into rooms for clearing them. We had no arrangement for illuminating the area. Beside a limited use of the 2-inch mortar at platoon level, it is generally planned at battalion and brigade level by using the battalion's integral battalion 81mm mortars or by artillery. We had nothing. We had everything but lying elsewhere, away from the battle field when it was badly needed! I was wondering, under such condition, whether it was prudent to undertake operations in built-up areas at night or during daytime. Each one, of course, has its own pluses and minuses.

"My thought process was interrupted by a loud and ear-splitting explosion. I had gone stiff; was waiting to hear the worst. I was expecting a call any moment. I did not know who got it, Maj. Ramcharan or Maj. Govind Sisodia. I was frantically trying to contact them. Suddenly the signal set crackled into life. It was Maj. Ramcharan. His voice was shaking. He reported that with the explosion 13 of his soldiers had fallen. He was the only person standing on the ground. He was yet to ascertain the seriousness of each soldier. But it became quite obvious that they were out from taking any further part in the battle, at least for the time being, and needed evacuation. The eerie apprehension came into reality. I immediately asked the Adjutant to send "Alfa" Company to reinforce the operations of 'Charlie' Company, inform the brigade HQ to arrange for evacuation, as I could not send any further troops for this purpose and further deplete my bayonet strength. I also informed him that I was going forward to meet Maj. Ramcharan. I was handicapped in not having a 2IC who could have taken over the administrative aspects and let me deal with the operational details. I instructed the battalion's Subedar Major, Nirmal Singh, to handle the casualty evacnation and other immediate administration. With this very large number of casualties, especially under the present circumstances of depleted strength, it was a big blow. I enquired about the progress of 'Bravo' Company from Maj. Govind Sisodia. He reported that he was facing stiff resistance from the LTTE. They were firing automatics at our advancing troops. So far luckily he was not welcomed with an IED. His advance though slow was steady, His objective was Cross Road. Holding that was very important for stopping the movement of the LTTE. I quickly narrated to him what had happened. Though he had guessed that something had happened, but he did not know the magnitude of it. I added that it might not be possible, with the present situation, to get *Ramu* (pet name of Maj. Ramcharan) going right then as he had no troops worth mentioning and it would take some time to reorganize them. I wanted him to positively take the Cross Road. Success with any objective was very essential at that stage. I told him I was placing "Delta" Company as his reserve but it would be available only in emergency as thereafter I would not be left with any reserve. I asked him to keep me informed about the progress of the battle. I decided to spend some time with 'Charlie' Company to reorganize them.

By the time all these were being done it was about 1 a.m. 21 October. There had been incessant calls on the radio from the brigade HQ, initially by the brigade commander, Brig. Manjit Singh, followed by Brig. Kulwant Singh, the Officiating G.OC., 54 Infantry Division. They had nothing else to say but to try to hurry up the operation. At one point of time I had to tell Brig. Manjit Singh, not to unnecessarily press me for the time being and let me fight my own battle. He could better organize far more important operational support like providing illuminating fire support, more automatic weapons, reinforcement, evacuation of casualties, ammunition replenishment, and if nothing else, some food at daybreak, as each one including my cooks and sweepers were fighting the battle, shoulder to shoulder with the other riflemen and were doing extremely well. After that he went off the air but the Deputy GOC was coming on again and again urging me to speed up! I wondered if they had forgotten the battle realities, battle drills and their professionalism. It appeared that they were being guided by only one thing: the word given by the Chief of Army Staff, Gen. Sundarji, to the Prime Minister that Srilanka would be cleared of the LTTE in seven days. They had nothing else in their armoury to give to their troops.

"On the "Bravo" Company axis, the progress was steady. The street was being cleared house to house. Progress was good at the same time casualties were sustainable. There were, till that time, only two wounded. Those were bullet injuries, that too walking casualties, and therefore could be evacuated without much problem. During the progress of the battle "Delta" Company was keeping the flanks and rear protected from any sniper firing or physical attack. This was a great relief to "Bravo" Company. They could surge ahead without looking back over their shoulders. On the "Charlie" Company axis first and foremost we had to organize evacuation of the casualties. There was no support from the brigade. I gave a forced pause to the operation, created an evacuation team, like before, out of the available troops, mainly from "Alfa" Company and a very small portion of "Charlie" Company. I retained that many troops which were the bare minimum requirement to hold the area that we had gained. We were basically holding the position with our automatics, by returning their fire and engaging LTTE positions, i.e., those being given away by their fire. We kept the same frontage so that the LTTE did not come to know immediately that the troops had thinned out. I was also worried that in case the LTTE could get to know that the advance on the "Charlie" axis was stalled they had two options. Either they could counter-attack us and regain the position, or they could reinforce the "Bravo" Company axis and try to stall their progress. Both were unacceptable to us. We had to take both the Road Junction and Ashoka Hotel objectives. Road Junction would have given flexibility of movement to us and denied the same to the enemy, and the Ashoka Hotel would have given us opportunity to dominate a fairly large area by fire and observation. During the pause that we had, I had a quick operational discussion with Maj. Ramcharan and Maj. Navin Bhatt, the "Alfa" Company Commander. Maj. Ramcharan was determined to lead the attack on Ashoka Hotel and capture it with his further depleted company. He would not have been left with more than 25 to 30 soldiers in his company. But he would not leave the honour to complete the given task. I fully appreciated his spirit and did not find any word to stop him, and why should I, I thought. I, however, kept "Alfa" Company as a reserve to carry out exploitation after the objective was captured. By the time all these were sorted out and the soldiers of "Alfa" Company and "Charlie" Company returned after evacuating the casualties, it was about 3. a.m. Fortunately we were allotted a detachment from 60 Field company of 3 Engineer Regiment, of the Madras Sappers and Miners, under Maj. Darshan Singh for helping us to clear mines, booby traps or explosives, whatever was encountered. "Charley" Company resumed its operation, closely followed by "Alfa" Company. "Bravo" Company was passing on its progress over the radio set. They kept themselves well dispersed so that even if an IED was activated the loss of human life would be kept to a minimum. They were moving hugging the houses to avoid IED's. This device is generally laid across the road and maximum impact is felt around the middle of the road. The atmosphere was very tense. I could hear my own throbbing heart.

The message of the first success came at around 4 30 a.m. on 21 October when Maj. Sisodia came on the set and gave me the news. My joy new no bounds. The best thing was that the casualties were kept to the minimum, only three soldiers were injured. They received bullet injuries while clearing the houses. Fortunately again these were not fatal. I told him not to feel complacent. They should cover and dominate the road junction in such a way that each road was covered. I released the "Delta" Company for exploitation. I also told Maj. Sisodia that he should hold the area as a sub sector, and being the senior-most there he will operate as a sub-sector commander till the battalion concentrates there. I asked the Adjutant to pass this information to the brigade HQ. I myself passed this happy news to Maj. Ramcharan and Maj. Navin Bhatt so that it raised their morale and gave them further impetus. Though I was not interfering in their conduct of battle but I was very near to them. The area of operation itself was not very large. After all the total number of troops involved was only approximately 60 though for the record two companies, i.e. half the bayonet strength of the battalion, were taking part. Our higher HQ were counting on us as battalion and companies and tasking us accordingly notwithstanding our incongruously low strength.

The operation that was being conducted at Ashoka Hotel was, however, more tricky and difficult. Ashoka Hotel was expected, as per the briefing, to be covered extensively with explosives. The troops just had a taste of explosive detonation which was absolutely a new experience for them. Its effect was devastating. One may sustain bullet injuries with lesser complication than explosive injuries. Explosives tear apart the limbs from the body frame unlike a bullet injury which generally causes perforation. In an infantry battalion, though handling of explosives is a part of the general training programme, they are generally handled by the Pioneer Platoon. At army level it is handled by combat engineers from engineer regiments. I instructed Maj. Ramcharan and Maj. Navin Bhatt not to be hasty, at the same time not to be unduly cautious: it was very difficult to discern between the two. However, this time the "Charlie" Company and "Alfa" Company group was advancing satisfactorily. After clearing the intervening houses overcoming stiff opposition from the LTTE, this group surrounded the hotel and first neutralized the small arms fire. A couple of rocket launcher rounds were fired through the main entrance and at suspected parts of the window. Enemy fire gradually lessened to a considerable extent. Maj. Ramcharan, Maj. Navin Bhatt and I had a conference over the radio set and discussed the latest situation. Time was about 4:30 a.m. Day was breaking and the visibility was improving. I told them that it was the right time to storm the hotel. Further delay might help the LTTE to reorganize. I instructed Maj. Navin Bhatt of "Alfa" Company to throw a ring around the hotel to act as a stop as well as denying any reinforcement by the LTTE, and to provide fire support to Maj. Ramcharan's "Charlie" Company, by creating a fire base by pooling a few automatics from his company. "Charlie" Company was to create three "storm teams" with engineers in each team, to assault the first three storeys and repeat the same till the entire building was clear. The entire operation was to be covered by fire by "Alfa" company.

The clearing operation started. The building had already suffered a good deal of damage. The engineers encountered a layout of explosives right at the entrance. They started clearing these while the storming troops gave them cover. While this was going on some movement was noticed at the backyard of the hotel. They were at once engaged. Within a few minutes they were silenced. Two AK 47s were recovered. It appeared that, seeing the inevitability, the enemy was withdrawing. Greater caution was taken while clearing the hotel. The ground floor was cleared room by room. There was no encounter. While the first group held the ground floor, the second group went for the first floor and started clearing it systematically.

There was also no encounter, only the fired cases of small arms were found there beside a few more explosive charges which the engineers were systematically clearing. In the meantime it became daylight and the operation, specially defusing of explosives became easier. Gradually, floor by floor, the hotel was cleared and occupied. By first light both the objectives, Ashoka Hotel and Cross Road Junction were in our hands. It was a good beginning. Brigade HQ were informed about it.

A wave of a sense of achievement, joy, as well as relief passed through the entire rank and file of the battalion. After much tribulation and sacrifice we had achieved the initial foothold on Jaffna town and had the LTTE reeling under our pressure. My tribute was to my felled soldiers and the brave fighting soldiers who against all imaginable odds made it possible. Other than throwing us into battle in the most un-soldierly and unprofessional manner, our higher HQ had made no contribution.

I conveyed my message of appreciation, at the same time I cautioned against any over-reaction. I was sure the LTTE would not be far and was keeping us under watch. It could be possible for them to inflict casualties at any time from anywhere, whenever they would find us less alert or off-guard. That was the first day we were inside the Jaffna town. It was their land and they could be anywhere and everywhere. Such battles had no borders. Our first task was to consolidate and secure our positions and link both the two company groups. They were operating at a distance of 500mtrs from each other. In a built-up area it was a large distance.

The immediate task on hand was to consolidate whatever we had gained. Though the strength of the battalion was very low, but we were being treated for all operational purposes as a battalion. We, therefore, should not be spread beyond our holding power. As much as I learned about the LTTE, I was sure that they were not going to take it lying down. Another two to three hours would be critical to us. I instructed the company commanders to take out patrols sub-sector wise. One patrol from each sub-sector should go out to exploit the success and try to assess the situation. They should try and estimate the presence of the civil population in that area. The presence of civilians would be detrimental to our security as it would be very difficult to distinguish between the two. At that time we had no intelligence system to gather information about the enemy intention where as they had. For all we knew they could be looking at us from the houses in the neighbourhood. The other patrol similarly from each sub-sector should move inward to establish a link up between the two sub-sectors. There would be a number of houses within this area. Each house could be a den of danger to us. I also told them to position sentries all around and they should remain extremely alert and not let any unknown person come near. They could open fire to stop them. We did not know the local language so we could not take a chance. Other than the patrols which were going out no one was to unnecessarily expose himself. While these activities were on, maximum rest was to be given to the troops to recover from the stress and fatigue and to be ready for the next round. I also informed them that after I set up my battalion HQ I would make rounds to each company location.

After all this I felt like sitting some place and having a hot cup of tea. That thought straightway took my mind to the urgent administrative needs. After the immense excitement that we went through during the operation subsided the stomach churned with hunger. Our own administrative echelon was not adequately functional as my staff was strewn from Jaffna to Lucknow. My JCO Quartermaster whom I left at the fort did not have any communications. Incidentally I did not get any call from the brigade commander or the Deputy GOC for the success we achieved. Perhaps they were still calculating the time plan and were not happy with the delay! How prophetic my thought was I came to know a couple of days later. I called up the Brigade DQ Maj. Jha of the Signals on the set and asked him what he was doing about our food and replenishment of ammunition. Luckily this time I heard some positive note from him that he was arranging delivery of food and ammunition to the battalion location in transport. I told him that I would send him the guide immediately. I also asked him to call my JCO over to the set so that I could talk to him as I had many instructions for him. After that I called up the BM Maj. Rakesh Sharma. He congratulated me. I asked him about the progress in the other sector. I enquired about the rest of the battalion about which he said he had no information. After discussing various other things I asked him to provide a radio set to my Administrative J.C.O. for the time being till I got my own radio sets and equipment. He said he would look into that. After that I spoke to Maj. Nikkam, the DAAG, about medical attention to my casualties. I also discussed about sending citation for gallantry awards. After I spoke to all of them I called my ever-smiling and tireless worker, Adjutant, Capt. Moti. In the absence of the QM, I asked him to look after and tie up administrative requirements in addition to his own operational coordination tasks. I asked him to be very particular about the sending of the situational report and to take recommendation for gallantry award on the radio from the companies and to send them by signal as early as possible. After that I told him to prepare an escort party for me to visit the company locations. I asked him to tie up with the companies to send guides for me which he said he was already tying up with the companies.

While I was busy in sorting out a few out of the innumerable problems, I received a call from Maj. Govind that his location had come under intense fire from LTTE. He had knocked off one vehicle full of LTTE. They, perhaps being unaware of our occupation of the Cross Road Junction, were shifting their position. It was a good catch. For this reason only I was keen to take this objective at the earliest. This would create a wedge into the enemy positions. After some time I came to know that the link patrol from Ashoka Hotel had also come under fire and was fighting back. The troops by then would be at the end of their endurance after fighting constantly for six days and nights with no rest, very scanty food and being under tremendous pressure. Extreme paucity of troops did not allow us to organize some rest in between. But they were braving all odds with equal amounts of courage and determination. But who appreciates such selfless dedication to the service and nation with supreme sacrifice if required? The shortage of maps made it very difficult to pin-point any location. The sound of firing in a built-up area is very confusing due to its echo effect. Though the difference in firing sound — the LTTE was using automatic A.K. 47's and we had our semi automatic Self Loading Rifle (SLR) — could give us a fair idea of their general location, but their shifting nature coupled with the echo effect was making it a little difficult to identify targets. But with complete daylight we were finding it easier to locate them. In absolutely a new town in a different country we were finding ourselves totally lost without direction and without maps. I enquired about the situation in the Ashoka Hotel sub-sector. There was no active interference from the LTTE I was told. I had no reserve with me which I could send and influence the battle in the 'Bravo' Company sub-sector. Anyhow, as the LTTE, had come into the open to confront us and give a fight, we had to take them on and defeat them. I had a feeling that the major portion of the LTTE would be on the run. This group of LTTE might be trying to stop us from further expansion and was buying time. By then Jaffna town was being invested from all sides by four more brigades. For the situation in front of me, I thought the only option I had to fight them was by encircling them. Now the question came as to how it was to be done. I could not lift troops from the Ashoka Hotel sector as it also might come under pressure at any moment. The only option that was left to me was to some how redirect any of the four patrols, preferably two of them joined together to form a greater strength, and send them to the rear of the enemy. This would definitely turn their rear and unhinge them. I had a feeling that by now heavy pressure of the Indian Army might be dawning on them as a physical load settling upon a person. But the question was how to do this without any communication set and a map. More number of groups operating would need more radio equipment and other necessities which we were extremely short. I contacted both the sector commanders and gave out my plan. They appreciated it. This would relieve the "Bravo" sub-sector from enemy pressure. Unless any aggressive action was taken this could carry on for an indefinite period. Eventually their positions might get reinforced and the task might get further difficult. On second thought I decided that instead of diverting the patrols which was difficult due to want of radio sets and maps, and more so because there was no spare officer available with any of the committed companies to lead the operation, I decided to launch "Alfa" Company for the task. I told Maj. Bhatt to take up this task. He immediately agreed with the modified plan.

Locating the patrols, it was felt, would be time-consuming and a dangerous proposition to disengage them in case they were physically involved in battle. It was decided that Maj. Bhatt would take his company, less his soldiers already out on patrol, who could join later after having returned. I also asked him to keep in his mind our next target which was Jaffna Bus Stand. He should, if possible, locate himself in such a way that would give us a firm base for our next objective. He needed half an hour to start his operation. In the meantime our administrative vehicle started reaching the positions carrying food, ammunition and some dry rations, specially tea rations, under escorts. My J.C.O. Quartermaster met me. I asked him the details of his holdings and instructed him to start indenting for all the items that were necessary.

While all these actions were going on, I got a call form the BM that a missile detachment was being sent to us. It was very timely and welcome news. This would help us to directly engage the targets and neutralize them.. It had longer range and much more effect at the target than the rocket launchers that we had with us. I warned Maj. Govind Sisodia to keep an escort ready to take the missile detachment once it arrived at the Battalion HQ.

After about an hour the situation tilted in our favour. The missile detachment was positioned in the "Bravo" Company sector and Maj. Bhatt also called to inform me that he was in location. The stage was set. The patrols also reached back to their respective locations without further incident. They reported that the streets and the houses were generally empty. Only one odd person was seen who would run away immediately after seeing the Indian Army soldiers. I asked Maj. Sisodia to plan on storming the houses after first neutralizing them with missiles. Inclusion of the missile detachment acted as a force multiplier. I wondered if the LTTE expected such force addition. The missiles landed with huge explosions and had great impact on the targets. Missiles were very effective with their deadly accuracy and impact. It was a good morale booster and an ideal weapon to neutralize targets. I asked both Maj. Sisodia and Maj. Bhatt to press home their attack from both directions and close our jaws on to the enemy. This called for a detailed coordination so that our troops did not become the victims of our own fire. Since the operation was impromptu there could not be a detailed planning and briefing. Things were being coordinated on the radio set. All things considered, the operation was progressing slowly but steadily and things were going in our favour. The engineers were also doing a good job in clearing room after room and houses after houses. We came across tell-tale marks of the LTTE vacating their places under pressure. There were a few dead bodies inside the houses which gave a good account of the missile firing. Our casualties were fortunately not fatal. It took about three hours to complete the operation. By mid-day we were in complete control of the area. We settled down to take stock of the situation and plan our next phase, which included the Bus Stand and the road to Point Pedro.

Some rest and reorganization became very essential. Ideally there should have been a reserve unit in the brigade which should have taken on the next phase, and we should have progressed in a leap-frog manner. It appeared to me that we had broken the main core of the LTTE defences in Jaffna town. The LTTE was on the run and they were fighting a rear-guard action to allow their main group to escape. Their use of IED and determined defensive battle was on the wane. This was my own assessment and feeling, which was dictated by my experience of the last few days of fighting, and from what I read in various battle accounts. The bite of the LTTE was becoming loose.

As I planned, I took a round of the battalion defended area. While we were fighting, the engineers had opened a route of maintenance. I was happy to see my jeep with the smiling driver waiting for me. The bond of the driver and the officer in the army is unimaginable in civil life. In the army we have the relationship of that of a family member. When we are out on duty they take full care of us. They would ensure that all our necessities are attended to. We depend a great deal on them. When I got into the jeep first thing he gave me after his salute was a hot cup of tea. God only knew, if at all he knew, from where the driver had procured the flask and managed to do all this. But it was his token of love for his superior which at that moment was very touching. Also, I badly needed that cup of tea.

I took five soldiers as my escort. We were seven in total. Our only problem was that we were in one vehicle only. One IED or a rocket launcher shot would have taken care of us. Ideally we should have had a minimum of three vehicles and moved as a convoy. As the engineers were also working on the road and our troops were giving them protection, it acted as my protection too. I was feeling extremely god to meet my soldiers and officers. They were looking tired and much reduced but as jovial as before. Sikh troops are known for their indomitable spirit. After talking to them and sharing a few jokes I sat with the officers and a few JCO's to plan our future course of operations. Our next objectives, Jaffna Bus Stand and the Road to Point Pedro, awaited us.

It would be pertinent to mention here that there were some disputes about some unfortunate happenings believed to have taken place inside the Jaffna Hospital. It was reported that some civilians were killed inside the hospital. First of all, the Jaffna Hospital was not part of our objectives. It was given to 5 RAJ RIF commanded by Lt. Col. B. K. Khanna to clear. It was said that the LTTE had built up the hospital with various arms and ammunition, taking it be a safe zone. It was the task of our neighbouring battalion to clear it. In the early morning Major Sisodia reached near the hospital while clearing the area on his way to the Jaffna Bus Stand when he heard the firing inside the hospital. Exactly who did it that was not known to us. Since LTTE was believed to have made the hospital as their base some casualties could have taken place in the crossfire. In fact since the LTTE also operated in civil clothes it was impossible to identify who was LTTE and who was not. The same morning when I was passing through that area I was surprised to see a couple of soldiers apparently of Indian Army huddled there. I was totally surprised. I had no information about anyone coming into my area of responsibility. Having gone near them I found they were all Indian Army officers of the Medical Corps, who were sent to provide medical cover. They were to activate the Jaffna Hospital. To my pleasant surprise I found that one of the doctors was Lt. Col. Maulick who had been the Regimental Medical Officer at our Sikh Regimental Centre where we had both served together. The complete team was at a loss. They had no wherewithal with them. They neither had any medicines with them nor any protection. It was a great surprise to me as to how they reached there and it was their sheer luck that they did not become victims to LTTE fire. How the LTTE missed them was also a surprise. This was another incidence of callous handling by the people responsible for planning. I shook hem out of their nervousness. They did not know where the hospital was, where to go, how to start, and last but not the least, how they were to protect themselves. They were carrying their personal weapons which were sten guns but I was not sure if they were carrying sufficient ammunition with them! I then and there provided a section of troops for their protection till they organized themselves and become self-sufficient.

Thereafter I did not see them again in Jaffna as we all got carried away by the flow of events. Once later I met Lt. Col. Maulick when he was commanding the Khadki Military Hospital near Pune as a brigadier in 2003-04. He remembered that day with fondness and gratitude.

Going back to the battlefield; the rest of the day we reorganized ourselves, maintained our weapons, replenished ammunition and equipment and rested for a while to regain enough energy to clear the rest of the western part of Jaffna town. Early the next morning we started operations for clearing the Jaffna Bus Stand and the Road to Point Pedro. The Jaffna Bus Stand was situated in the middle of the Jaffna market area. The area was full of shops, though those were all closed and no person was seen in the area. From time immemorial the biggest sufferers in any war or conflicts are always the civilians. They get it from both the sides. All these people had either fled into the nearby jungles or had taken refuge in the refugee camps that were set up all over the area. The responsibility to capture the Bus Stand was given to "Bravo" and "Delta" Companies and the Point Pedro road junction area to "Alfa" and "Charlie" Companies. Due to the crippling shortage of troops, on each axis both the companies were grouped together into a task force and they were to undertake the task as a joint operation. It was planned to provide cover by fire and then clear first the high-rise buildings around the objectives and hold them before going for the actual objectives. This would provide protection, wider observation and depth to the objective. The targets, however, did not themselves have any tactical value as such. These were the part of the over-all plan for the occupation of the town by securing and holding important localities, to give credibility to our possession, and at the same time denying the LTTE access to Jaffna town.

The night of 21/22 October passed off peacefully without much intervention from the LTTE. We had intensive perimeter patrolling, had as usual posted sentries adequately. Full precaution was taken against any surprise attack or any surreptitious grenade throwing or firing of any explosives from close quarters to cause us casualties. On the morning of 22 October, the second phase of our operation started. Both the columns took different routes to reach their objectives. I was keenly monitoring the progress. It appeared that the enemy's will to fight at that moment and place was diminishing. Other than a couple of innocuous shots nothing much was encountered en route. The enemy was on the retreat. The combined weight of the Indian Army present there would have been too much for them to bear. But I was constantly reminding the company commanders not to throw caution away and to follow the battle drills that we had successfully developed in such a short time.

By about 11 a.m., I was informed that both companies were in their respective positions. I heard the cheerful voices of all the company commanders on the radio sets. It was time to shift my battalion headquarters and reorganize the deployment. I instructed the Adjutant, Captain Moti, to move the battalion HQ to a suitable place preferably near "Bravo" Company to get inherent protection. We did not have enough strength in the battalion HQ to fend for ourselves. With this instruction to Moti, I took my precious jeep and an escort of four jawans to go around the companies. I was to get a first-hand idea as to what Jaffna was like, see the condition of the civil population, re-site the battalion, and plan the expansion phase with the company commanders. Like any other town it had an old congested area and a new growing and affluent area. It was well-connected with axial and lateral roads. Overall it was a decent city but at that time it looked deserted."

### *The Jaffna Hospital Incident*

On 21 October occurred the contentious clearance of the Jaffna Civil Hospital area. The hospital was located near the Jaffna market and the bus terminus, and had been declared a "no-war zone." However, the LTTE, who respected no codes of conduct rushed in, evacuated all LTTE members admitted there, and began firing from within the building. The doctors and employees of the hospital protested, but the LTTE brushed them off, leaving the hospital moments before troops of 5 RAJ RIF stormed the premises, throwing grenades into rooms as they entered as per standard practice. As per M.R. Narayan Swamy, "Some 50 doctors, nurses and employees were crowded and cringed in the radiology department. Several patients and visitors were also there. The LTTE firing had died down by then. But the Indian troops opened fire indiscriminately, mowing down at lest 21 doctors and staff. Most of them were killed inside a room where they were cowering or on a cemented path leading to the Medical Superintendent's office. Soldiers quickly fanned out throughout the building. The next morning, a senior consultant pediatrician arrived at the hospital in white robes accompanied by two uniformed nurses. When he saw an Indian soldier, he said aloud in English, "I am a doctor, I am a doctor" and started climbing the stairs. But the soldier calmly picked up a rifle and shot him dead.

"Yes, the soldiers killed them" admitted Brigadier Ravi Inder Singh Kahlon.* "There was no way of knowing they were civilians. It was the fog of war." Kahlon said the hospital massacre was due to the heat of the moment and the extreme provocation to the soldiers who had witnessed the death of scores of their colleagues."

On 22 October, 72 Brigade's 13 SIKH LI cleared the axis Urumparai-Kopai North. Central Jaffna town was secured on 24 October by the two severely under-strength battalions of 41 Infantry Brigade, 19 RAJ RIF and 16 SIKH, while 5 RAJ RIF captured Jaffna Railway Station, Hindu College and Hindu Ladies College, all in building-to-building fighting in built-up areas. 13 SIKH LI of 72 Infantry Brigade captured Jaffna University on 24 October in the face of tough LTTE opposition, completing the capture at 4 p.m.

*Brig. R.I.S. "Risky" Kahlon, of the Grenadiers, was Deputy GOC of 54 Infantry Division from 15 October onwards, and was later appointed Town Commandant of Jaffna during the period of the IPKF administration.

Shyam Tekwani, a photographer of the weekly newsmagazine *India Today* was the only Indian media photographer present in the area of operations during the last stages of the battle for the capture of Jaffna. He spent five days with the LTTE till 28 October, having first met the LTTE at Vavuniya on 24 October and asked them to be taken to Jaffna and the combat zone. On 26 October he had been taken to the LTTE Deputy Commander Mahattaya outside Jaffna. Mahattaya's first question to him had been: "Are you here as an Indian or a journalist?" He was present on the LTTE side during an engagement at Kokkuvil where 18 Indian soldiers died, and watched two teenage LTTE guerillas, barefoot and in short pants, Babu, 18 years old, and Keethan, 17 years old, arguing about who would get to finish off the two remaining Indian soldiers of the group, and then cutting down these two men in a hail of gunfire. He was also present with the LTTE at Chavakcheri where an engagement was actually on, and when helicopter gunships strafed LTTE positions during the firefight. His pictures of dead Indian soldiers lying on the road at Kokkuvil, which appeared in the *India Today* issue of 15 November 1987, caused considerable loss of morale among the families of troops at peace stations from where units had been hastily inducted, such as Lucknow and Gwalior. *(See Appendix)* He was also taken blindfolded to meet the few Indian soldiers taken captive, and not brutally killed by the "tyre treatment" – burning tyres put around the necks of captives. They were 17 men from 8 MAHAR who had run out of ammunition and were forced to surrender after their last four trucks in a convoy got separated from the rest at Chittankerni near Vaddukodai on 16 October, and the sole survivor of the abortive raid on the LTTE HQ from 13 SIKH LI, Sepoy Gora Singh, all kept captive in chains. He witnessed Mahattaya sending LTTE men into battle, reminding them of their three main considerations: stealth, speed, and surprise.

An interesting episode is recounted by Lt. Col. M.K. Gupta Ray of 16 SIKH.

"After my visit to the company locations, I was returning through the main road along the Jaffna Bus Stand. It was a deserted road. Suddenly I saw that a lady clad in black 'burkha,' her veil lifted, was beckoning me. I was in two minds whether to ignore the call or try to find out what she had to say. Under the prevailing situation no lady would come out unless the situation was desperate. I asked my driver to turn the vehicle towards her. When I went near her I could see her more clearly. She was a good-looking woman about 40 years of age, who appeared to be a Muslim lady. She was standing at the entrance of her house. When I went near her she pointed me to go inside the house. This was a predicament for which I was not prepared at all and I did not know how to react. It could be a source of some valuable information or a death trap. In a helpless manner I looked at my driver and the escort commander. The driver spoke out and said *"Sab tusi andar jao. Dekho ki whoeya."* ("Sir, you go inside and see what has happened.") Very reluctantly I got down. In no way was I prepared to be killed at the hand of a woman or to be caused to die at her instance. We heard many such stories where women had killed unsuspecting soldiers, including the C.O. of a battalion. He was shot at by a 10 year old girl and was killed on the spot. In the fight between valour and discretion, the valour won. I decided to go inside with my heart in my mouth. We were six of us including myself. I kept the driver and two guards outside to take suitable action should something happen to us. I was equally worried when I left them outside. They should not be bumped off. I had half a mind to take all of them with me so that we all could face the situation together. But keeping the single vehicle by itself was equally risky. The vehicle could be either stolen or booby-trapped. Both were equally dangerous. I could face the LTTE squarely, but here I was at a loss. Anyway, four of us started following the lady. Amongst us in that situation, I found one of my escort was the bravest. He took the lead and physically guarded me behind his huge frame of over six feet height. The lady led me to the first floor and then through the veranda to a corner room. The room was a fairly big one. She indicated to step in. I kept two soldiers outside the room. The escort and I entered the room. All the time I was surreptitiously holding my rifle tight. In battle I always prefer to carry a rifle rather than the sten-gun which is authorized to an officer. On entering we found a group of ladies quietly sitting around a pretty lady, presumably mourning. I saw no male. At that point of time the lady who brought us here started talking. She said "All the male members of this house have fled to the refugee camps to save themselves from this carnage. This is a big joint family. We have got account of most of them accept the husband and the child of this lady who is sitting in the middle. They have come from the Middle-East where her husband is employed." After saying this she gave a pause. This statement confused me more as I could not discern till then as what was my role under this situation. What was I supposed to do? She would have understood my mind. She continued with her narration. She continued to say "Her husband and her son went to the market when this carnage began. The firing started. Like all others they had also fled towards the refugee camps which are generally located alongside the mandirs so are generally spared from firing. We tried our best but we have not been able to locate them. We want your help." This further confused me. I myself did not know how could I could help them under such a situation when I was not certain of myself. While I was engrossed in my thoughts, the lady came out with what she wanted of me. She continued saying "All that we request is that you give us a letter of permission to be free enough to go from place to place in search of these two persons." I still was a confused person. Very politely I was trying to explain to her that the whole town was not under me. So I did not know how it would help her. She said in reply "Indian Army is seen in other parts too so this being the last resort and there being no other way we beg of you to give us an authority letter." I realized 19 RAJ RIF would be carrying out similar task like us. Though I did not know how much it would help them, but I had no face to say no. I realized that LTTE might be using this method to control the movement of population so they were accustomed with this. I asked for a pencil and a pen and wrote an authority letter to allow this lady and another companion to go anywhere they wanted to go. First time in my life and perhaps never in future when my writ was to run in a foreign country. It never happened in my own country.

After that touching moment, the type of which manifests the futility and sufferings of humanity on account of useless violence, I started for my headquarters. On reaching there, to my extreme delight, I found our Commanding Officer, Col. A. K. Chatterjee, had arrived and was taking a briefing from the Adjutant. A great deal of load was taken off my shoulders. I was also feeling happy for the reason that I, despite all odds, had not let him down. I had given him Jaffna town. It could have been possible that had he been present things would have been better, but could not have been easy as well. I greeted him. I could understand that it would take him some time before he would settle down to this new environment. I briefed him in detail from the beginning to date and my further plan of action. It was now his turn to formulate his own plan. I took over my original position as the battalion's Second in Command.

Next day we started expanding our hold on Jaffna Town. We went and linked up with Jaffna University. This was the place where the seed of this war of attrition had been sown. Here the Sinhalese Government tried to impose their arbitrary rule to restrict admission of the local Tamil students scoring higher marks by making a rule wherein a Sinhalese student scoring lesser marks could get admission and not the Tamil student. This rule out of all others became the turning point and indirectly gave impetus to the growth of militancy. Many militant organizations sprang up. At the initial stage of our present operations a brutal fight had taken place between a detachment of IPKF consisting of a team of para commandoes and a platoon of 13 Sikh Light Infantry and the LTTE. It had been a very daring plan. Success of this plan would have led to capture or elimination of almost all the top LTTE leaders including their chief Prabhakaran. But as the link-up did not take place and the Air Force withdrew their helicopters, the troops ran out of ammunition. Ultimately they charged with their bayonets. The LTTE dealt with them brutally. They hung burning tyres around our live soldiers. They kicked our wounded soldiers. They dishonoured our dead. That was the haunted place where we went to link up with 13 Sikh LI. We met the C.O. It was almost a silent meeting. I realized how the commanding officer feels when his troops die, that too in such a helpless state. It would probably haunt him all his life.

After we got back to the battalion HQ I was told by the Adjutant that I along with Lt. Col. Mukherjee and the Deputy Commander S. K. Singh had been asked to report at Palali airfield. A helicopter was waiting for us. I already visualized that the brigade commander would have something waiting for us. When we reached at the airfield we were told that we were to be posted out with immediate effect. The charge against us was that we were "dragging our feet" while advancing to link up with Jaffna Fort and that was why the link-up with the Jaffna Fort got delayed! Every one up the channel forgot that while four full-fledged brigades with much larger forces could not make any headway, and got stuck on their way to Jaffna, it was us with much lesser forces and with a host of innumerable problems did the job. While the other two officers were excited about such wrong treatment being bestowed upon us, I was not much perturbed seeing the various twists and turns in lives of so many innocent people, serving in Jaffna or elsewhere; getting further promotion or not had no bearing in my mind. I knew for certain that in our hierarchy no one would be seriously bothered about what had happened to us. We were inconsequential pawns to be dispensed with any time after the work was over. However we were trying to contact the Divisional Commander, Maj. Gen. Harkirat Singh and also the Army Commander, Lt. Gen. Depinder Singh. Somehow the

Army Commander prevailed, and, by nightfall, we were informed that the posting order had been cancelled and we could go back to the brigade. Next day we again went back to our units. There I was told that Lt. Col. Handa was being posted as the new 2IC. By then I was fed up with the intrigues of Brig. Manjit Singh and the callous handling of the Army Headquarters. They were located too far away and out of touch to know about the ground realities. Manjit Singh was nothing but a self seeker and in the Army there is no system of separating the chaff from the grain. As events unfolded, Brig. Manjit Singh managed to get himself a Mahavir Chakra, and eventually he prevailed in his plan and after two months when I went on 10 days of casual leave to Lucknow, I received initially my attachment order to the HQ Lucknow Sub Area, followed by a posting order as General Staff Officer Grade 2 to HQ 16 Infantry Division. The same were the fates of Col. S. K. Singh, the Deputy Brigade Commander, and Lt. Col. Mukherjee, who were also initially attached in Lucknow and later posted out to various formation HQ. But as luck would have it once the truth about Brig. Manjit Singh came to be know, he was asked to put in his papers and go home. Fate and justice took a complete circle. And after twenty years I got the opportunity to write what I wanted to write twenty years ago. God has his own way of dispensing "justice."

By the time we cleared Jaffna University and beyond, the ferocity of the Jaffna battle had diminished to a large extent. Clearing of the rest of Jaffna was no longer a big deal. We started to rebuild Jaffna town. The civil population who were hiding in jungles or had taken refuge in various safe places started returning. We started creating various entry points. The idea was to check the credentials of the people who were returning and try to stop the LTTE infiltrating in disguise. But how could we distinguish them and how could we stop the sons of the soil from entering their own homes? It was not possible. But in the process, I came to witness untold sufferings of umpteen numbers of innocent people who were oppressed from both sides: SLAF and LTTE—but who cares? I in my own small way tried to assuage their feelings. I instructed my troops that unless otherwise indicated no one was to be treated badly and all the doubtful cases were to be brought to me, at any time of the day or night. The biggest barrier in this was language. We could not follow each other's language. I could be of some help to the people who could speak English. Anyway things were going on smoothly. I was only worried of the LTTE inflicting casualty to our soldiers taking this opportunity to mix with the crowd and coming closer to us. I tried to keep as much vigilance as possible. There was one odd incident of firing but nothing much to write home about. Subsequently when the "Town Administration" was set up we started distributing rations and various other essentials to the civil population.

It is customary for the military to take over the administration of the towns cleared by them in the course of the operations conducted by them. I had read about it while studying military histories. The classic example is of Japan which was administered by General MacArthur after he captured the entire Far East including Japan. He had administered for the initial five years which helped Japan a great deal to attain today's success. We had first-hand experience of it when the administration of Jaffna town was taken over by the IPKF. Brig. R.I.S. Kahlon was appointed as the Town Administrator. He was flown into Jaffna for the purpose for taking over a brigade. He flew in with us in the same plane. Incidentally he and I had the opportunity to serve in the same brigade decades ago when he was a major and I was a captain. After Jaffna town was cleared of the LTTE, I found him appointed as Town Commandant. A few I.A.S. officers were also posted to assist him. Col S.K. Singh after having been returned from Palali Airfield was posted as Assistant Town Commandant. Before the IPKF took over the administration, it was the LTTE who used to run it. Contrary to popular belief, the LTTE had, beside a military wing, its own administrative, and judiciary departments and other administrative elements. It used to have the entire infrastructure that any administration needs. Other than defence, finance, foreign affairs, industries, and supplies, all were being handled by the LTTE. Now there was a great vacuum. Nothing was available and no system was functioning. With the refugees being allowed to return, the first thing that was needed was food and cooking gas or kerosene oil. People used to line up before us. With the combined effort of the Government of India and the Red Cross very soon we coped with the singularly most essential aspect that was food. We divided the whole are into Zones and placed them under each rifle company with the company commander as the zonal chief. Each company commander was told to create a liaison and coordination cell with the civilians for a dual purpose. Purpose One was to ensure proper distribution of the essential supplies, and Purpose Two, was to obtain as much information on the LTTE as possible. This helped us to be forewarned on many occasions thus saving precious lives. We used to organize civil-military liaison meetings in each locality. I shall narrate my unique experience in one of such meetings. It was being held inside a church. The hall was quite a big one and about 200 people attended. The turnout was very impressive. It was being attended by the Mayor of Jaffna Town, the Divisional Commissioner and many other local dignitaries. When I entered there I found that there was only a single piece sofa on the dais and no other chair. All the dignitaries were sitting on the floor. On enquiry I found that they were not sure how would I take it in case they sat on chairs or sofas on the same dais. Then and there I instructed that maximum chairs were to be brought, and since each one could not be offered a chair, at least the dignitaries were to sit on sofa/chair along with me on the dais and only then would the meeting commence. This gesture was well appreciated and as a result we could get lots of information on the LTTE and their likely movement and intentions, thus avoiding casualties to a great extent. I used to walk or move in a vehicle through the lanes and alleys of my part of the Jaffna town and tried to meet as many locals as possible. Though it was fraught with danger but it was also worthwhile for the task that was given to us.

In one of such trips, one day I came across the same lady whom I had met near the bus stop, and had gone inside her house at her behest. I then and there halted my vehicle near her and asked what had happened after that and why was she here? She was accompanied by couple of ladies and girls. She broke into a laconic smile and said that the man was found killed but the boy was found alive and they were just coming out of the burial ground after performing the last rites! One of the girls she pointed out was his daughter who was at that time staying at Colombo with one of their relatives. I had nothing to say, fumbled with a few words and could at best offer them for a lift up to their residence which they readily accepted. Subsequently as a gesture of goodwill and friendship we sent some rations to that family.

From then on till I came on leave in December, we were basically busy in bringing back normalcy to the town, helped opening the roads, communications system, schools, shops, restoring electricity etc. On many occasions I was called for arbitration also. But our main task, behind all these activities, was to locate hides and gain maximum information regarding the LTTE. Due to the close rapport that was built up and good intelligence that was set up at our level, Maj. Govind Sisodia could locate a place where he found a two-seater plane and associated workshop, way back in 1987. It could have been the beginning of the inception stage of the LTTE Air Force.

Among these activities I came home to Lucknow on a short leave, never to return to Sri Lanka again. 16 SIKH continued to stay till the end of the IPKF operations and returned only when the IPKF formally came out of Sri Lanka when they were withdrawn by the Government of India.

Thinking back, my impressions, observations and recommendations from my experience in Operation PAWAN are:

1. Proper mobilization is the essential part of any successful operation. The forces should be properly balanced for the given

task before it is launched. All resources of the nation must be commandeered to enforce it. This would only be possible if a proper mobilization plan is made covering all contingencies and early warning is issued at the national level. The troops should also be given proper warning time to organize themselves. Since the time the first telephone call was received and as the things proceeded nothing seemed to have been the work of professionals.

2. As mentioned the before the battle indications should have alerted the military planners to take anticipatory actions in alerting the troops well in time. A minimum of one month's warning period could have been easily given to the troops to prepare. It is one thing for the 2IC to take over the command in war due to the CO becoming a war casualty or any other operational need. But to start the operation in 24 hours without its permanent incumbent at the very outset is unthinkable. If a mobilization period had been given, the result would have been much happier for the IPKF. Even if it was not possible, the 54 Division, which was said to be dispersed in small detachments, as commented by Lt. Gen. Depinder Singh in his book "The IPKF in Sri Lanka," could well have been concentrated within Sri Lanka and held as battalion groups for at least ten days to a fortnight to allow for proper mobilization.

3. At the initial stage 54 Division was so hurriedly inducted that it had to shed most of its heavy equipment and supporting arms back in India. Artillery, armour, mechanized infantry and engineer support is very essential, like any other battle, to reduce casualties. While facing bullets it should be dealt with as much professionally as possible by employing full fire power. America's "Operation Desert Storm," the first Gulf War was completed in record time using a very high superiority of fire power. All types of fire power, i.e. land, air and naval, were combined to create effect. And everyone knows the result. As I always used to tell my soldiers, in battle there is no second position. Either you win or you loose. It is your choice. If you have to strike then strike hard. Though there are factors of civilian casualties, which can be taken care of by target

selection and forewarning them to vacate the battle zone. That is unfortunate but part of the game.

4. Administrative back-up plays a very major part in success of any operation. There are a number of issues that are to be considered and administrative echelons are to be set up at all levels. It was totally missing in the Sri Lanka battle. If at all it was existing we did not see it operating. There was no arrangements for supply of food, ammunition, evacuation of casualties, medical facilities, reinforcement of troops and a host of other things. It appeared no one had any time to look into this aspect. Probably the planners had a wishful thinking that either this was not required or that this would happen on its own! Administrative planning is the core issue of any operational planning. This process starts much earlier. This involves setting up of administrative echelons and dumps at various locations at various formation levels.

5. Most surprisingly, in this operation, troops were launched without very basic things e.g. maps, supporting weapons, supporting artillery fire, engineer support, medical cover, signal communication, proper mobilization, launching units or formation without even minimum operational strength, interpreter as we were confronting people with different language, administrative back up, intelligence cover, proper operational order or even operational briefing etc. It was just collecting some uniformed personnel and throwing them in front of the enemy to be mowed down. One cannot put one's own soldiers in the battle without any training and preparation. Training for such operations is not contained in common training programmes. It has to be special in nature. Lack of mobilization time and transportation means made us to land with only 210 soldiers as opposed to the authorized strength 850 of an infantry battalion. I still can not believe that such a thing could happen.

6. There was an agonizing mismatch in weaponry between the IPKF and the LTTE. The Indian Army's basic infantry weapon was the semi-automatic version of the 7.62 mm FN rifle (the FAL) designed in Belgium and produced in India under

license. It is a single-shot weapon with automatic reloading, and thus named the self-loading rifle (SLR) in India. The idea behind this perhaps was an emphasis on individual marksmanship and saving of ammunition. Against this, the LTTE had an array of automatic weapons of different calibres and makes. It had the AK 47 assault rifle (using the short Soviet 7.62 mm cartridge), German G3 rifles (using the same 7.62 mm NATO ammunition as the Indian SLR), American M 16A1 (of 5.56 mm caliber), the Chinese T 56 version of the AK-47, and LMGs and HMGs of .30 (7.62 mm) and .50 caliber respectively. With a large number of automatics, they could bring down a murderous volume of fire on the target as opposed to the single shots of IPKF solders. In the Indian Army an LMG is authorized at the scale of one per section or 10 soldiers. That makes only nine LMGs per company of 120 -130 soldiers and two MMGs, both of 7.62 mm (NATO). It was too inadequate to face the LTTE fire power, especially since the numbers of men available in each sub-unit was very low. The LTTE could also compensate for their lack of strength with increased firepower. The firepower of the LTTE was further augmented by their dexterous use of explosives in terms of mines, booby traps, and IEDs against which the IPKF was not particularly trained at that time. The LTTE were also quite competent enough to manufacture certain weapons at their own bases.

7. The lack of training made the IPKF soldiers remain hugging the roads and tracks. This suited the LTTE in their use of automatics and explosives. IPKF, specially, at initial stage, sent large patrols which could not avoid detection. It was, however, not without reason. It was the direct result of lack of training, orientation, maps, signal equipments and very importantly lack of proper composition of units and sub-units. These operations are generally done at section or at the maximum at platoon level. Section level and platoon level training are very personal. Each person in a section is given a specific task to perform in such type of minor tactics. Each one knows exactly what to do under a specific battle situation. They

know who and how to give cover and fire support at what point of time and how to progress. There are field signals both conventional and improvised to execute the task. But due to the very faulty mobilization plan troops at all levels got mixed up. I had three to four persons per section, out of an authorized ten, and that too merely for the sake of numbers. Many of them were non-combatant administrative personnel. In most of the cases the section commander, the most important link in such operations, who knows the traits and strong and weak points of each individual, was not present. Why I am elaborating this is to make one realize that mere naming one as an army does not make it functional. It also has its components essential to function like any other well oiled machine. It is not just a mass of armed people. When the army is mobilized it should be in its full strength to be able to deal with changing situations. Because there is nothing to employ thereafter, so no chance should be taken in hurry.

8. The ground reality should travel from the lower to the upper and not from the upper levels downwards. The plan should get modified from time to time depending the ground situation and a rigid plan dictated by non-tactical compulsion, should not be thrust upon the troops on the ground. I still can not believe my ears when Brig. Manjit Singh told me that we should move out even during the daytime disregarding the entire ground situation, disregarding the likely high casualties, just because the Chief of Army Staff, Gen. Sundarji, was believed to have told the Prime Minister, Rajiv Gandhi, that the battle would be over in seven days.

9. However in the case of 54 Division it was a total case of command and intelligence failure. Taking the enemy at face value, despite all the adverse indications from Prabhakaran from the time he was in Delhi and the intervening two months that Indian Government and the Army had at their disposal, was a mistake. Things should have been mended.

10. The IPKF was even less prepared for peace enforcement as per the accord. Their initial movement as on 30-31 July 1987 was

hurried enough with scattered deployment of the division all around the island. When reinforcement was rushed to Sri Lanka to participate in the in "Operation Pawan" the confusion was even greater! At the divisional level the brigades were shuffled and re-shuffled just like playing cards. The 54 Division in Jaffna started commanding the brigades normally under 36 Infantry Division: 18 and 72 Brigades and its own 91 along with 115 Brigade from elsewhere. It also had 41 Brigade from 4 Infantry Division. That left 36 Infantry Division with 54 Infantry Division's other two brigades 47 and 76 along with 340 Independent Infantry Brigade. The ensuing battle of Jaffna town raised a serious question as to whether it was a realistic operation when the Indian Army had never been involved in urban warfare and did not have the time to train itself.

11. The best way to fight insurgents is to fight by deploying a number of columns at a time, taking advantage of superiority of force, thereby surrounding the insurgents. This will give them a feeling of being encircled and also outflanked and prevent them from using the concept of a battle of interior lines. In this concept the enemy can switch troops depending on the threat perspective. But if numbers of columns are deployed at one time, firstly, it would automatically provide flank protection, thereby, protect from being surprised and, secondly, unhinge the enemy's own plan of action. Nobody likes to be encircled. These tactics with some modification can be applied both in jungle as well as built up areas. I could successfully employ this tactic against the LTTE on a number of occasions and got good results. This will neutralize to a great extent the enemy's advantage of ability to switch from axis o axis, taking the advantage of his home ground, as he is surrounded. While employing this tactics, as far as possible, stops should be positioned, if available jointly with armour or mechanized infantry. The plan should be to throw a ring around enemy locations. Para-dropping at certain locations will be more effective to hasten the operation and totally encircle the enemy. We must try to neutralize the advantage of the enemy who is

fighting in his own area which he knows so well, by coordinating employment of our superior force in combination of all arms and sister services, be it Air Force or Navy or both.

12. Application of these tactics is possible if the troops are very well trained to operate independently in small detachments. They should be well trained in good map reading, handling explosives, accurate shooting, handling of all types of weapons, calling and directing the [artillery] fire, camouflage and concealment, stalking, signal communication, field signals, first aid and sustainability under very adverse condition. Under such circumstances, at times the operating small detachments may also feel isolated and surrounded. Since the possibility in getting involved in such type of battle is more often than the conventional one, such training should become a part of regular training along with the major operations of war. In fact anyone who masters such minor tactics, it would not be difficult for him to get himself molded in the major operations of war, but the reverse would be difficult.

13. As a corollary to the above, raising of special units for this purpose with special authorization of manpower, arms and equipment, may also be considered. They should be as light as possible and should most of the time operate in conjunction with helicopters. They should not have heavy equipments, but their basic weapon must be automatic rifles and not semi-automatic as we had in Sri Lanka. Authorization of LMGs and MMGs should be more than of the regular infantry. The regular infantry relies on bayonet strength whereas these special units will have to fight on their own firepower. All other types of support should be provided. These units should be able to operate in the jungles for a long time at a stretch. Their maintenance should by air.

14. We have a very unfortunate system where a state can virtually go in the opposite direction of the national plan. When the IPKF was bleeding in Sri Lanka, political leaders in Madras including MGR, Karunanidhi, Maran, George Fernandes and various lesser mortals were providing all kinds of support to the

LTTE ranging from cash funds to supplying arms, deadly explosives and detonators: those were being produced in that state and were maiming our own soldiers. The wounded LTTE cadres were getting treated in Madras, going back and killing our soldiers. The same George Fernandes later became the Defence Minister, perhaps having achieved his political goal over the dead bodies of our IPKF soldiers. One should imagine the frustration that the IPKF had.

15. I shall take this opportunity to quote one example which should be a case study. I quote this from the book of Lt. Gen. Depinder Singh, "The IPKF in Sri Lanka." In that he mentioned that in his operational order he had specified that Jaffna (he did not mention whether it was the entire peninsula or the Jaffna town) was to be cleared in four days. Whether he meant the Jaffna peninsula or the town, it was a very ambitious target for any battle condition specially when this involved clearance of large part of jungle and built up area. This under no circumstances could be a realistic task, specially, considering the prevailing condition at that time. Indian Army was not ready for the task from any angle. Though with the God's grace we did manage to come somewhere near to achieve that task with our most under-strength unit, but the overall scenario did not reflect the attainability of such ambitious task. I am sure he was under pressure. Under normal military situation he would not have issued such order. The subsequent incidents that unfolded proved this. This can only be possible in a highly mobile operation undertaken by fully mechanized formations in *blitzkrieg* types of operation. The important lesson is that operational order, as much as possible, should be realistic.

16. Things could not have been worse than what we experienced during the employment of IPKF in Sri Lanka. You name it and it was there. There was no preparation, relevant training, advance intimation, proper mobilization, tactical concept, administration, communication, grouping and employment of arms and services, use of other two services, command and control and last but not the least proper

leadership at higher level They either were not capable at the worst or put up a blind façade at the best to face the reality. The list could be unending. I am trying to bring out the relevant tactical issues that could be further analyzed and a concept formed.

17. The IPKF had done many good jobs to restore the civil administration. After the assault on Jaffna the IPKF was also tasked to hold provisional elections and other administrative duties like running essential services and keeping the roads open. They manned banks, post offices, railways and vehicular transport. These jobs were carried out with distinction by the IPKF. This part of the story somehow never got publicity or praise. It was a Herculean task, done with the typical thoroughness that is the hallmark of our armed forces.

*Army Commander's Interview*

Lt. Gen. Depinder Singh, OFC IPKF and GOC-in-C Southern Command answered questions put to him on 29 October 1987 by the Chennai Correspondent of the newsmagazine *India Today*, S.H. Venkatramani, as under:

Q. *What were the main hurdles that the IPKF faced in the battle for Jaffna?*

A. Initially, there was a paucity of troops. When the battle broke out, there was only one brigade in the whole of the Jaffna peninsula. There was half a battalion at the front, one at Point Pedro and one west of Palaly. Actually we had not mobilized for war. And each battalion available had only 50 per cent strength; people had gone on leave or for training. Secondly, the LTTE's use of human shields was a constraint. Thirdly, to avoid damage to civilian life and property we did not employ our full range of heavy weaponry.

Q. *What weaponry did the IPKF use?*

A. We used small arms and light mortars only. Later, when we encountered heavily fortified bunkers and resistance from concrete houses, tank guns were used only to knock out bunkers.

Q. *What are the Mi-24 helicopter gunships being used for?*

A. Helicopters carrying troops came under sniper fire. So we had to give orders that they should bring down suppressive fire in turn. I wish to state, categorically, that we did not use offensive air power in the operation to free Jaffna town.

Q. *But the helicopter gunships were used in Chavakcheri.*

A. Yes. One or two helicopter gunships were used. But we had confirmed military intelligence that the Tigers were present in strength in Chavakcheri. Also, we had two companies of our soldiers east of Chavakcheri, and there were two battalions of the Madras Regiment in Navatkuli. The idea was for the battalions in Navatkuli to link up with the two companies east of Chavakcheri, but we met with strong resistance from the LTTE. So we were forced to use the gunships. We have only four or five helicopter gunships in Jaffna. There were admittedly a few civilian casualties in Chavakcheri; the death toll was 27.

While mopping-up operations continued, the LTTE continued to take a toll of the officers in particular. For example, Maj. Ashwani Kanva of the Army Medical Corps, with the 93 Field Regiment (artillery), was shot thrice and died on 3 November, when he rushed out of his tent with his medical kit to provide first-aid to his tent-mate, Maj. Gurpreet Singh, who had been wounded nearby by a sniper. Maj. Kanva's body was among the few bodies that were returned to their families in India for cremation.

Clearing of many areas around Jaffna with search operations and house-to-house fighting took up to 8 November, with all the available strength of all the infantry battalions of the five brigades being engaged. 5/1 G.R. of 115 Infantry Brigade cleared and captured Manipai town on 8 November. After this, the LTTE started breaking off action whenever a proper assault was mounted on its positions.

Shekhar Gupta, Special Correspondent of *India Today*, in its issue of 31 January 1988, aptly described this part of "Op PAWAN" by commenting that "If there had been less political haste, victory could have come easier."

Lt. Gen. S.C. Sardeshpande comments on this period:

"The IPKF had to be strengthened with the whole of 36 Div and a couple of other brigades of other divisions through airlift at Palali. The fly-in went at breakneck speed, evoking awe, but violating all principles of affiliations, equipment levels, command and control structure, briefing, tasking and mental preparation. Troops were disorganized, ill-equipped, unprepared and ill-trained. The suddenness of violence, alien land and Jaffna's watery maze struck a kind of terror among troops and petrified them. For a time—a long time perhaps—they did not overcome the fear of operating in small numbers, withholding of the overuse of heavy fire support, and getting out of the safety of slow movement. Basic minor tactics were thrown overboard. That resulted in casualties, delay and more morbid fear of the hidden IED and lurking LTTE. A three-day mandate given by the Chief to capture Jaffna took almost a fortnight and considerable casualties from nearly four brigades that finally cleansed the area of major LTTE concentrations. The LTTE escaped to Vanni and continued the fight."

There was some criticism about the fact that numbers of LLTE cadres escaped. This charge is unfounded, because attacking columns cannot be easily and quickly re-organized into a cordon with stops, tasked to prevent escapes, which even in that case would have happened unless there was an organized body of men trying to fight their way out, which could be stopped by an organized road-block force. The incident that was publicized by the LTTE, of the IPKF firing into the Jaffna Hospital, occurred during this period. Troops did indeed assault and take the hospital, from where the LTTE had been engaging them, and into which some LTTE mortars had been moved. As regards causing of civilian casualties, any LTTE body recovered by the IPKF was labeled by the LTTE as a civilian casualty, since the body would have been recovered wearing a *lungi*.

It is worth noting that the LTTE always kept at least one, generally more, unarmed cadres along with every armed one.

Their tasks were to keep the firer supplied with ammunition, to recover any weapon from a downed IPKF soldier where possible, to carry away the firer or his body in case he was hit, and to pick up his weapon and ammunition and carry on engaging from another location. If the house was stormed by IPKF troops and the body could not be taken away, all that would be found was a dead body in a *lungi*. As per LTTE propaganda all their killed were "civilian casualties."

*Command and Control Arrangements*

The command and control from the divisional level downwards to brigade and down to battalions and further down to their rifle companies was by the standard army communications equipment and network, which follow the chain of command. A weakness already existed in the quality of radio communications between the company HQ and the rifle platoons, which becomes even more critical in situations where the platoons have to move out and operate independently, as in operations in built-up areas and jungles. But this tended to affect the tactical operations of the company and below. The serious flaws in the command and control arrangements were at the levels above the division. The IPKF, in theory, was being commanded by an "Overall Force Commander," but whose authority and responsibility extended only to the army component. He was the Army Commander Southern Command whose office was in Poona, but who also had an "ad hoc" office at Force HQ in Chennai. However, the actual operational orders were being given to the IPKF Force HQ directly by Army HQ, thus, in effect, making the OFC himself redundant.

*Casualties and Recoveries*

Casualties incurred by the IPKF in the operations and LTTE recoveries from 11 October to 30 October were:

*IPKF*

*KILLED:* 17 officers, 26 Junior Commissioned Officers (JCO's), and 276 Other Ranks (OR)

*Wounded:* 53 officers, 67 JCO's, and 919 OR.

*LTTE*

*Killed:* 1100 cadres
*Weapon Recoveries:* 23 machine guns, 167 rifles, 17 Sten carbines, 8 rocket launchers, and 70 mortars of different calibres.

- Two of the major lessons of this phase of operations in Sri Lanka were regarding the lack of numerical superiority (i.e., of adequate strength), and an inadequacy of medical facilities to treat the casualties. 54 Infantry Division could have kept one battalion uncommitted to ground and held concentrated as reserve in its initial deployment itself.
- A lack of basic tactical judgement at the company and battalion level was noticeable in some instances. It was sometimes compounded by *"a degree of petrifaction at all levels—company, battalion, and brigade. Defensive mentality overpowered all...."* Lt. Gen. Sardeshpande said that *"We were to make such basic mistakes in our approach, execution and conduct throughout our stay in Sri Lanka."* Such mistakes of poor tactical judgement were made by the officer cadre, but the troops of all regiments continued to display courage, stoicism, and endurance.

### *Dispersal of the LTTE and Consolidation of Trincomalee Sector*

The LTTE survivors of the IPKF capture of Jaffna melted away in two's and three's, primarily into the Vanni jungles. Some wounded were undoubtedly moved to Tamil Nadu across the Palk Strait, to receive treatment and to recuperate at the expense of the state government, a shameful contradiction. At this stage the local Tamils of Jaffna were not really angry with

India or the Indian Government, except immediately after helicopter gunships were used against a confirmed LTTE stronghold in the capture of Chavakacheri, which left 27 dead, amongst whom how many were LTTE and how many genuine non-combatants was impossible to tell.

***Trincomalee Sector:*** The Trincomalee Sector, in the east, had initially faced a somewhat different set of problems from those of the Jaffna Sector. The problem in this area arose from the fact that Sinhala colonization, with government sponsorship, had been taking place in the narrow area that formed the boundary zone between the Northern and the Eastern Provinces, and had been a cause of disquiet for all the Tamil separatist groups. Sinhala policemen and SLAF personnel in the Eastern Province saw themselves as the protectors of the Sinhala minority from Tamil violence. The provision of the ISLA which confined the SLAF to barracks was greatly to their dislike. From the beginning of October stray incidents of petty violence against IPKF personnel had begun, carried out by Sinhala policemen and even some SLAF in civilian clothing. From the 5 October onwards there were LTTE atrocities against Sinhalas and reportedly also against rival Tamil groups. As already brought out, HQ 36 Infantry Division was inducted during October, and its GOC, Maj. General R.P. Singh, took command of all IPKF troops in this sector, which were deployed as under:

| | |
|---|---|
| 47 Infantry Brigade | Vavuniya-Mannar |
| 76 Infantry Brigade | Batticaloa-Amparai |
| 340 (Independent) Infantry Brigade | Trincomalee |

**Other troops available in the sector were:**

65 Armoured Regiment less one squadron

An artillery regiment

Two companies of mechanised infantry of 25 Mechanised Infantry

36 Division was tasked to keep the LTTE in their sector under sufficient pressure to prevent these from reinforcing the Jaffna Sector. They were also tasked with keeping the road Trincomalee-Vavuniya-Elephant Pass open, to allow stores,

vehicles and personnel arriving by sea at Trincomalee to be moved to the Jaffna Sector. This involved very careful convoy moves and road clearance and protection, as the LTTE were mining the road and laying ambushes and road-blocks which had to be fought through and cleared. The mines were extremely powerful, and were selectively remote-detonated by just one man at a distance choosing the vehicle he wanted destroyed. For example, a BMP was lifted almost 10 feet into the air, and all inside killed, its doors torn off and flung away by the force of the blast, and a 3-ton lorry with 22 men destroyed with no survivors.

*Changes in IPKF Command Structure:* In end-October 1987, with two divisions now in Sri Lanka, Maj. General A.S. Kalkat (later promoted to Lieut.-General) was appointed GOC IPKF, with authority over both divisions, 54 and 36, in their two respective sectors. The Army Commander, Southern Command, Lt. Gen. Depinder Singh, retired in February 1988. The new Southern Army Commander, Lt. Gen. A.K. Chatterjee, had the IPKF under his command for administrative purposes, whilst operationally it remained under Lt. Gen. Kalkat. This arrangement had in-built scope for friction at the highest levels, and affected the promotions of a number of officers who performed well exercising their respective commands in operations in Sri Lanka, numerous colonels and brigadiers, and seven major-generals, who were thus denied further promotions.

Chapter 5

# 'Operation PAWAN' – Phase III: The Counter-Insurgency Campaign

On 5 November 1987, a fresh directive for the subsequent phase of operations was issued to the IPKF from the Army HQ, more troops were inducted into the IPKF with four separate divisional HQ controlling the four sectors. By this time, Army HQ had created a new Military Operations Cell for Sri Lanka (MO-SL), and had begun to issue orders to fight company and even platoon battles to the General Staff at IPKF HQ in Palaly. These orders were being issued by Brig. V. P. Malik* or Brig. V.R. Raghavan, or even at times by a Duty Officer in the Operations Room in the MO Directorate (DGMO). The OFC, Lt. Gen. Depinder Singh, issued only verbal instructions, and thus it is claimed that the MGGS in Southern Command HQ, Maj. Gen. A. S. Kalkat, could hold formation commanders and unit commanders responsible for any acts or omissions, without having to take any share of the responsibility upon the General Staff (GS) at Southern Command HQ. This includes the two major sub-branches the GS (Operations) and the GS (Intelligence), which are supposed to issue written Confirmatory Orders for the Army Commander's verbal instructions as well as issue and disseminate Intelligence Reports and Intelligence Summaries.

In November-December 1987, operations to further degrade the LTTE potential continued commenced. In December 1987, the 9th Para Commandos under their C.O., Col. Katoch, based on

*Later to become Chief of Army Staff, which he was during the Pakistani Kargil incursion and consequent conflict in 1999.

information given by RAW, were tasked directly by Army HQ to raid a hospital overlooking the beach in the northern Vadamarachchi area where Pirabakaran was believed to be. The GOC IPKF, Maj. Gen. Harkirat Singh, had to use his personal rapport with captains of the Indian Navy ships present to enforce a blockade of the area. The LST's required to take the commandos to the beach were not made available till after midnight, losing much of the valuable hours of darkness, the mission proved abortive, and the commandos had to be withdrawn from the beach after first light, because in spite of naval gunfire support the beachhead could not be held in the face of heavy fire from the LTTE who were dominating the area. HQ IPKF were unable to influence the outcome because they had neither any additional infantry nor any additional supporting arms, no were there any armed helicopters available.

In November 1987, in order to make up some of the deficiencies in manpower in infantry battalions caused by a full mobilization not having been ordered, some infantry regiments resorted to sending reinforcements from other sister battalions to the battalion deployed in 'Operation PAWAN.' 5/1 G.R. thus received 10 OR each from its sister battalions of the 1st Gorkha Rifles*, who were distributed to the four rifle companies, and were later regrouped to help form a fifth *ad hoc* company ('E' Company) for the requirement of maximum tactical maonoeuvre sub-units needed for counter-insurgency (COIN) operations. Not ordering mobilization permitted normal Army courses of instruction to continue at the permanent training establishments, while routine administrative and non-warlike temporary duties also continued.

From after December 1987 the IPKF was in full control of the Jaffna Peninsula, including the Vadamarachchi area. It was not in

*Since men do not like to leave their own battalions permanently, even if they are moved to other battalions of the same class composition and of their own regiment, they were returned to their parent battalions on the return of 5/1 G.R. to India. To form the fifth 'ad hoc' company one platoon each from 2/1 G.R. and from 4/1 G.R. had been sent to the battalion by early March 1988.

complete control of the central districts of Vavuniya, Mannar, Killinochchi and Mullaitivu. The assessment of the Indian High Commission at this point was that the IPKF had completed the major portion of its task and the LTTE could be militarily neutralized in another eight to ten weeks provided it did not get financial and other warlike assistance from Tamil Nadu.

*Command and control problems, political and military problems, political and diplomatic manoeuvres, twin-track and triple-track*

From end-1987 numerous problems of command and control, and of political and diplomatic policy formulation and implementation, had begun. There were differences of opinion between the GOC IPKF and Deputy OFC, Lieut. General A. S. Kalkat, and his immediate superior, the OFC and Southern Army Commander, Lt. Gen. Depinder Singh. The use of "liaison officers" at each divisional HQ to send information direct to Army HQ meant that there were misunderstandings caused by misinterpretations of information that reached Army HQ without going through the two intermediate HQ and commanders, IPKF and Southern Command. There were differences of opinion between the Prime Minister's Office (PMO), the Ministry of External Affairs (MEA), the Army, and the external intelligence agency RAW, and there was a lack of rapport between the Prime Minister and the Army Chief. RAW advocated a "Triple-Track" policy wherein a line of negotiation was maintained with the Tamil militants, in addition to the other two official "tracks" of military action and diplomatic negotiations with the Sri Lankan Government. This "triple track" policy suggested by Mr. Anand Verma, head of RAW, also included the provision that they should be authorized to make direct contact with President Jayawardene, without involving the MEA or the Ministry of Defence, with regard to the devolution package to be given to the Tamils. Rajiv Gandhi generally agreed to these suggestions. The Sri Lankan Government threatened to go back on its commitment of merging the Northern and Eastern Provinces into one unit with devolution of some powers, if

India resumed talks with the LTTE. The Tamil Nadu Government continued to provide the LTTE with arms, material and moral support, and by providing treatment to wounded cadres, in spite of the demoralizing impact of this on IPKF troops being pointed out to the Indian Government by the army. Rajiv Gandhi was convinced that military operations against the LTTE were to continue, a view shared by almost all his advisers, except the RAW chief, Anand Verma, and some politicians, especially from Tamil Nadu. In Tamil Nadu, the politicians Gopalaswamy and P. Nedumaran, of the Tamil Nationalist Movement, remained vocal in support of the LTTE.

In January 1988, Maj. Gen. Harkirat Singh was transferred away from 54 Infantry Division, evidently because the initial operations had gone badly. As per him, the next Chief of Army Staff, Gen. V. N. Sharma, had bluntly told him later: "The commanders who initially launched the campaign have to pay the price for it, and in this scenario, Harry, you had become the prime target."

Lt. Gen. Sardeshpande explains the military situation:

"In January 1988 two more divisions – 4 and 57 – were brought in, with two more brigades from 23 Div. There were nearly 15 infantry brigades, 50 infantry battalions, an engineer brigade's, a mechanized brigade's worth of armoured elements, a commando brigade's worth of Special Forces, an artillery brigade's worth of gun support and a civil affairs administrative brigade's worth in the form of the Town Commandant, Jaffna, and his staff. There was a strong airlift capability of Mi-8 helicopters and AN-36 transport aircraft, and adequate naval support for logistics.

The LTTE was subdued, worsted and knocked about everywhere, except in the Vanni jungles. It was paying a heavy price, but fought on gallantly with guile and grit, resolve and motivation, that were indeed impressive if not remarkable. In the maze of jungle and water inlets between Mulaithivu and Kokkilai four major battles were fought, identified with Alampil (swamp), Nayaru (lagoon), Nittikaikulam (lake) and Kokkilai.

All were inconclusive, and given up a wee bit prematurely, for reasons I do not understand. We lost a lot of weapons—enough to equip an infantry battalion worth. What we captured was negligible. Our search missions of early '88 came to naught by June 1988 as intelligence dried up following the Indian Government's talks with the LTTE leader Kittu in Madras, though they proved abortive. The last source of countering the LTTE on their home ground disappeared."

The sectors now were:

- *Jaffna:* 54 Infantry Division, now commanded by Maj. Gen. S.C. Sardeshpande
- *Trincomalee:* 36 Infantry Division, now commanded by Maj.-Gen. Jameel Mehmood
- *Batticaloa:* 57 Mountain Division commanded by Maj. Gen. T.P. Singh
- *Vavuniya:* 4 Infantry Division commanded by Maj. Gen. Gupta

The tasking of the IPKF changed to counter-insurgency operations, and by the end of the year, the IPKF had broken the control of the LTTE in the urban and semi-urban areas. At its peak, during the elections of November-December 1988, a total of 54,802 personnel were deployed as part of the IPKF in Sri Lanka.

Throughout 1988, from February onwards, the IPKF maintained pressure on the LTTE by launching a series of combing operations, e.g., *Op-Trishul* in April. *Op-Viraat* in May-June, and *Op-Checkmate* in July, with the same restrictions on the use of force and weapons as in the initial stage. However, during these COIN operations there were inevitably some casualties among the troops and their officers. For example, Capt. Pramod Jolly of the 12$^{th}$ Jammu and Kashmir Rifles (12 JAKRIF) was killed on 13 September 1988 while advancing in a group of three who were all killed. The operations in July, in particular the battle at Nitikaikulam became the turning point, by effectively neutralising the LTTE. This provided the appropriate security environment for the holding of elections.

## IPKF DEPLOYMENT 1988-89

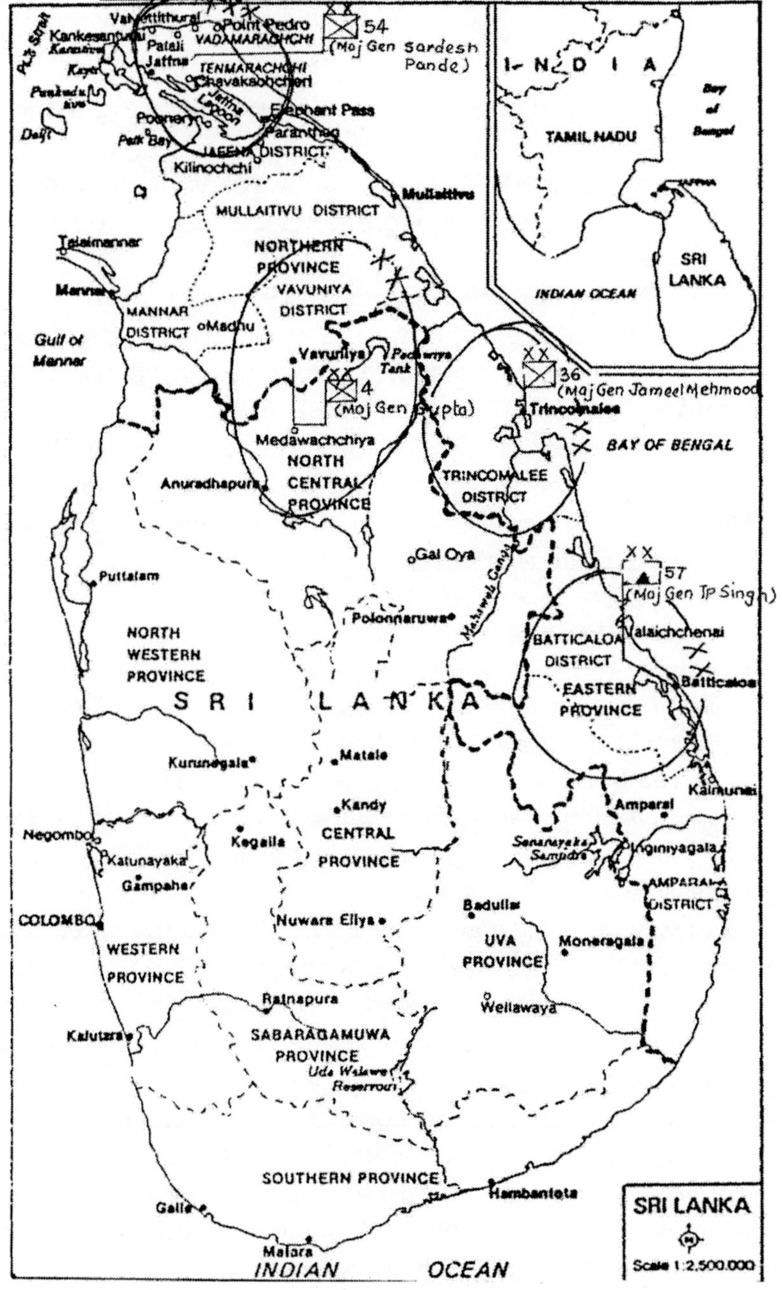

COIN operations of a more routine nature continued through 1989.

*Tactical Problems*

Among the tactical and other practical problems experienced by the IPKF were:

1. Infantry tended to operate along roads or prominent and well-defined tracks, and were consequently prone to being ambushed.

2. LTTE snipers with sniper rifles, firing from concealed positions on roof-tops, and from seats tied at the tops of coconut palms, invisible from a distance, took a heavy toll of infantry on the move, often holding up the advance of a patrol.

3. Weaknesses in signal communication capability were experienced, since it was not found possible to communicate with smaller patrols, due to the normal scaling of the appropriate radio sets in infantry battalions. This led to an odd situation: *Every time a patrol went out from any one of the widely-dispersed deployments, the nearest temple or church bells would ring. The number of times the bell rang would indicate to the LTTE the number of men on the patrol. A little girl or boy, un-noticed by the patrol, would run ahead of the patrol for a short while, till relieved by another child, sometimes on a bicycle, and so on, as long as the patrol was out. The arrival of such a child would warn the LTTE by then waiting in ambush. Thus ambushes were common.* While the patrol's progress was being monitored by the LTTE, their radio networks would keep all other LTTE stations informed. Higher echelons in the IPKF were able to monitor the patrol's progress by continuously intercepting the LTTE radio network, but the patrol's own sub-unit HQ would often be out of contact with its own patrol.

4. Partly due to such reasons, there was a tendency to use larger numbers of men on a patrol, born out of the "security-in-numbers" syndrome. It would have been more effective to have a much larger number of smaller patrols dominating a larger area, thus keeping the LTTE off-balance.

5. If an IPKF patrol was ambushed, a number of young children would rush in to quickly take away the arms and ammunition of any wounded who could be safely reached.

6. Wounded IPKF soldiers taken captive by the LTTE were often burnt alive with a rubber tyre put around their waists which was filled with petrol and set alight. Since the LTTE themselves were also trying to monitor the IPKF's radio networks, there would often be times when a message would be received on an open administrative network that an IPKF prisoner was burning at such-and-such a place.

In May 1988, Maj. Gen. S. C. Sardeshpande, in command of the critical Jaffna sector under his 54 Infantry Division, maintained extensive contact with Jaffna's Tamil population. He said in his only interview, given to the AFP correspondent M.R. Narayan Swamy and the UNI correspondent P. Jayaram at Palaly, that 99 per cent of the population was with the Tigers, stating that: "The majority of the people still support the LTTE. Our effort is to loosen that. Total eradication of this is not possible. They have no faith in India, in the Accord, in the IPKF. They find something fishy in the whole thing. They think we are playing the Sri Lankan game." Since this assessment was not shared by the Government of India, the remarks attributed to the general were denied, a rare occurrence, and IPKF commanders were told not to interact with the press. The IPKF achieved considerable success in the Batticaloa sector, where Indian soldiers kept up the pressure, finding and destroying LTTE hideouts and bases in villages and forests, the officers maintaining strict discipline among the troops so that civilian complaints eventually dried up.

In this period, units with superior levels of individual training in field craft and fire control, and in small sub-unit training, such as in anti-ambush drills, laying ambushes, and in section and platoon tactics were able to dominate the LTTE, with some units proving outstanding, such as 4/1 Gorkha Rifles, 5th Madras, 4th Assam, and 10th Para Commandos. Even though, by and large, Indian infantry tactical skills were just about adequate, their hardiness and their ability to grimly do the necessary tasks were wearing down the LTTE. Sri Lankan military commanders were amazed at the hardships the Indian infantry could withstand.

It was during this phase of "Operation PAWAN" that a Battle School was opened at Chennai, and infantry battalions being inducted were given pre-induction counter-insurgency training, which paid dividends. At the height of these counter-insurgency operations, the peak period of the Indian Army's involvement in Sri Lanka, nearly one-fifth of India's infantry battalions were deployed in Sri Lanka, or being rotated in or out.

Some battalions of practically all the infantry regiments of the army were deployed in Sri Lanka during this phase of "Op PAWAN," engaged in the various necessary tasks in an insurgency-affected area. The experience of 1/11 Gorkha Rifles can be considered typical of the period. The battalion was inducted by sea in January 1989 and deployed in the general area of Batticaloa District as part of the COIN grid, with its Battalion HQ at Vakarai. It spent 10 months in this area, being engaged in numerous smaller operations and duties such as long range patrols, laying ambushes, road opening duties, and security of dockyards. On 16 August 1989, a long-range patrol of its 'B' Company fell into an LTTE ambush, but the instantaneous reaction, the aggressive counter-ambush drill adopted by the patrol, resulted in the patrol killing six LTTE members while suffering only three fatal casualties of their own. The battalion was moved to Trincomalee on 11 October 1989, where it continued with COIN operations against the LTTE. Its tasks there included coastal security patrols in motor boats, searching the Trincomalee-Colombo train, and providing security to the Indian Army helipad at Trincomalee.

Maj. Gen. Ashok K. Mehta, who took over as GOC 57 Mountain Division recalls (in August 2007):

"I arrived in Batticaloa in June 1988 and was received at the Sri Lankan Army (SLA) guarded military airport by my predecessor, Maj. Gen. T. P. Singh. On the drive to the divisional headquarters nearby in the Christian Seminary hugging the lagoon, I sensed an air of tension and disquiet. The size of my escort and the security enroute indicated that the Tigers' threat was still serious. As I was coming from the Defence Planning Staff in Delhi, I was conversant with the big picture in Sri Lanka, therefore only the area-specific nuances of the situation had to be understood. At the time, GOI was trying to persuade the LTTE to join the political process and offering them the moon to fight the provincial elections. But Prabhakaran had other ideas, foremost, being Eelam. He knew Indian troops would go back sooner than later.

57 Infantry Division's area of responsibility stretched from the Verugal river halfway between Trincomalee and Batticaloa to Pottuvil in the South and included the districts of Batticaloa and Amparai. Batticaloa is known as the Land of the Singing Fish - a keen ear can supposedly hear fish making music below the Batticaloa Bridge spanning the lagoon. Batticaloa has a mixed population of Tamils and Muslims with the latter comprising nearly 40 per cent of the population concentrated in distinct pockets.

Kathankuddy is the largest Muslim habitation in Sri Lanka and has the largest concentration of mosques and *madarsas*. The biggest massacre of Muslims—more than 300—took place in August 1990 after IPKF's departure by the LTTE. Amparai consists of Muslims, Sinhalese and Tamils, approximately one third each. The bulk of the people live along the coastal North-South Highway.

57 Mountain Division had three Infantry Brigades located South to North along the coast at Kalmunai, Batticaloa and Vantramullai (24 Brigade was in Kalmunai and 76 Brigade in Batticaloa). T 72 tanks, 75/24 field gun-howitzers *(guns)*, engineers and logistic elements were in support and emphatically employed in the infantry role in spite of heavy opposition. A helicopter was located 24x7 in the divisional headquarters.

57 Infantry Division's tasks were:

- Assist State Administration in law and order
- Marginalise and keep LTTE on run
- Create conditions for Presidential and Provincial elections

- Assist Sri Lankan Government in organizing and conducting elections in November-January. (These were the first ever Provincial elections held in the east and recorded the highest voter turnout averaging 70 to 80 per cent)
- Assist in restoring democratic institutions
- Engage in small scale development projects from within divisional resources
- Wage a hearts and minds campaign

57 Infantry Division achieved these tasks efficiently. In his book, Assignment Jaffna, this is what Lt. Gen. S.C. Sardeshpande says: "A proper CI battle plan based on relevant themes and well-meditated CI philosophy had been attempted and was evident in the Jaffna and Batticaloa sectors. In Batticaloa, every LTTE stronghold was disturbed and scattered by establishing substantive IPKF posts and vigorous search operations which seldom permitted LTTE to breathe freely and stabilize. Most of the LTTE's executive—level leaders in Jaffna and Batticaloa sectors were killed while our communications with the people, their pacification and efforts to rejuvenate administration were maximum. These Divisions (54 and 57) on their own, followed the tenets of CI operations." Karuna who has become famous for assisting the SLA in liberating the East from the LTTE is from Kiran in the Batticaloa sector and despite our best efforts, could not be caught in the net.

The biggest detriment to the IPKF's success was the Indian government's dual approach-fighting the LTTE while keeping the doors open for negotiated settlement. The secret RAW-LTTE talks in Chennai did a lot of damage to the IPKF operations, as the opportunity was well used by the LTTE for their own political and military purposes.

*The Political background: Hardening Sinhala attitude and Elections to the New North-Eastern Provincial Council (NEPC)*

President Jayawardene had withdrawn the general amnesty to the LTTE, Prabhakaran included, at the outbreak of hostilities. He also indicated that until the LTTE fulfilled its obligations under the ISLA, he was not going to proceed with the devolution of powers to the Tamil provinces. The senior Sinhala politician Premadasa publicly questioned the wisdom of having a foreign military force fighting separatists in Sri Lanka, and demanded that the SLAF should be given the task. On the first anniversary of the ISLA on 29 July 1988, the Marxist JVP launched a massive and vicious campaign against the Accord, branding it "a betrayal of the motherland," and gunning down political opponents who refused to support its protests. (The LTTE too called for a *hartal* against what it called "the enslavement of the Tamils of Sri Lanka by the IPKF)."

A 5-day ceasefire was declared by the IPKF from 15 September to 20 September, 1988, to give the LTTE an opportunity to join the democratic process. The ceasefire was declared due to immense pressure from the Tamil population in Jaffna who were confident that the LTTE would respond. In response to the public pressure, the ceasefire was also extended by another five days but the LTTE refuse to participate. Polling was conducted on 19 November, 1988. The overall polling percentage was 62.71 per cent and the EPRLF-ENDLF combine obtained a clear-cut majority.

After the successful conclusion of the Provincial Council elections, Varadaraja Perumal was appointed as Chief Minister of the North Eastern Province and was sworn in by President Premadasa in Colombo. Subsequently, four other Ministers were also sworn in by the Governor General, Lt. Gen. Nalin Seneviratna and the Government formally assumed office by end of November, 1989. There was reluctance on the part of the Sri Lankan Government, to devolve necessary powers to the Provincial Government, which led to its losing credibility with the local population.

### *Sri Lankan Presidential Elections*

Jayawardene did not contest the Presidential election in 1989. An anti-India posture was adopted by Premadasa and some of his Ministers to play up to the feelings of Sinhalese chauvinism for political gains.

Thanks to the presence of the IPKF, elections were held in both the Northern and Eastern Districts on 19 December, 1988 along with polling in the rest of Sri Lanka. Premadasa defeated Mrs. Bandarnaike by a narrow margin and was elected President. The voter turnout sector-wise was as under:

1. Jaffna - 22%
2. Vavuniya - 19%
3. Trincomalee - 53%
4. Batticaloa - 60%

Premadasa became the President in January 1989.

*Decisions on the De-induction of the IPKF*

The IPKF's operations were carried out to create normalcy. With the Alampil operation of September 1988, the LTTE's remaining strength had more or less disintegrated. With the IPKF in place, the situation was almost normal. People wanted schools and colleges to open. Shops and banks were functioning and mail delivered. The IPKF provided security to banking transactions; public places had been rebuilt by the IPKF engineers. In Jaffna, the IPKF provided the civic administration through the office of the Town Commandant. People came to the IPKF for assistance. The IPKF achieved a situation in which militants were no more capable of operating as an effective force in both the North and the East. The IPKF had almost achieved the tasks it had been given in November 1987, and the middle-order of the LTTE had been decimated. In 1989 President Premadasa's stand against the IPKF's continuance in Sri Lanka, and his government's deal with the LTTE, made the ISLA more or less defunct. The Sri Lanka Government itself began to supply arms to the LTTE, and began to militarily support it in actions against other Tamil groups. They were united in wanting the IPKF out of Sri Lanka, and the NEPC dissolved. The Sri Lanka Government began to delay the actual granting of powers to the NEPC, thus making the North-Eastern Province Government ineffective. President Premadasa even threatened to declare war against the IPKF and to use the SLAF against it if the IPKF did not withdraw by 29 July 1989. In a televised speech, he said, "After the end of July they have no business whatsoever on even an inch of land in my country." Lt. Gen. Kalkat, the OFC, IPKF, had to resort to the threat of ordering firing on Sri Lankan soldiers if they stepped out of their barracks. He unofficially let it be known to the Sri Lanka Government that any hostile act against the IPKF by the SLAF could lead to offensive operations against the Sinhala heartland and Colombo. This had the desired effect.

State Assembly elections in 1989 brought the DMK to power in Tamil Nadu, with its leader, M. Karunanidhi becoming Chief Minister. Karunanidhi had been critical of the IPKF role in Sri Lanka, and was not in favour of its operations against the LTTE. He has stated that he was not opposed to the induction of the IPKF as long as it was a peace-keeping force, but believed it should not have been used for anything else. At the national level, the Opposition was opposed to the IPKF solely because it had been sent by a Congress government. As the Indian Parliamentary elections drew closer, the External Affairs Minister, a member of the ruling Congress party, Natwar Singh, hastened to make clear that the LTTE had not been labeled as an "enemy," so as to retain as much support as it could get in Tamil Nadu. The IPKF was losing its political support both in Sri Lanka, and at home in India, which was very unfair to the troops sent abroad by the nation to carry out a difficult task under numerous non-military restrictions. It was clear that India was still an immature country where the use of military power in furtherance of national political aims was concerned. The IPKF no longer having any formal political validity, since the provisions of the ISLA had been broken by the Sri Lanka Government itself, which wanted the IPKF withdrawn at the earliest practical date, the Rajiv Gandhi government ordered a phased withdrawal, to be completed in March 1990. The IPKF 's main political task, that of creating a Tamil-majority North-Eastern Province in Sri Lanka, with sufficient autonomy to feel secure, remained unfulfilled.

After the Parliamentary elections of 1989, the Opposition Coalition came to power, and V. P. Singh became Prime Minister with a "Leave Sri Lanka to its own affairs" policy. The gradual phased de-induction of the IPKF, as planned under the Rajiv Gandhi government, continued.

Lt. Gen. Sardeshpande recalls this entire period: "Our intense interaction with the civil population of Jaffna and certain pockets in Trinco and Batti sectors indicated a genuine desire on their part to meet the LTTE leadership and persuade it call off violence. Accordingly at the insistence of GOC Jaffna Division, the Army HQ and the Indian Government agreed for a temporary ceasefire in August 1988 to enable movement of civilian representatives and LTTE leaders. But the LTTE, expectedly spurned the people's initiative and harangued them to keep up the Eelam struggle. Our efforts to persuade the LTTE failed; but at least we had convinced the people of our genuine intentions in deference to their request. We proved to the people that we were amenable, but the LTTE was adamant. We tightened the rope again. The killing game continued.

Then, once again, at the insistence of the IPKF, the Government of India was agreeable to hold provincial elections to the Tamil Provincial council. The SLG also rose to the occasion. These elections were held under the political, legal and constitutional provisions of Sri Lanka and supervised and certified by an international observer group. The IPKF officers studied their constitution, distributed and propagated the provisions of the ISLA, argued, discussed and attempted to impress the people about the importance and benefits of participating in elections, and following a line clear of the violent and fascist methods practiced by the LTTE. It was a frantic, hectic effort to be interacting with the unwilling, fearful, suspicious, hypnotized people, totally under the LTTE's thumb. Alas, what a sad curse this—we had to do same in Kashmir in less than eight years!

Then followed the Presidential and parliamentary elections, with permissible levels of peacefulness and participation. But the content of devolution of power granted by the SLG did not satisfy the Tamils. The EPRLF-dominated Provincial Council (PC) was not accepted by the Jaffnaites and the Vavunians at all. The people had little faith in the SLG. They fell back to the LTTE as their sole saviours. The Village Volunteer Force (VVF) was reluctantly raised by the SLG at the IPKF's prodding; the Tamil response to join it was eminently poor. But the RAW painted rosy pictures of the whole venture as it perhaps suited the PM. Finally with the change of government in late 1989 it was decided to dump the PC and the VVF and withdraw.

It was around this time that the Sri Lankan President Premadasa, got together with the LTTE, bypassed India and the IPKF, and asked it to quit, ordering his forces, the SLSF, to come out of barracks and take over. Now the LTTE was in direct confrontation with the SLSF, while continuing to operate against the LTTE. All kinds of offensive plans were made, including landing in Colombo to rescue the High Commission staff there. Air forces and additional army formations moved closer to Bangalore. The Navy got ready with its carrier component. However, the SLSF sagacity in not obeying their President's orders averted a showdown."

Maj. Gen. Ashok Mehta remembers this period: "The IPKF was forced to withdraw before completing its mission due to the breakdown of political will and failure of coercive diplomacy. This does not absolve the military from the self-inflicted foul-ups that confounded the operational performance. There was a terrible disconnect between the political realities of the time and the thinking of the IPKF. As Prabhakaran had forecast the IPKF was forced to leave Sri Lanka in March 1990."

Chapter 6

# 'Operation PAWAN' – Phase IV: De-Induction of the IPKF October 1989-March 1990

The initial decision to de-induct the IPKF was taken on the successful culmination of the election process, and two brigades were accordingly de-inducted between April and June, 1989. However, the belligerent stance adopted by President Premadasa consequent to the resumption of the SLG-LTTE dialogue, left no option other than ordering a freeze of de-induction to protect the IPKF's interests. Subsequently, after signing of the Indo-Sri Lanka Joint Communique on 18th September, 1989, the de-induction commenced. The outline plan for de-induction of the IPKF area-wise was in three broad phases as under:

(a) Amparai and Batticaloa Sectors by 30 November 1989;
(b) Mannar and Mullaitivu Sectors by 31 December 1989;
(c) Killinochchi and Vavuniya Sectors by 31 January 1990;
(d) Jaffna and Trincomalee Sectors by 31 March 1990.

The withdrawal of the IPKF had to be carefully carried out, particularly since some force had to be kept deployed to cover the non-tactical de-inductions of other units and formations, the most tricky being the last. There was no guarantee that the de-inducting troops would not be attacked. The Chief Minister of Tamil Nadu, M. Karunanidhi, sent a message to the LTTE supremo Pirabakaran, through the Indian High Commissioner in Colombo and thereafter through the Sri Lankan President, Premadasa, that the de-inducting IPKF should not be interfered with, and apparently received the assurance that it would not. The IPKF clearly remained more a political issue than a military

## OPERATION PAWAN DE-INDUCTION PLAN
## <u>OCTOBER 1989 - MARCH 1990</u>

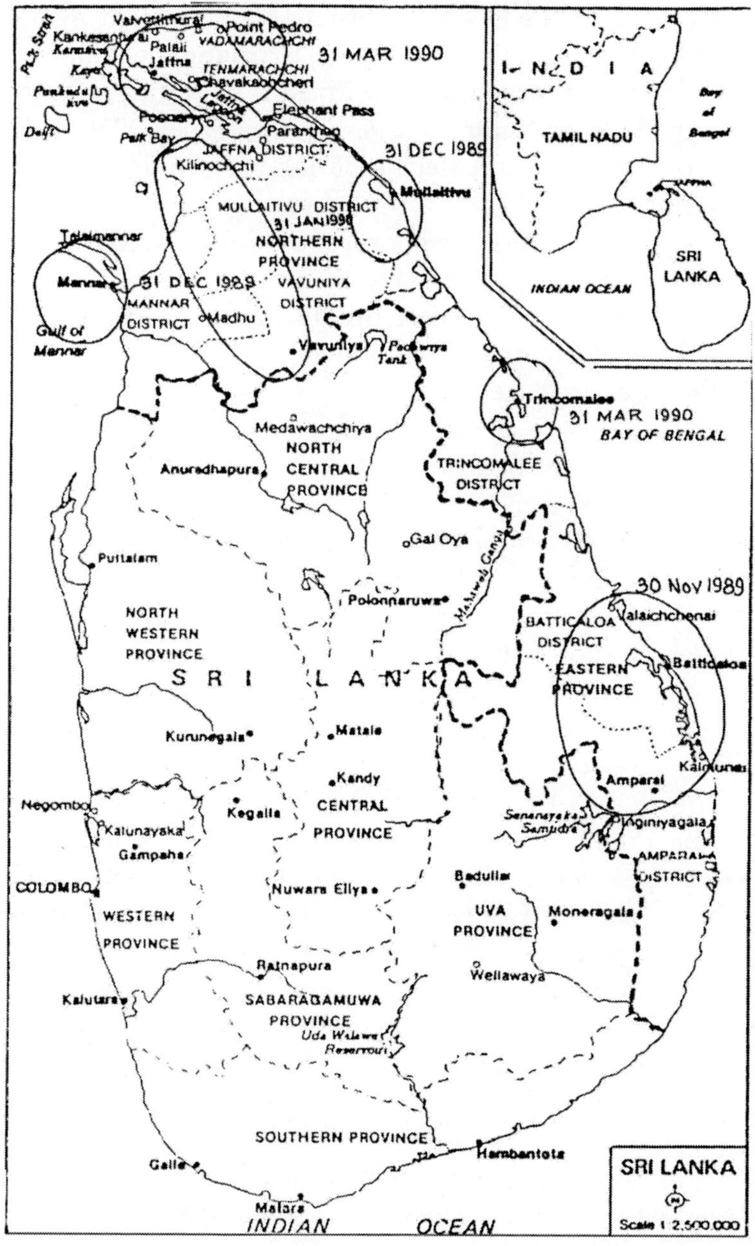

one. Nevertheless the IPKF itself took all tactical precautions till the last man was embarked.

Maj. Gen. Mehta continues: "The vacation of territory and deinduction of IPKF was a formidable operation against the unlikely eventuality of SLA and LTTE driving the final nail in the IPKF coffin. Amparai Brigade withdrew to Batticaloa and so did the Brigade from Vantramullai. 57 Infantry Division moved by road to Trincomalee replacing 36 Infantry Division which had sailed out."

1/11 Gorkha Rifles, commanded by Col. P. K. Rampal, was in Sri Lanka from October 1989 to the time of the pullout from the island. The battalion's experience during this period was typical of the kind of infantry task involved. Col. Rampal* tells of his battalion's experience:

"After a year's active Counter Insurgency Operations in Batticaloa District (Vakarai Area), it was in October 1989 that orders for 1/11 Gorkha Rifles were received to move to Trincomalee, as part of the 59 Mountain Brigade of 57 Mountain Division, which as an entire division was moving to take over responsibilities for the Trincomalee sector. 59 Mountain Brigade was made responsible for safeguarding the coastal road to Nilaveli area, the roads leading to Anuradhapura and to Colombo, the Trincomalee Airfield and the Lagoon.

The obvious and most difficult task, being to guard Trincomalee Airfield, the Air Force Academy, the Lagoon Area and the Prema Jetty, was allotted to 1/11 Gorkha Rifles. The onerous task was performed with classical élan and enthusiasm by the '*Kirantis*'**. However, towards Dec 1989, the de-induction of other formations started. It was at this stage that the affiliation of 1/11 Gorkha Rifles changed from 59 Mountain Brigade to 72 Infantry Brigade. The unit was responsible for the safe passage and de-induction of all units.

*Presently Lt. Gen. P. K. Rampal, AVSM, and Colonel of the Regiment, the 11th Gorkha Rifles

**As the soldiers of the 11th Gorkha Rifles are known, who are mainly from the broad *Kiranti* community of eastern Nepal, which primarily comprises the Rai and Limbu communities of hill-farmers.

By end February 1990 when most other formations deployed in the hinterland had been de-inducted, with the progress of the pull out, the anxiety level of our unit also started rising. There were reports about a likely nexus between the LTTE and some elements of the STF trying to act against the last contingent of IPKF. As the day approached for final de-induction, actions even in areas as far away as Nilaveli and Muttur appeared virtually next door. A planned action of the LTTE on the Air Force Academy was thwarted by good intelligence and effective denial of the routes leading to it.

Gradually all the troops pulled out from Sri Lanka and on 24th March 1990, the final phase consisting of an armoured squadron, with its 'A' vehicles, of 65 Armoured Regiment, a team of 10 PARA CDO, and the *Kirantis,* boarded the I. N. S. Magar and M. V. Akbar. A convoy of five other ships also sailed away from the shore. The anxiety levels remained high till the ships moved well away from the Sri Lankan coastline."

Maj. Gen. Mehta remembers the event at Trincomalee: "On 24 March 1990 at 1100 hrs the IPKF was given a ceremonial send off by the Sri Lankan security forces from Trincomalee harbour. INS Magar was the last ship to set sail from Koddiyar Bay. Defence Minister Ranjan Wijeratne walked to the nearest telephone in the harbour and informed his Supreme Commander, President R. Premadasa: "I have good news. The last foreign soldier has left Sri Lankan soil." That is the short tale of 57 Infantry Division and IPKF."

Lt. Gen. Sardeshpande concludes: "Finally, in March, the last elements of the IPKF sailed out simultaneously from K.K.S. and Trinco. GOC IPKF, Lt. Gen. Kalkat's last message from aboard the flagship was historic, prophetic and dramatic. To the Army Chief he signaled for the last time, "The IPKF has done its duty" and closed down. It had a Nelsonian touch. And that is all the IPKF did — "their duty."

The IPKF had been in Sri Lanka for 967 days at a cost to the nation of 1155 soldiers dead, over 4,500 wounded, and an expenditure of Rs. 300 crores.

The flotilla reached Chennai in the afternoon of 25 March 1990. The Tamil Nadu Chief Minister, exhibiting very poor taste, pointedly did not come for the reception ceremony arranged for this last IPKF contingent to return to India. As Maj. Gen. Ashok Mehta has commented, "By the time we reached Madras the next day, IPKF had become ITKF – Indian Tamil Killing Force."

Lt. Gen. Kalkat was interviewed in March 2000, 10 years after the de-induction by Josy Joseph of the internet newsmagazine *Rediff.com,* and gave a very comprehensive overview of the last phase of the IPKF's campaign in Sri Lanka. The relevant part needs to be read by all military officers to understand the complexities of the time from the viewpoint of the top commander.

*The Most Difficult Part was Managing the Withdrawal*

Q. *So that was the game plan of the LTTE and Premadasa?*

A. This was part of the same game plan. The two of them decided that if the IPKF remained there, then neither could cheat the other on the Accord. And each one thought that he was cleverer than the other. So both were playing a game to double-cross each other. Who could prevent them from doing it was the IPKF. Our stand was [that] it was not over and if they do it, they will end up killing each other. That is the reason why the IPKF remained there. Because we were sure that it would not work. And it was apparent that both sides would not do what they were saying. Their priority was, Let us get the IPKF out.

For the LTTE their concern was that as long as the IPKF was there they could never get away with their demand for an independent Tamil Eelam. For the Sri Lankan government, or the Sinhala government of Premadasa, it was quite clear that we could insist that the Sri Lankan government honour its part of the agreement.

Q. *You had a lot left to be done.*

A. There were so many things to be done. The land reforms. There were illegally occupied lands, they had many areas where the demographic pattern had been changed. In the northern province certain area was made a separate territory for the so-called experiments in irrigation, but basically the Sinhala convicts were resettled there. It was a convict's colony. They were trying some arid agricultural experiments etc. Those land belonged to the Tamils, it was part of the Tamil homeland. There were many issues like that.

Q. *But Premadasa pushed you out.*

A. Both felt that it was not in their interest to honour the Accord. Particularly after Jayewardane stepped down and Premadasa took over. He had always opposed the agreement. In that he was backed by a large chauvinistic group of Sinhalese. So both of them felt that let us get the IPKF out, then we will sort out the other guy. So the IPKF came out on March 24, 1990.

Q. *When did you get orders to leave Lanka?*

A. I was told that our government gave a commitment that by the 31st of March the IPKF would withdraw. So I was given the charter. By that time it was apparent that the LTTE and the Sri Lankan government had joined hands. When I say the Sri Lankan government—I would like to clarify that not all governments have been like that—I mean Premadasa's government and not of his predecessor or his successors.

Q. *You came across proof of the LTTE-Sri Lankan government collaboration?*

A. The collaboration between the LTTE and the government had started around October 1989. It came to our notice, and we brought it to the notice of the Sri Lankan government and our government also. I myself took it up at the highest level, with the President.

Q. *But the Lankan government never accepted that?*

A. Of course, it was denied. There was nothing that they could do. I am literally accusing them of collaborating with or sleeping with the enemy. The whole scenario changed soon after President Jayewardane decided that he will not stand for elections. The presidential election was held around, I think, December 1988, and as soon as President Jayewardane decided that and nominated Premadasa to be his successor, the bureaucracy and government started naturally behaving in the interest of Premadasa. So he started working on it earlier, and as soon as the announcement came the tilt was slowly and slowly taking place.

Q. *You interacted with the Sri Lankan army closely. How did they react to Premadasa's decision to tie up with the LTTE? Did the army also change its tune to suit the new president?*

A. Obviously, the last organization to be affected by the tilt was the Sri Lankan army. They were professionals, they were dedicated. But over a period of time that also gets affected when the government gives you certain orders. Slowly and slowly they started replacing those officers who would not play ball with Premadasa. Because it was hurting them also, because the Sri Lankan army had been fighting the LTTE. They had lost a lot of people. And then suddenly to ask them to collaborate with them and assist them wouldn't go well. In fact, to the extent that Premadasa faced a revolt within the army at that time.

Q. *You could feel that revolt?*

A. I could feel that revolt simmering. And there was talk in Colombo that they might press a coup. The [*Sri Lankan*] army chief that time was Hamilton Vanasinghe. But it was not one person, it was simmering across the board with generals because they were not happy. Because on the one hand they were asked to go easy on the LTTE, and on the other hand they had been asked to give them weapons.

A lot of officers would say We are giving them weapons today, and they will be used against us one day. So he was in a precarious situation. I think for him getting past it, he owes it to his late foreign minister who was assassinated, Ranjan Wijayarante. He was also the minister for defence, because he was liked by the army and he supported their action. What he did was since he could not go in any way against his president on the IPKF issue, he got clearance from the president for the Sri Lankan army to go against the JVP.

They were facing two problems. The JVP, the leftist Marxist movement in the South, and the LTTE in the North. Therefore, he got the clearance that the army would have a free hand against the JVP. And as you know, within three months they had virtually destroyed the JVP. They just destroyed it. Of course there were no human right activists there that time, otherwise it is a matter that would have come up. Those times, the visual media wasn't like it is today, so a lot of it did not come out. Today, there is a lot of transparency in military operations; at that time it was by and large close. With that the army, and every one got a respite.

Q. *You haven't answered my question: Was it the right time for the IPKF to withdraw?*

A. It was preordained. There was no option. It had been announced by the new government in India in 1989. Once it was elected, the IPKF had to withdraw. We were told the time.

Q. *Once the withdrawal was announced, what were your concerns?*

A. The main thing I was concerned about was that the Sri Lankan government was hostile to us to the extent possible. Not that they were fighting us, but they were abetting the fighting. I did not want my soldiers to be caught like what happened in Vietnam or in Afghanistan. I wanted to make sure that every soldier came home safely. I did not want to lose lives during the withdrawal.

Secondly, I wanted the withdrawal to be with dignity, not as in Vietnam where people were running away, hanging on to helicopters. Those thing would be terrible for the morale of an army. I was quite determined that as we went in with our flag flying high, we would come out with our heads high. So certain plans had to be put into action.

The most difficult part of my entire command was managing the withdrawal of the IPKF. At one stage we had 70,000 troops, we slowly brought them down to 50, 40, and then to 30,000. When you are in a narrow bridge head, with the LTTE all around and you getting militarily no assistance from the Sri Lankan army and the LTTE free at that stage, the prime concern for me was the lives of my soldiers.

Every day we withdrew certain amount with ships at Trincomalee and Kankeshanthurai in the northern province of Jaffna. We had planned the de-induction. Each day a battalion would withdraw; over three days that would complete a brigade and that was how it was done.

The last day a ceremonial send-off was given by the Sri Lankan army guard of honour was given at Trincomalee. The foreign minister came there, then the three service chiefs of the Sri Lankan armed forces, senior officers of the armed forces and, of course, the media was there to see. While we were pulling back, we had our party standing by on all sides to make sure that someone did not double-cross or conspire against our soldiers. We had even helicopters on board standing by to extricate.

We did not want to leave behind a single item of equipment because it was costly and they were heavy equipment which had to be phased out. We had heavy vehicles, tanks, armoured cars, which was useful. Now, we needed them there, we wanted to keep them till the last, but then to keep them till the last and pulling them out on a ship takes hours. So you had to have a fine balance, take them as late as possible but not too late.

And ultimately, of course, the infantry solider was on his own. For these kind of problem one did make arrangements for some kind of naval guns to support, if we can call. This kind of management, tactical planning was done.

Q. *Did any trouble happen during the withdrawal?*

A. No. If anything, we were over careful, and things went off as we planned.

Q. *While withdrawing did you not think that you could have brought complete peace, disarmed the LTTE?*

A. There are a couple of things. Disarming the group cannot be an ongoing task. You can disarm a group, there are no arms today. But you cannot guarantee that they will not acquire them in future. So it cannot be a job in perpetuity. It should be time-framed. The military part is disarming, the LTTE was disarmed to that extent, their holding became negligible once we were able to hold elections. But then they continued to get arms. That is why they went to the Sri Lankan government and got arms.

Now, that task cannot be given to the military, to prevent the government from arming them. Because the implications of that are far more serious. To prevent that I have to go at the personnel arming them, I cannot go at the Sri Lankan government.

The second part is, what about peace? Can you bring in peace? Let me say this: Application of military force will never bring peace, anywhere in the world. I know I am making a categorical statement, but I stand by that statement. Application of military force can never bring about peace. Peace in the minds of the civil population is the perception in the minds of the common man on his environment, on the kind of governance he has, on his basic needs being met, on his rights being protected.

These are all political matters, not one of them is a military matter. So it is a fallacy if anyone thinks anywhere that by sending in the military you bring in peace.

The military can only create a condition for the political actions to take place. It can neither take political action, nor take on the role of the political system.

Q. *So did you complete your task? The popular perception is that you did not.*

A. If the IPKF was deemed a political weapon, obviously *[it did not]*. If it was deemed a military weapon, the task was completed the day election was held and the government could be installed. Thereafter there were no dispensations that the IPKF could give out. We could not give them independence, we could not give them devolution of powers, we could not give financial control to the chief minister, we could not give the provincial government what it took them to be a strong credible government.

I agree that we could not prevent the Sri Lankan government from arming the LTTE. But I could have done it, I had the strength to do it. That would have meant to forcibly preventing the Sri Lankan government from arming the LTTE.

Q. *You could have done that?*

A. You know what that means. That means, taking over the country.

Q. *Did you think of taking over Sri Lanka any time?*

A. No, no. Because we cannot be involved in it. It was not me, in fact nobody in India could have done that to force the Sri Lankan government not to *[arm the LTTE]*. Because what do you do with the Sri Lankan government still doing it? What do you do? You go to war.

## Chapter 7

# Results, Analysis and Lessons

Dr. Norman F. Dixon was an officer in the Royal Engineers, the British Army's combat engineers, before taking premature retirement in 1950 and becoming a psychologist, going on to earn laurels in the world of science and academics. His seminal work, "On the Psychology of Military Incompetence," first published in 1976, written when he was a Reader in Psychology at University College London, became a world-wide "must-read" for its insights into the normal learning disabilities of all militaries. His explanation of "strategic incompetence" should therefore have been well-known to General Sundarji, the Indian COAS, an extremely well-read officer. Yet the Sri Lanka misadventure provides a perfect text-book example of strategic incompetence.

Strategic incompetence refers to incompetence at levels beyond the military, occurring when the decisions made in deploying or withdrawing the use of military force. Often this incompetence takes place at the political and national level. As explained by Dr. Dixon, the five situations listed below constitute separate examples of strategic incompetence. In Sri Lanka, from 1987 to 1990, India managed to display or commit four out of the possible five simultaneously.

1. Sending a military force to a situation without a clear mission or objective.

2. Sending a military force into a situation without the legal ability to defend itself or the mandate to fulfill its role effectively.

3. Leaving a military force in a situation where it becomes progressively more committed, to the point where it is unable to withdraw safely, or when resources and lives have to be continually poured into a situation with no clear end.

4. The lack of political will to sustain losses, or an unrealistic political definition of "acceptable losses."

5. Withdrawing a military force before the successful completion of objectives.

### *Analysis*

M. R. Narayan Swamy* believes that:

"What burned India's hand in Sri Lanka war the lack of a clear politico-military goal. No one was clear (and at times various arms of the Indian government appeared to be working at cross-purposes) about the role the IPKF was assigned. Was the LTTE to be crushed without reprieve? If so, how long was the Indian army going to carry on fighting? What would happen when the LTTE was a spent force? Why was the IPKF waging a war at all? Some questions antedated the IPKF's arrival. Why did New Delhi arm and train the militants? To carve out a separate state in Sri Lanka? Or to teach Colombo a lesson for whatever it was worth? If India did not want a LTTE Eelam, was it ready to accept an EPRLF Eelam?"

He continues: "This lack of clear-headed political approach resulted in unseemly frictions within the Indian establishment. The differences were evident to, more than anyone else, the Sri Lankans themselves. Pakyanathan Rajarattinam of the ENDLF, who witnessed the shadow boxing from close quarters, complained: "Indian officials would say that the Tamils should be united. But there was no unity in the Indian government. All agencies—RAW, foreign ministry, Tamil Nadu police and later the IPKF—spoke ill of one another."

Both Indian diplomats in Colombo and the IPKF held the RAW in contempt. There was no love lost between the IPKF and Jyotindra Nath Dixit, the Indian High Commissioner in Colombo. Indian diplomats believed that the IPKF was fighting a half-hearted battle. The anti-LTTE Tamil groups (EPRLF and

*In "Tigers of Lanka: From Boys to Guerillas," Konark Publishers, Delhi, 1994, 3rd Ed. 2002.

ENDLF in particular) frequently complained that the IPKF was too soft on the LTTE and that sections of Tamil soldiers of the IPKF were sympathetic to the Tigers. The LTTE, on the other hand, threatened families of IPKF personnel who hailed from Tamil Nadu. It was a frustrating experience for the IPKF, whose morale and discipline were affected. Indian soldiers also repaired temples and buildings, dug wells, laid roads, protected railway tracks, restored power and telephone lines, and treated the sick and wounded civilians. But in the bargain they paid for it with their lives and were vilified." *(The LTTE enjoyed a safe run in Tamil Nadu protected by the Tamil Nadu police, while the IPKF battled them in Sri Lanka).*

India's High Commissioner in Colombo, Mr. J. N. Dixit, has said: "... the IPKF restored order and stability in the northern and eastern parts of the island. They were the main factor enabling elections in the Tamil areas of Sri Lanka and the creation and establishment of a Tamil provincial government. They were an equally important factor assisting the Sri Lanka government to hold the presidential and parliamentary elections in 1988 and 1989. By the end of 1988 and the beginning of 1989 they were in the final phase of containing and neutralizing the LTTE. It is my *(the High Commissioner's)* assessment that had the IPKF been allowed to stay on in Sri Lanka for another six months or so, the LTTE would have been under sufficient pressure to give up violence and join the mainstream in politics."

Jaswant Singh, presently a Member of Parliament, who has been India's Finance Minister in one government, but is probably better-known for his being India's External Affairs Minister in another and even for a short while India's Defence Minister in addition, and who is a former Army officer himself, writing about India's IPKF experience has said: "Some fundamentals of peace-keeping operations need to be outlined. Obviously there must be a clear definition of the role: keeping peace or warring parties apart, or enforcing it by employing military force? About this there must not be any ambiguity, as so self-evidently there was in the case of the IPKF. Where after, such a "force" must be despatched only if there exists a broad enough acceptance of it from the local population, even the warring elements of it. It must then be for a specific period announced in advance so that a withdrawal route and date is always available as an option in case of change of circumstances. Such a force must retain its military character and not attempt too many additional responsibilities, for example, policing, or civil administration or even relief, as the IPKF was so confusingly required to shoulder. A force such as the IPKF must conjunctly with local forces, as a force that assists, in contrast to one that occupies or pioneers."

*Political and Diplomatic*

The political decision-making and the diplomatic handling of the implementation of the Indo-Sri Lanka Agreement were seriously flawed. There should not have been a "Triple-Track" policy: the IPKF, the diplomatic channel consisting of the Ministry of External Affairs and the High Commission, and the "intelligence agencies," principally R&AW, each evidently pursuing its own agenda. Instead, there should have been a "Single Track" national policy, with the IPKF, the diplomats, and the intelligence agencies, all functioning as strands of the same policy, with actions complementary to each other. A good rapport between the Prime Minister and the Army Chief was essential, which did not exist, providing yet another example of the traditional Indian disunity, in its most modern form.

*Organization of the IPKF*

The military organization of the IPKF, its command and control structure, its induction, and its operation on the island, all needed to be structured differently. There should have been a "Joint Overall Force Commander" appointed, who could have been a senior officer of any one of the three services, with a formal headquarters established. Since this required the magic "government approval" (as if the three armed services are private bodies), the planning group headed by the Prime Minister should have ordered the Ministry of Defence to set it up or create it at the outset. The basic reasons for such "Joint Commands" not getting set up, even when obviously needed, are again the well-known Indian lack of cooperation with each other, inevitably leading to failure or lack of success. If, for reasons of finance or doubts about its future employment, this could not immediately be created, then one of the army's existing Corps HQ should have been shifted to provide the command and control structure, and requisite staff elements of the Air Force and the Navy formally attached to it, AND placed directly under the "Joint Overall Force Commander," who needed to be given air and naval elements placed directly under command. It was even possible to have a separate OFC for the induction phase, from the Navy perhaps, since this was the country's first major overseas operation, to be relieved by one from the Army after the inducted force had settled down. In all circumstances, such an OFC should have had Deputy OFC's from the other two services.

*Command and Control*

For the conduct of the ground operations, to have a Deputy OFC and GOC IPKF (in the person of Lieut. General A.S. Kalkat), receiving major operational instructions directly from the Indian Army Chief at Army HQ in Delhi, made a nonsense of the position of the OFC, who happened to be the Southern Army Commander. This issue needed to have been resolved before its functional repercussions began to affect the infantry divisions operating in Sri Lanka. Additionally, the "Liaison Officers" deputed from Army HQ and located with each of the divisional HQ, reporting directly to the Army Chief in Delhi, created misunderstandings, and also led to the undermining of the authority and the flexibility of action of the intermediate commanders; viz., the GOC IPKF, and the OFC, while not diminishing their responsibility in any way.

*Logistics*

The logistical planning and preparation upon which the success of such a venture as the IPKF/'Op Pawan' depended should have been much smoother and more professional. As it was, it functioned, just about. The Army Maintenance Area (AMA) that was set up at Chennai, under the GOC Madras (formally GOC Andhra Pradesh, Tamil Nadu, Karnataka, Kerala and Goa Area) as Commander AMA, needed to have the requisite staff who could function with commitment, rather than having staff sent on rotation on temporary duty from other formations and units of Southern Command not committed to the Sri Lanka operations. The OFC and Southern Army Commander, Lieut.-General Depinder Singh, has given "security" as the reason for both the inability to pre-position the requisite stores at Madras, and for not asking the Government of India for sanction to raise a full-fledged headquarters as HQ IPKF. This explanation does not hold water, since Sri Lanka would almost certainly have been anticipating Indian military intervention once they began military operations against the Tamils in May 1987, and would have had this apprehension even when they decided to act militarily against the Tamils of Jaffna. The High Commission and the intelligence agencies should have been able to inform the decision-makers of the Sri Lankan apprehension, which in fact was the case, well beforehand. If so, then the charade need not have been maintained, and the military preparations made much smoother and more efficient, making the operations on the ground much more efficient, and prevented loss of life in cases where troops ran out of ammunition, and suchlike.

*Infantry Weapons and Equipment*

The infantry of the Indian Army is its basic arm, which seems to get forgotten, even by Army HQ and the Ministry of Defence, let alone the Prime Minister and the Cabinet Committee on Security. The fact that the infantry needs to have the most up-to-date weapons and equipment seems to be only grudgingly accepted, and that too only after a serious set-back. The old World War I pattern bolt-action .303 rifle, the SMLE No. 1 Mark III, along with its Second World War version, the SMLE Rifle

.303 No. 4 Mark I, the well-known *Three-nought-three,* was used to fight the Chinese Army in 1962, when the rest of the world was using semi-automatic and automatic infantry personal weapons. It was the soldiers who carried out India's foreign policy adventure ("the Forward Policy") and diplomatic blunders (Nehru's "I have ordered the Army to throw them out") of the time, who paid the price. In Sri Lanka more foreign policy immaturity and diplomatic blunders were paid for in blood or with their lives by soldiers using the 7.62 mm Self-Loading Rifle (or "SLR"), which was introduced as a result of the 1962 debacle. In the closer confines of urban and jungle warfare, the short and much-lighter, fully-automatic and quicker- and easier-handling AK-47's and American M-16's, with their light ammunition, of which many more rounds could be carried, proved much more effective than the Indian infantry soldier's SLR. Therefore the LTTE could produce a much greater volume of fire than the same number of Indian infantrymen. *(The AK-47 uses a short-case 7.62 mm cartridge, and the M-16 fires a small-calibre 5.56 mm bullet)* The LTTE'S radio communications reaching down practically to the lowest level, was more effective at ground level than the Indian infantry company's signal communications, which in any case existed only down to the platoon. The personal equipment an Indian infantryman wore on himself in 1987, to carry his ammunition, water, and other bare essential field necessities were of the British 1937 pattern, and the larger pack, larger than the haversack, continued to be of the British 1908 pattern, still officially known as the "Pack '08," (called the *Pack 'O'-Eight,* or *Pack Zero-Eight*). Just for the sake of comparison, Britain discarded the 1937 Pattern for the 1944 Pattern, which again was discarded for the 1958 Pattern, presumably for improved infantry functioning.

*Inadequate Professionalism in the Infantry*

The Indian infantry in Sri Lank has been criticized by two of its own generals for lack of professionalism in some vital areas. It has been criticized for poor fire discipline, lack of basic tactical fire and movement, unimaginative tactical operation at the sub-unit level (company and below), a tendency to operate only along the roads, a tendency to patrol in large groups, even up to company-sized, instead of spreading out in small groups of three to five men each, and of not being able to transform itself mentally from the attitudes of peace-time soldiering to the more practical requirements of operations. Regarding the tendency to send out large patrols, Lt.-Gen. Depinder Singh, the OFC and himself an infantry general commented, *If each (Brigade) Commander could have his own way, he would have preferred to send at least a rifle company, if not a complete battalion on each mission.* Infantry battalions and formations (brigades and divisions) have also been criticized for unimaginative operational planning and execution during the counter-insurgency phase of the operations. All this is true, but were all indicative of the general level of professionalism of the Indian infantry as a whole at the time, not merely in Sri Lanka. Also, the generals of the Indian Army, in their various capacities, had over a period, been responsible for allowing things to get to this low level. It is absolutely true that, had the infantry been able to deliver, whether in the initial few days of active operations in Jaffna, or quickly later during the counter-insurgency stage, India could have achieved its political objectives in Sri Lanka. If Pirabakaran were to have been eliminated, the problem in Sri Lanka would have been over, there would have been a functioning North-Eastern Province with sufficient autonomy to meet Tamil needs for security, self-governance, and respect. The faults were caused partly by the urge for "paper qualifications' that furthered the individual officers" careers, at the cost of the efficiency and effectiveness of the infantry units. There were two other factors also simultaneously at play, which got exaggerated due to the preoccupations of the officer cadre with matters other than those of low-level effectiveness, such as individual marksmanship, fire control and fire discipline, field formations during tactical movement on foot, field signals, field craft, section battle drills, platoon tactics, and ambush and counter-ambush drills. The first of these two diluting factors were the "cadre review" appointments, in which sections began to be commanded by Havildars (Sergeants in English, as in the Air Force) instead of by Naiks (Corporals), with additional higher appointments all the way up to Lieut. Generals, made in the interest of improving everyone's promotion prospects. The second was the increase in regular service for ordinary soldiers who did not get promoted to NCO (which starts at the junior-most level with promotion at about 8-11 years' service up to Lance-Naik (Lance-Corporal, who wears a single stripe, or chevron). If a soldier (an ordinary Sepoy) was not capable of being promoted to that first stage, he used to retire at 10 years' service in earlier times, with a 5 years' "reserve liability" during which he could be called up in a national emergency. In the interest of career continuity, and also the impracticality of calling reservists every year for "reserve training," as well as the impossibility of recalling them in the case of a "short warning period mobilization," this "colour service" was increased, and "reserve service" abolished. After a few years, the colour service was increased to a near-automatic 17 years, and then to 18 years. The effects on the effectiveness of the infantry company were not long in coming. The average age of the *jawans* of the rifle platoons and sections, which make up the fighting strength or "bayonet strength" of rifle companies, went up from an average age of 23 years to close to 30 years! The fighting *jawans* of India were no longer so *jawan* any more. The companies of fighting *jawans* of the 1971 war became companies of youngish family men with little children back home. There was a sea-change in the basic ethos of the men of the infantry rifle company, which could only be offset by careful conditioning and the bolstering of regimental spirit and unit pride, allied to hard and serious basic training, and all-round basic field competence at the sub-unit level. But this could only be done by the "Company-grade Officers" *(the Lieutenants and Captains)*, who were in short supply, and were mostly preparing for the Staff College entrance examination, under the careful guidance of the "Field-grade Officers" *(Majors to Brigadiers)*, who themselves were actually mostly striving hardest at trying to become "General Officers" *(Maj. Generals, Lieut. Generals, and only one General, the Chief of the Army Staff)*. There was no change in either the design (the organizational structure) or the method of employment (the basic tactics) of the instrument (the infantry battalion), consequent to this change in the raw material from which it was made. All the three factors, acting upon each other, and thus compounding the problem, were the root cause for the Indian infantry's apparent lack of adequate professionalism, which has been commented upon by two of the infantry generals who were themselves deeply involved in Sri Lanka. These root causes were further acted upon by the factors already mentioned, of hasty and ill-prepared induction, lack of psychological conditioning, units and sub-units being under strength, no maps, lack of intelligence, lack of supporting fire, and weapons and equipment being not quite good enough. The two generals who have commented on the infantry's general lack of professionalism are the first OFC, Lt. Gen. Depinder Singh himself, and the professionally highly-respected Lt. Gen. S.C. Sardeshpande, who as a Maj. General commanded 54 Infantry Division in the Jaffna Sector from November 1987, and was thereafter Deputy OFC.

*Ethical Issues*

(a) *The actions of the successive AIADMK and DMK Governments of Tamil Nadu, and the utterances of prominent people:* When a nation's armed forces, including men from that very state, were fighting an active military campaign, and lives were being lost, could these actions by an elected state government, a responsible political party, and by citizens of India not constitute an act of treason? The state government of Tamil Nadu continued to provide material and moral support to the LTTE even AFTER the IPKF had started to take action against it. What would have been the action of a government in a liberal western democratic country, the systems which are held up as role models for India's democracy? Would such a situation have been legally allowed in

France, the fountain head of western democracy, Britain, the parent of the Indian system, or the United States of America? Most probably not. In this case, the state government needed to have been formally warned, the provisions of the Constitution of India brought into play, and the state government dismissed if need be, for treasonable activity while the nation was at war. A Tamil Nadu under President's Rule would greatly have helped the prosecution of the IPKF campaign against the LTTE, and boosted the morale of the country's soldiers, instead of them and their families having to read in the media about wounded LTTE cadres being evacuated to Tamil Nadu, enjoying state government treatment, and returning to fight the IPKF bringing warlike stores purchased in Tamil Nadu with money given to them by the state government.

The Chief Minister of the state, Karunanidhi of the DMK, the party in power at the time of the return of IPKF, pointedly did not come for the ceremony welcoming the last of our troops back to India, which was commented upon in the media, but needed to have been censured in Parliament, and by the President of India.

(b) *Reporting by the Media:* The reporting by the Indian media in at least one instance lacked sensitivity; by being clinically impartial, it let down the Indian soldiers fighting in the field and their families. With the families of many officers and men seeing the images of dead Indian soldiers and reading the words, the reportage was in very poor taste, and damaging from the point of view of morale: including national emotions regarding the armed forces, morale of the families of army personnel, and the morale of the troops themselves. Was such clinically impartial reporting ETHICALLY correct from the nation's point of view. Should the print media not evolve and exercise some form of internal censorship of its own, as measured against a code of conduct that lays down the dividing line between what is journalistic ethics as well as patriotic, and what is not? And if some specific reportage, audio and video, electronic or print, is not patriotic, should it be deemed treason and triable in a Court of Law. Who would be responsible for the treasonable act, the reporter or the editor? These are some of the ethnical issues that need to be identified and resolved at the national level, BEFORE any such operational situations where Indian armed personnel are involved in future.

### *Lessons*

The strategic lessons of the IPKF episode in Sri Lanka are that policy-makers who wish to use the armed forces as a foreign policy instrument:

1. Must understand the capabilities and limitations of the forces sought to be employed, and task them accordingly, in terms of both timings and broad tasking.
2. Must create and use a simple and straight-forward command and control structure using the existing channels of command (instead of complex *ad hoc* structures).
3. Must clearly define the tasks given to the armed forces, which should be militarily practical.
4. Must use the existing and defined diplomatic and armed forces advisory channels for national policy-formulation and diplomacy, instead of "twin-track" or "triple-track" diplomacy, which inevitably creates uncertainty and confusion.

**The over-riding operational and tactical lessons of the Sri Lanka fiasco are:**

- That the Indian Army continues to remain prone to discarding its own laid-down drills and procedures when pressed by "higher headquarters." This was as true in 1988 as it was in 1962. The results are often chaos, and more time taken for the units to become operationally ready, than would have been the case if they had taken the little extra time to follow their own mobilization drills and proper battle procedure.
- Another lesson, again a repeat of 1962, is that "higher headquarters" themselves should consider the results of their orders, or their un-protesting acquiescence of unprofessional demands from their own superiors. The little extra time taken in moving units with their "first-line" scales of

ammunition would have paid dividends arrival in Sri Lanka, instead of having infantry with arms but little ammunition.

- Yet another unlearned lesson from 1962 is that, as far as possible, units should be moved in their full formations, under their own formation commanders, at least at brigade level, if brigade-level operations are considered a distinct possibility, rather than have individual units moved "piece-meal" to form *ad hoc* brigades, under *ad hoc* brigade commanders. This would greatly improve both the administration and the coordination of subsequent operations at the new operational location.
- Lastly, the lessons of the "aged army": in a counter-insurgency campaign, where ambushes and sudden encounters, rather than set-piece battles, are the name of the game, instant offensive reaction is the only answer to prevent taking more and more casualties. There is a natural tendency for troops to go to ground when suddenly caught in fire; the reluctance to get up and charge as per the standard drills, is very great when the infantryman is recently-married or is a new father, and even more when his family responsibilities are beginning to weigh on him. This factor has to be recognized, acknowledged, and as much remedial measures as can be taken, organizational and motivational, be seriously attended to.

## *GEN. SARDESHPANDE'S ANALYSIS AND LESSONS*

### *Analysis and Lessons Learnt*

By Lt. Gen. S. C. Sardeshpande, AVSM, UYSM (Retd.)

*Politico-Military:* On this plane it is very confusing to think what made the powers that be to take the decision of military intervention, as all factors were against it. The people and the militants were not supportive. The Sinhalas detested it. The international community did not bother about this South Asian backyard. The ISLA provisions indicated a no-win situation.

Peacekeepers thus turned warmongers. Erstwhile protégés became viciously inimical. India's serious limitations to pressurize either the Sinhalas or the LTTE were clearly identifiable by anyone with open eyes. The Indian government had undertaken a military commitment which could not force political solutions that satisfied the opposing parties. In Barbara Tuchman's definition this march of folly qualifies to be labeled as "Asserting a power you know you cannot exert."

What kind of military advice was given? And accepted? Could a National Security Council have analyzed and offered more sober, mature and realistic advice?

*Military Advice:* The military leadership of the day, I suspect, was greatly obsessed with the "projection of power abroad." One repeatedly heard of airmobile division, RAPIDs, amphibious brigade, etc. Sri Lanka fell into their lap. The Army Chief appeared to be hell-bent on grabbing the opportunity of power projection and giving the country and its military the benefit of a tested regional power, and its readiness to project it outside. Nothing else seemed to matter. Although the venture failed politically in all its goals, it showed Indian military ability to mount such a big operation across the sea and to sustain it for 32 months. It opened the eyes of the international community perhaps, and cleared most cobwebs and reservations of our own defence services. It crystallized a core of immense confidence in them. But this side effect cannot detract from the folly of inopportune, over-enthusiastic military advice.

*Strategy:* In the Indian Army strategic thinking has remained a polio victim. The chief operational commander, the GOC IPKF, Lt. Gen. Kalkat, was beset by so many agencies—the three armed Services, the Core Group, the Army Chief, the MEA, the RAW, the Indian High Commissioner in Colombo, the notional Sinhala Supreme Commander J. R. Jayawardene, Headquarters Southern Command, etc., that he hardly seemed to have had time enough to think, evolve and implement matching strategy. After the initial Jaffna battles of late 1987 and early 1988 the strategic balance had shifted to the Vanni jungles, where the IPKF did not concentrate adequately at any stage, not even half as much as we did in Jaffna even later. In fact Jaffna had become an obsession. Failure to grasp this change and act on it, in my view, was a strategic error. Secondly we did not pose challenges to the LTTE and the people by strategically changing our pattern of operations and deployment, pursuit of objectives, and incorporation of measures other than military, namely, economic reconstruction, psychological operations, diplomatic pressure, and interaction with people to convince them of our *bona fides*. Thirdly, we left a big hole across the sea, the navy unwilling to operate in "brown waters" as they did not have the necessary craft and manpower, they said.

*Organization for Operations Abroad:* Just picking up a standard infantry division couldn't do the trick. Our intelligence capability was nil, language a monumental problem, our link and wherewithal for meaningful interaction with people inadequate, our knowledge of their constitutional, legal, political and economic issues—as important in this situation as the military issue—nonexistent. We had few advisors or staff to deal with these vital subjects. For a venture of this nature the military force earmarked must have the following elements integral or assured to it:

1. *Tri-service Commend set-up:* Not merely advisory cells. It must have firm allocation of resources from each service, with full tri-service cooperation and integrated staff down to divisions.

2. *Liaison Cell* — of political, diplomatic, and economic advisors.

3. *Communications Cell:* To establish communications within the force, with the diplomatic representative of the country, the government and the Services Headquarters at home, intelligence agencies and home bases of Service formations. It will have to include members of the Department of Telecommunications.

4. *Intelligence Cell*—with representatives of RAW, Intelligence Bureau (IB) and Customs; interpreters and interrogators; integral intelligence units of the Force and of the Military Intelligence Directorate; cipher and decoding units and signals intelligence detachments.

5. *Psychological Operations Cell*—having experts for propaganda and counterpropaganda, representatives of the media management, liaison, and specialists for evolving and executing psychological operations themes, their appraisal, revision and recasting.

6. *Civil Affairs Cell*—with advisors in policing and civil control, medical services, reconstruction and rehabilitation, handling civil complaints, organizing public distribution and essential services.

7. *Media (PR) Cell*—with advisors and representatives of the media—TV, Radio and Press; to arrange press releases, press conferences and the like.

8. *Transportation Cell:* To handle and organize transportation of civil supplies, maintenance and construction of roads, railway facilities, harbours, jetties, airfields, helipads, bridges, ferries, labour, storage facilities and billets for troops.

9. *Command and Control Set-up:* (i) A commander (of the dominant service, preferably) of the overall force commanding all the integral and allocated resources; with; (ii) A well laid out chain of access, and clear levels of responsibility; having minimum links to the top decision-making body, making it the shortest possible access; (iii) Having above it a top decision-making body (the Core Group, for example) to translate government policy into actionable roles, goals and objectives for all participating components; to supervise and periodically assess developments; to identify suitable and favourable political situations act of developing military operations.

### *Training, Motivation and Leadership*

I am grouping them together because they are closely interrelated and interconnected. We found that there emerged some fundamental features of counter-insurgency (CI) operations:

(a) Application of force while retaining people's goodwill, or retaining people's goodwill while applying force. The combination is absolute, inseparable, but the nuance dictates the preference in the mix of the two. This is the very foundation of CI operations, and the most difficult part.

(b) Emerging therefrom is the next one—that the use of force therefore is highly restrained, highly selective, highly accurate and highly speedy. These are generally violated—because of lack of specific education and training; and self confidence and discipline of troops and leaders. This is actually what is meant by fighting with one hand tied. Violation of this feature results in the use of excessive force in the forms of heavier fire power and larger numbers, or pain and simple avoidance of action, delaying of action, or premature breaking off of action. It is strange but true. That is how human rights violations, "got away" stories, jungle-bashing exercises and mass scale cordon and search inflictions become *mantras*.

(c) In operations of this nature the best, the most visible and the most convincing ambassador of the country, the true representative of the country and its people, is the *Jawan*—on patrol, on checking duty, on guard duty, on observation posts, on missions, and even "off duty." Each *jawan* is a mini-ambassador! Military, he, as an individual as well as a member of the smallest group, is the strongest and the forward-most pressure point; as the fastest carrier of that pressure. This generally is not realized. The individual soldier and his smallest group actually, physically, carry and apply force; and also retain people's goodwill.

(d) Lastly, the senior officers of the military must evolve strategies, devise tactics, arrange intelligence, harmonize all agencies involved—military, psychological, political, economic and diplomatic, and arrive at suitable progressive steps in solving the problem, as military operations bring about changes in situations. This is a very cogitative, intelligent, imaginative, bold and timely orchestration, fine-tuned, alert and persuasive. In the Indian military's romance with apoliticality, a euphemism for keeping mum all along, our nostalgic indulgence with military life-style of a *Burra Saab,* smug cantonment mentality, and sumptuous pleasure of power over our own subordinates, I felt we had failed to develop the directness, forthrightness, boldness, persuasion and expertise to deal effectively, firmly and perseveringly with the political superiors, bureaucratic colleagues, intellectuals, wealth creators and the media. The seniors, instead of making things easier for the *jawan* and his small group in applying force and yet retaining people's goodwill, had failed them, distanced themselves from them and limited their contribution to daily routine and to routine intervention.

### *Training*

We suffered badly-*because,* we failed to fully grasp the basic factors and specific education of the soldier and the senior officer as mentioned above; *because* we almost forgot our basic military training - minor tactics—use of ground and weapons, patrolling and ambush; *because* we did not emphasize individual and small group actions, self-thinking and self-activation; *because* we were found quite weak in jungle operations despite the 30 year old Counter-Insurgency and Jungle Warfare School, and in boat-craft in the lagoons.

We did not quite succeed in evolving a operational philosophy and a technical philosophy for the employment of para commandos, mechanized forces and shallow-water ventures.

Formations back home largely failed to train and prepare units on their ORBAT *(order of battle)* which were earmarked for Sri Lanka. Many units broke off from golf-course working and flag-staff house guard duties and landed up in the Vanni jungles and Jaffna lagoons. This indeed was despicable. The few COs who took the trouble of zeroing their weapons and preparing their men did well.

### *Leadership*

Junior leadership—at platoon and company level; young officers and JCOs - bore the brunt. Surprisingly the JCOs did well in this long struggle of over two years. The casualty figures bear testimony (officers: 23 per cent, SCOs: 12 per cent, OR: 3 per cent). Barring a few exceptions, the training of units generally was not sharp enough; it seldom raised the standards of operation to higher planes of imaginativeness, innovative, rapidity, opportunism and initiative. These are the decisive elements, best exercised by, and most relevant at, junior levels. The junior leaders need careful nursing, breeding of greater self-reliance and self-actuation, and habituation of thinking and acting on their own within the superiors' broad parameters in a CI environment.

Unit level leadership was by and large adequate, but nothing much to write home about. Only a few volunteered to be bold. There were some very serious failures. Their units suffered very badly.

The senior leadership, brigade command and above, did not quite measure up. I shall sum it up in one sentence—it failed to inspire. Many seniors slogged, moved around, but did not inspire. Some, through flamboyance; some, through their reluctance at communicating; some through their manic strictness and terrorizing method; most distanced themselves from the troops and the hazards and discomforts of forward areas. Heli-hopping helped and increased this distancing. In such cases the helicopter is a curse. Maintaining very close links and identity with troops and frequent direct communication with them gained enormous importance, as operations progressed. As levels and intensity of force were orchestrated by increasing or decreasing pressure, posing fresh challenges and alternatives to the opponent, it had to be explained to the soldier and the junior leader, and their level of keenness maintained. This is a vitally important and awfully painstaking task for seniors. They had to keep changing operational formats, deployment patterns, pressures and pressure points, and keep the opponent guessing. This is possible only if they rise above the level of floor supervisors in a factory that tends to manufacture military history only reactively.

### *Motivation*

The domestic front exerted negative influence. The internal political-ethnic front in Tamil Nadu was unfriendly. Several intellectual, political, and bureaucratic luminaries were openly critical of the IPKF. National intelligence agencies like RAW, IB, and the State intelligence units of Tamil Nadu stood aloof and often played on IPKF nerves by their unrealistic assessments and non-cooperation in many spheres; they were of little use. Even regimental spirit often gave way. One battalion disintegrated leaving behind their C.O. to die. Another failed to galvanize its own sub-unit to rush to the assistance of its own neighbouring sub-unit. There were piecemeal massacres of sub-units due to lack of spirit and alertness. One unit developed the habit of going into harbour at sunset when even the armoured corps had given up this noble practice since 1965. Almost all units lost a few weapons to the LTTE in ambushes, but captured negligible numbers from the LTTE. In this formidable environment what, in my opinion, held units together and kept then going *was the simple and perhaps the most enduring factor of our army's professionalism*—the duty of the soldier being to fight.

In fact the heavy tail of regimental reputation built over old doddering battle honours, long dirges of regimental histories, and the magic spirit supposed to ooze out of annual rituals of regimental celebrations tend to prove inadequate on the highly elusive, circular battlefield, where the ghost-like opponent is invisible, indistinct, unknown but yet hits so hard unexpectedly as to shatter the glory and image of that peacetime reputation. This peacetime reputation tends to lead average units to *status-quoism*, drive them into defensive attitudes and render them psychologically unprepared to strike out.

The IPKF did its duty, as a true professional army. It showed it could take plenty of beating, and give it back too. Its combat strength lay more in this endurance of brawn than the sharpness of its brain. Its rank and file remained phlegmatic, but capable, and needed higher levels of training by way of specific education on vital issues, and of preparing them to think independently and act on their own, boosting up their self-reliance, self-actuation and initiative. Senior officers needed to revise their leadership horizons, content and philosophy, as they were found wanting in communicative and persuasive skills, inspiring subordinates, tackling political masters and bureaucrats, intellectuals and the media, and in building strategies that lessened the soldier's burden and made it easier for him to work harder, faster and with lesser damage in achieving his goal.

Projection of power outside the national confines is a very serious matter. A group of wise and competent men needs to be put in place to evaluate and assess situations and policies better, and offer better national security advice to the political leadership which is in a tearing haste; and contain military chiefs who are over-enthusiastic. A second string of such competent professionals, forming a core group, should translate policies into roles, tasks and objectives for all participating agencies, oversee their execution and performance, relate progress and results to determine the direction and level of success, and orchestrate goal-achievement efforts. Organizationally the designated military force must comprise of relevant armed Service, civilian and intelligence agencies.

Internal security and CI operations demand their own specific education, specific skills, mental preparation and stricter discipline, alongside a strategy integrating several non-military departments, and an intimate, forceful interaction with the political leadership, civil bureaucracy, intelligence agencies and the people.

## Chapter 8

# Post-Campaign Views

## Interview with Pirabakaran in 1990 after the Departure of the IPKF

An interview given by the enemy chief needs to be read to see how the LTTE saw the IPKF campaign after it had ended.

*Time Magazine Interview*

Pirabakaran gave an interview to the *Time* magazine's correspondent Anita Pratap, from Mullaitivu. This interview, which appeared in the *Time* of 8 April 1990, was posted on the internet in full by Sachi Sri Kantha.

In this interview, Pirabakaran reflected on the strengths and weaknesses of the LTTE, what he gained from his confrontation with India and what his motive is in peace talks. The words within parentheses were in the original text.

Q: *What made you confront India?*

A: India claimed to have intervened in Sri Lanka to secure Tamil interests. In actual fact, India came to secure its own interests. There was never any genuine attempt to understand and solve our problems. India deliberately aggravated Sri Lanka's ethnic crisis. It destabilized Sri Lanka [by training and arming Tamil militants, including the Tigers] so that it could play a dominant role in bringing Sri Lanka within its sphere of influence.

What I can't forgive is the way India claimed to have intervened to protect the Tamils and then launched this war against our people. On the third day after the war started, I sent an appeal to India to stop the attack because of the civilian casualties. But India mistook it as a sign of weakness and pressed ahead with the offensive, thinking they could crush us.

Q: *But isn't it true that India has consistently stood for a united Sri Lanka?*

A: India used this excuse to impress the world that it was the protector of Sri Lanka. By adopting this line, India ensured that other powers were excluded from interfering in this region.

Q: *You knew India was using the Sri Lankan problem to pursue its interests, but didn't you also use India by taking advantage of Indian training and arms?*

A: Yes, we also used India. We were aware of India's strategy but made use of the opportunity to strengthen ourselves militarily.

Q: *What gave you the courage to take on the world's third largest army?*

A: India failed to secure the release of twelve of my area commanders who were arrested by the Sri Lankan security forces. [When the captives later swallowed cyanide] their suicides made me determined to confront the Indian army. Some of my top colleagues cautioned me against it and wondered how long the LTTE could hold out. I gave them the Vietnam example—a small nation can fight a superpower with determination and dedication. When I was deciding to fight, the thought of winning or losing didn't bother me. What you have to assess is whether you have the will to fight. People cannot give up their cause, their rights, for fear of defeat.

Q: *Is there a lesson in this for India?*

A: That however formidable a military power you may be, you cannot impose upon a people anything against their will.

Q: *What guerilla technique was most useful to you?*

A: We used land mines to great effect. They caused a lot of Indian casualties.

Q: *What did you consider were the Indian army's main strengths and weaknesses?*

A: Their strength—and their weakness—was their huge manpower. It created difficulties for us. It restricted our mobility. But because they came in large numbers, they suffered many casualties. Also, they wasted a lot of time, energy and money on providing logistical support. Another major weakness was that the Indian army was not motivated. The soldiers didn't know why they were fighting. They were confused. They came to protect Tamils, and then they had to kill them.

Q: *And what in your judgment were the LTTE's own strengths and weaknesses?*

A: Our strength—and our weakness—was our overconfidence. Sometimes our cadres took impossible risks, like ambushing an Indian patrol at a point where there were no escape routes. This cost us casualties. We were sometimes careless. But also because of our overconfidence, our boys carried out some amazingly brave attacks.

Q: *The Indians say they fought this was with one hand tied behind their backs because they wanted to minimize civilian casualties.*

A: If they could indulge in such atrocities against our people with one hand tied behind their backs, I shudder to imagine what havoc they would have unleashed if both hands had been free. They used every technique—aerial strafing, dropping 250-kg bombs, artillery bombardment, harassment of civilians. These are excuses peddled by a defeated army.

Q: *Some 6,000 Tamil civilians were killed in the war with the Indian army. Was it worth it?*

A: Yes. We have proved that we will not allow any force to interfere with the freedom and independence of our people.

Q: *But what have you gained?*

A: I have gained self confidence, courage and the support of my people.

Q: *What made you start negotiations with Sri Lankan President Ranasinghe Premadasa?*

A: Our people thought India would give us Tamil Eelam [a separate Tamil state]. Instead India [reached an agreement] against our will. So we thought it would be better to talk to the Sri Lankan government and work out a better deal. Besides LTTE will not allow a foreign force to intervene and dominate our people. Premadasa articulated the same viewpoint. He was determined to end the foreign intervention.

Q: *Now that the Indian army has gone, many fear that confrontation with the Sri Lankan government — your historical enemy — is again inevitable.*

A: We have had a long history of state oppression against our people. Earlier, the Tamils negotiated and were repeatedly betrayed, and so the armed struggle was born. If the Sri Lankan government resorts to state oppression against the Tamils and Muslims, then we will fight. But we hope the current peace will continue.

Q: *How sincere do you think Premadasa is about solving the problems of the Tamils?*

A: We started the negotiations on the basis of trust. We have that trust.

Q: *How serious is the LTTE about participating in the provincial council elections?*

A: We are very serious. We want to show India and the world that we are the authentic representatives of the people.

Q: *Have you given up the demand for an independent Eelam?*

A: We have not.

Q: *Then what are you talking to Premadasa for? How can you enter the democratic mainstream if you still cling to your separatist cause?*

A: We are entering the political mainstream. Our demand for self-determination will not be an impediment for us to enter the political process.

Q: *Many people feel that your peace talks with Premadasa are only a tactical move.*

A: We have not cheated or betrayed anybody. At the same time, if we are cheated or betrayed, we will react. But if somebody trusts us, then we will reciprocate.

This interview with Pirabakaran was 17 years ago, but Pirabakaran has not shifted at all from his professed goal. This adamancy, and what the scientist-inventor Thomas Edison called *stick-to-it-iveness* (in his formula for success) is what makes Pirabakaran a successful and dangerous military commander.

*Views on Induction and De-Induction of the IPKF*

Different views have been expressed on the induction and de-induction of the IPKF. They are worth reviewing for an overview of the political dimensions of the campaign, after it was concluded.

Lt. Gen. A. S. Kalkat, who held key positions throughout the entire IPKF operations, first as MGGS HQ Southern Command at Pune (Poona) directly under the Overall Force Commander, and later as Overall Force Commander himself, has said that the IPKF was close to restoring normalcy when it was withdrawn.

In an interview to Prabhu Chawla of *India Today* for its issue dated 15 September, 1988, on being questioned regarding the Alampil Operation, he said that one unit of the IPKF came across this camp with about 150-200 Tamil Tigers as part of the operations to disarm the militants. The operations were a success. More troops were placed to isolate this area since it was of importance to the Tigers. With this Alampil Operation, the Tigers disintegrated. He further said that the IPKF had brought the situation close to normal but in some areas there was still some struggle. In the East, the people wanted schools and colleges to open. Shops and banks were functioning and mail delivered. The IPKF provided security to banking transactions; public places have been rebuilt by the IPKF engineers. People came to the IPKF for assistance. Operations were carried out to create normalcy. On elections, Gen. Kalkat said that IPKF will ensure that there is no coercion, no threat in the conduct of polls and it will provide full security. IPKF was there only as a catalyst in the political process.

Gen. Kalkat deposed before the Jain Commission that during the first ten months or so, the IPKF achieved a situation in which the LTTE militants were no more capable of operating as an effective force in both the North and the East.

J.N. Dixit has stated, "Shri M. Karunanidhi was critical of the IPKF and supportive of the LTTE when he was the Chief Minister. V. P. Singh's reaction was to respond by withdrawing the IPKF. His view was that even without completing its task, the IPKF should be withdrawn. He said that he deduced it from the chain of events and took his policy decision. AfterV.P. Singh came into power, the decisions taken appear to confirm the assessment that M. Karunanidhi and V. P. Singh thought alike on the IPKF.

There were two strands of thinking shared by the Tamil population in Sri Lanka after October, 1987—one that it is unfortunate that the IPKF has been compelled to operate against the LTTE, the second stand was under no circumstances should IPKF leave Sri Lanka till the situation was stabilized because the Sri Lankans were afraid that both the LTTE and the Sri Lankan Security Forces would unleash violence against them. IPKF was the only safeguarding factor. This continued not only till the withdrawal of IPKF but even thereafter."

Karunanidhi claimed on 23.11.1996 that, "my views in the matter are that the peace keeping force to Sri Lanka was for making peace and not for any other purpose. I did not give any press release opposing induction of the IPKF. I believe that the IPKF was sent as a peace force. I did not oppose the very idea of sending the IPKF."

On the induction of the IPKF in Sri Lanka, V. P. Singh, who became Prime Minister after Rajiv Gandhi, has stated: "I was not in the Government at the time of induction of the IPKF in Sri Lanka. I demitted office in April, 1987." He further said, "about some elements in the DMK being unhappy about the induction of IPKF and on the activities of the IPKF, I am aware some were unhappy and such unhappiness was not only limited to some elements of DMK alone but shared by other political elements. I think his (Karunanidhi's) reservations were political on the ground that perhaps it was not proper to induct IPKF. Janta Dal, as such, also held that view that induction of IPKF was not very wise. My personal opinion regarding induction of IPKF was that it was not a well thought out decision in terms that there were no adequate preparations regarding collection of ground information, logistical needs, ability of the opponent, the necessary resources which we could command, all these strategic considerations were not gone into in detail and finally we ended up in confronting the Tamil population as well as the Sri Lankan Government. The objectives failed, not only in achieving the objectives and also in results, that is to say, diplomatic objective or military results."

How far is the above statement of Shri V. P. Singh correct? His views are not in conformity with the statement given by Lt. Gen. A. S. Kalkat. It cannot be denied that the goal of Indo-Sri Lankan Agreement was not achieved; but whether the failure in the achievement of the goal can be attributed to wrong induction of the IPKF is debatable.

J. N. Dixit has expressed his views. By the signing of the Indo-Sri Lanka Agreement, it was expected that the LTTE as well as the Sri Lankan Government would continue to faithfully implement the Agreement. But they colluded to destroy the Agreement.

Justice Jain has said: "The circumstances in which the IPKF was inducted also cannot be lost sight of. When once President Jayawardene committed himself to the concessions for devolution, the Agreement had to be signed without loss of time and a request was immediately made for sending the IPKF. That request was acceded to being a stipulation in the Agreement. The Agreement brought happiness in the beginning but things took a different turn after some time. So, under the circumstances, it cannot be said that induction of IPKF was an unwarranted step in the given situation."

V. P. Singh has also deposed about his views on withdrawal of the IPKF. He deposed that the order for withdrawal of the IPKF from Sri Lanka was made by Rajiv Gandhi and out of eight districts, withdrawal had taken place in six districts during Rajiv Gandhi's time.

About his concerns for withdrawal, V. P. Singh has enumerated as under:

(i) to keep the word of the Government of India as committed by Rajiv Gandhi;

(ii) in our security strategy, any military commitment in Southern zone would have meant new military commitment and over-stretching our defence resources;

(iii) militant problem had broken out in J&K and also in Punjab situation was very delicate;

(iv) national concern was to secure the country from any military adventure from the West.

(v) The Army committed in Sri Lanka was needed on this side. Therefore, it was necessary to withdraw the IPKF by preponing the date.

V. P. Singh said that he got the goodwill of Sri Lanka and also strengthened the defence of the country in the Western sector and other places. He deposed before the Jain Commission that during his tenure as Prime Minister, after the de-induction, President Premadasa sent a communication of appreciation of the Sri Lankan Government to the Government of India. This is also indicative of the fact that the Government of India had nothing to do with the LTTE; otherwise President Premadasa would not have sent his appreciation; he would have sent complaints.

At the time of de-induction, V. P. Singh further said "Karunanidhi also contacted Mehrotra, High Commissioner in Colombo to open a dialogue with Prabhakaran via Premadasa so that at the tail-end of the de-induction, attacks are not made on the Indian Army. Premadasa did contact Prabhakaran and conveyed to the High Commission that he has obtained the assurance of Prabhakaran that LTTE will not attack the Indian Army because we made it very clear to Premadasa that if the India Army is attacked, we will not withdraw in dishonour. Then we will have to make further military commitments. This was my stern warning. It paid off in the sense that except for one minor incident, Indian Army came out not only safely but honourably. This was the positive result of contact by Karunanidhi."

There was a phased de-induction of the IPKF as the Indian Government of the day had taken a decision in the light of its policy. Irrespective of the consequence on the island, IPKF had to be withdrawn in view of the stand taken by the Sri Lankan Government headed by Premadasa.

Although before the Commission, different views have been expressed by J. N. Dixit and S. C. Chandrahasan, Chandrahasan has said that it was an unfortunate decision and J. N. Dixit has said that withdrawal of the IPKF was a mistake.

The Government of India was not at all interested at any time for its prolonged stay in Sri Lanka. But it also did not want to bring IPKF back without fulfilment of its commitment and without achieving its objectives of restoration of peace and normalcy.

The IPKF could not remain in Sri Lanka against the wishes of the Sri Lankan Government and the Indian Government had no option. Premadasa should have respected the bilateral Agreement under which on the request of President Jayawardene, the IPKF was sent and it was at the behest of the President that it started its operations. Sri Lankan Government headed by Premadasa on the other hand started a proxy war against the IPKF by arming and funding the LTTE. Premadasa had given unilateral ultimatum for de-induction of the IPKF. As a result of de-induction of the IPKF, the fears and apprehensions came out to be true and the areas which stood evacuated from the holds of the LTTE again fell back into its hands. The rival militant groups were completely decimated and the LTTE established its sole authority over the areas evacuated by the IPKF.

When the IPKF reached Madras shores, the Chief Minister of Tamil Nadu M. Karunanidhi did not receive the last contingent. Karunanidhi, in his statement, to the Jain Commission deposed:

"My view in the matter is peace keeping force to Sri Lanka for making peace and not for any other purpose. I did not give any Press release opposing induction of the IPKF. I believe that IPKF was sent as a peace force. I did not oppose it to the very idea of sending the IPKF. When IPKF ceased to keep peace and when they themselves went to the battle ground, I started opposing the IPKF. Due to conflicts between Sinhala and Tamil forces and due to violations of Indo-Sri Lanka Agreement, the IPKF identified itself with Sri Lankan Army and launched attacks not only on the militants but also on innocent Sri Lankan Tamil civilians. I did not go and receive the IPKF. Normally, a victorious cricket team is received and not a losing team. Since the IPKF failed in its mission in keeping peace, on their return, I did not go to receive the IPKF. It is not my intention to denigrade the Indian Army and compare it with a cricket team. In fact when there was an exhibition in Tanjavur by the LTTE supporters, where the Indian Army was denigraded, I banned the exhibition." That news is reported in *The Hindu* on 7 June, 1990, marked Exhibit 566. Karunanidhi was asked the reason as to why he did not go to receive the IPKF, was it because that Rajiv Gandhi sent the IPKF to Sri Lanka, was it that there was no advance study before sending the IPKF or was it for the reason that the IPKF committed atrocities against the Tamils? The answer of Karunanidhi was: "I did not go and receive the IPKF because a force which was sent to keep peace in Sri Lanka created chaos and confusion there. I also believe that the proper course for sending the IPKF was not adopted and in Sri Lanka the IPKF did not do what it was intended to do. I do not remember whether V.P. Singh, the then Prime Minister, terms my action of not receiving the IPKF as an unfair action. The news item in the *Indian Express* of 14 May 1990 is the opinion of V. P. Singh and I have nothing to say about that. V. P. Singh's statement is "Describing Karunanidhi's attack on the IPKF as "Unfair." V. P. Singh said the previous Government has made a political mistake in sending the IPKF to go to Sri Lanka. But it must be remembered that the armed forces were only carrying out the assignment given to them by the political authorities. It is therefore unfair to run down the Army."

"I never questioned the intentions of Rajiv Gandhi, but I only criticized the way the Agreement was signed. Prabhakaran was never made to commit by signing of the document. If he had made to commit perhaps the objective of the Agreement could have been achieved. My statement should be understood in that spirit. I read from the newspapers that the Indian Government held talks with all the Sri Lankan militant groups prior to the Indo-Sri Lankan Agreement."

If Sri Lankan Agreement would have been implemented, it would have satisfied both the parties. If the Agreement had satisfied both parties, it might have succeeded.

Rajiv Gandhi had an occasion to express his views on de-induction of IPKF, in the interview he gave to Vir Sanghvi in *Sunday* dated 12-18 August 1990. On page 53 under the caption "Sri Lanka," his interview reads: "Ques. On Sri Lanka, you were planning to withdraw the IPKF by 31 December 1989. The new government withdrew it by 31 March, 1990. But you appear to disapprove: what is the difference between what you wanted to do and what they did do?"

Ans. I had very long talks with the Sri Lankan government when it came to India in September (1989) last year. I think it was the longest that any delegation had remained in another country. They were here for three weeks and I spent something like ten hours or 12 hours talking with them and I was able to convince them that it was not just a question of withdrawal. It was a question of what happens after withdrawal and how to give stability.

I met the Sri Lankan delegation that came to India—this was a few weeks ago, and one of the members had also been there at those talks. And he told me that everything I said was coming right today.

So we were not just talking in the air. We had linked the withdrawal of the IPKF to two things: devolution-economic and political devolution to the North Eastern unit, and the security of the Tamils.

We had in fact worked out formulas on how devolution was to be, or who was to define devolution. Because I said, "I cannot define it." It has to be worked out there. Who is going to define "Security"? And I said, "neither can I and neither can you define that. It is the Tamils who have to say, yes we are secure."

But this Government didn't follow up on that. In fact, there was an agreement on 18 September or something like that—a joint communiqué which lays down the whole thing. This Government gave up all that and that is why we are back to square one. And here I would like to point out that the IPKF in Sri Lanka was not fighting for the Tamils against the Sinhalas. It was not fighting for the Sinhala against the Tamils. It was fighting for the unity and integrity of Sri Lanka. It was fighting for a certain stability in our region without other people interfering in our area. And the definition of that stability was a joint definition by Jayawardene and myself. It was not something that India had unilaterally laid down.

The problem that is going to come up with the line that this Government is taking, with the capitulation this Government has one is that all that is going to be lost. Today I find they are saying, "We will never send Indian troops anywhere" or something like that. That is ridiculous.

If a friendly country needs help, what will we do? Maldives asked for help. Were we supposed to say no and let the United States send people to the Maldives? Because, in effect, this is what it means. If it wasn't the United States, it would be somebody else.

This Government is totally abrogating its responsibility in the region, and to our friends, it is creating a vacuum the others will fill." From the aforesaid interview it would appear that Lankan delegation had met Rajiv Gandhi in September 1989 and he had discussions with the delegation about 10 hours or 12 hours during its stay of 3 weeks. According to him it was not a smooth question of withdrawal, it was a question of what happens after withdrawal and how to give stability. When another delegation came just few weeks before the interview, one of the members of the delegation was also there, in the earlier talks and he had told Rajiv Gandhi that everything he said was coming right. Rajiv Gandhi expressed that the Government had linked withdrawal of IPKF to two things. Devolution-economic and political devolution to the North Eastern unit and the security of the Tamils.

With regard to defining security, his view was that the Tamils have to say that they are secure. He also expressed that "IPKF in Sri Lanka was not fighting the Tamils against the Sinhalese nor it was fighting Sinhalese against the Tamils. Fighting for the unity and integrity of Sri Lanka and was fighting for a certain stability in the region without other people interfering in this area. And the definition of that stability was a joint definition by Jayawardene and myself. It was not something that India had unilaterally laid down."

The IPKF was sent under the political decision taken by the Government at the Centre, following the political decision of signing a bilateral Agreement between Sri Lanka and India. The Indian Army performed to its best under the orders of the Indian Government. Every Indian national should be proud of the Army's role which it performed after great sacrifices without going into the question of correctness or incorrectness of any political decision, as deposed by Shri V. P. Singh.

The IPKF had to be withdrawn after the stand of the Sri Lankan Government was made known to India.

(*The Jain Commission Report,* Volume VIII, Chapter 11, Paragraph 21.2).

## Chapter 9
# Conclusion

It would be illustrative to touch upon a campaign which is at times referred to in the context of the Sri Lanka campaign, terming the IPKF operation in Sri Lanka as India's Vietnam.

*Vietnam War*

Topographically Sri Lanka is only 32 KM away from India at the nearest point between the two countries. Both the countries have common ethnic connections including the two warring factions in Sri Lanka: Tamils and Sinhalas. India has a direct stake in the political, military and economic mismanagement in Sri Lanka. Any injustice on Sri Lanka Tamils has direct repercussions on the large number of Tamils living in India and abroad. India would thus not like to see political, economic and military instability in Sri Lanka and would not accept the hegemony of any other country on her sensitive neighbour. Sri Lanka is located on the very important marine route used for strategic and commercial purposes.

Contrary to this, America and Vietnam had no commonality. American involvement was purely the fall out of the cold war and the mutual suspicion between communism and capitalism. America was physically, emotionally and economically far away from Vietnam. It had no stake to claim but for ideological differences. The world at that time was divided in two camps based on capitalism and communism. Each was trying to establish its own hegemony. American involvement was also to some extent caused by the ultimate defeat of France at the hands of communist forces under the political leadership of Ho Chi Minh and the military leadership of Gen. Vo Nguyen Giap. Vietnam was divided into South and North Vietnam under communist and non-communist rule respectively along the 17th parallel. France withdrew. A hundred years of French colonialism ended. South Vietnam under Ngo Dinh Diem felt threatened by North Vietnamese Communist activists. America slowly got drawn in. Initially President John Kennedy started by providing advisers and other non-active support. But under President Lyndon Johnson, various incidents forced it grow into full scale military involvement. But despite full military and logistic support from America, the combined force of South Vietnam and America could not defeat the communist forces. America was forced to withdraw its forces in 1972 and South Vietnam gradually gave in to North Vietnam offensive operations. Vietnam was formally reunified in July 1976, and Saigon was renamed Ho Chi Minh City. U.S. casualties in Vietnam during the era of direct U.S. involvement (1961-72) were more than 50,000 dead; South Vietnamese dead were estimated at more than 400,000, and Viet Cong and North Vietnamese at over 900,000.

Compared to this, despite initial hiccups, the IPKF gradually captured almost all major pockets of LTTE strong holds. They were driven into a small pocket in Mallaitivu jungle. If President Premadasa had not joined hands with the LTTE and compelled the Indian Government to withdraw the IPKF for another couple of months, the history of this part of the sub continent could have been different. The IPKF was in a dominant position. The major difference was, despite having support from Tamilians from all over the world including Madras, the LTTE did not have the magnitude of support enjoyed by the Viet Cong of South Vietnam and communist forces of North Vietnam. Communist China was also a next door neighbour with a common boundary with North Vietnam. The casualty figures given above gives the immensity of the battle.

*Foreign Policy Failure*

The recent history of Sri Lanka up to 29 July 1987 had "made extremism the currency of the day, and the IPKF was sent in to ensure its devaluation," in the words of Manoj Joshi of the *Frontline* newsmagazine in November 1987. In this effort the IPKF did not succeed.

As a foreign-policy exercise, the less said about the outcome of the IPKF campaign the better. Political complexities aside, as a tri-Service regional power-projection exercise, it forms a stark comparison to the British Falklands/Malvinas campaign, which was mounted almost exactly five years before "Operation PAWAN," and in which a number of warships and combat aircraft were lost on both sides. What is worth noting is that this successful British campaign was launched by a mature medium power across 13,000 km of cold and hostile ocean, a three-week one-way sailing time for warships at average speed, and not just across a 35 km strip of sea. Part of the difference lay in the vast historical experience of the British people and armed forces, their ability to learn from their history, and in the inherent national characteristics of the two different cultures.

A good example of a smooth power-projection exercise also existed from India's own neighbourhood, when the Soviet Union invaded Afghanistan on 25 December 1979. Examples and comparisons apart, the Chief of Army Staff, Gen. Sundarji himself had been BGS* of HQ 33 Corps during the Indo-Pakistan war of 1971 and thus held a key appointment in the eastern theatre, from the preparation stage onwards, and should have remembered the necessary wait to prepare, from March 1971 to November-December 1971. His discarding of the laid-down battle procedures and logistical preparations of the army's own teachings is, therefore, inexcusable. His handling of the campaign at the topmost level in the Army was an almost complete negation of everything taught at the Defence Services Staff College in Wellington, which is designed to prevent exactly what actually happened. Troops being sent in piece-meal, without adequate logistical support, and with the infantry arriving to operate

*Brigadier General Staff, the senior staff officer who heads the General Staff Branch in a Corps HQ, and heads the intelligence and operational functions as well as the operational coordination in warlike situations and war.

immediately on arrival with no proper intelligence and operational briefings and mental preparation, and not even that most basic of intelligence requirements, proper maps, would be incredible if it had not actually happened.

Another factor brought to light was that the Indian Army had only been paying lip-service to counter-insurgency (CI) theory and practice. Ever since the gradual cessation of active hostilities in some of the north-eastern states, where the erstwhile insurgents had either joined the political mainstream, or a "peace accord and cease-fire" had been reached, classic CI had taken a back seat, in spite of its low-key persistence in Kashmir. A case in point was that the Army's Counter-Insurgency and Jungle Warfare School (CIJW School), set up by Eastern Command in 1969 at a temporary location in Vairangte, Mizoram, had never got shifted to what was intended to be its permanent location, on 100 acres of suitable land near Haflong in the North Cachar Hills District of Assam. This land had been negotiated for and had been agreed to be handed-over to the Army by the *gaonburas* (the village headmen) concerned, but was not finalized because the Army did not pay the money agreed upon.

The IPKF episode in Indian history showed that a basically sound strategic political decision, the ISLA, was unable to be implemented primarily because of the inability of the Army, and in particular its infantry, to deliver the required goods within a suitably short time-frame. The implementation of a good aim also did not succeed because of inept handling of the whole operation by the Government of India itself, and by the inability of its three subordinate military arms, the three armed forces (which in every other country of the world are considered part of the Government), to combine to form a joint operational HQ, or otherwise to sufficiently cooperate with each other. India's esteem in the eyes of the world went down due to this failure which was both political and military, and certainly its standing as a regional power was greatly diminished.

India lost the straight leverage it could certainly have gained in Sri Lanka, in spite of its bungling on the political decision-making and diplomatic front, because of the inability of India's infantry to quickly and effectively break the LTTE's power. The infantry's failure was clearly due to a lack of professionalism which had resulted in poor performance on the ground level basics: field craft, fire control and fire discipline, section leading and platoon tactics. These deficiencies were aggravated by prior organizational error in allowing the infantry rifle companies to be saddled with aging manpower, rather than having a bayonet-strength of predominantly young men in the 19-25 age group; real *jawans*. In Sri Lanka these rifle companies were already under-strength due to lack of prior preparation and undue haste in induction.

In their hurry for promotions and the desire to get on to "better" things, the very foundations of India's military strength had got neglected and were rotting away due to this neglect. It had become unfashionable for a unit's (i.e., the battalion's) main emphasis, to be the men's individual training cycles and their standards of weapons proficiency (e.g., annual range classifications, and fire control practice at field firing exercises). The entire army's focus seemed to have shifted to major high-level collective exercises (also known as "manoeuvres" or "schemes" in earlier military parlance). It didn't seem to matter any more whether the individual men, or the lowest, teams and sub units, such as the scouts from one section leading a platoon, or a 2-man LMG team, or an entire section, knew how to fight well. But it was precisely these on which the effectiveness of the whole force depended—as the LTTE was to prove to the Indian Army in Sri Lanka.

However, due to the obscuring of this basic military fact in the various higher-level explanations that emerged after 1990, India's government, and its people, continued to remain unaware of this. So there was no national introspection on the subject. What introspection there may have been regarding this failure remained confined to the Army.

Had but India's infantry been able to deliver the goods, the political equation would have fallen into place and stayed firm till today. The evidence clearly shows that till 1987 India had undoubtedly not learnt that to attain political objectives through military means, it needs the best possible infantry it can produce, in terms of manpower, arms and equipment, and training. To be able to do that requires a great deal of thought and political will. The IPKF in the Sri Lanka episode has conclusively proved, if there ever was any doubt, that the infantry's rifle companies are the cutting edge when national aims have to be achieved militarily. If the rifle companies cannot perform, then all military tactics, operational plans and strategy, and national geo-political plans will fail. By 1987 India had forgotten this, and its cutting edge was not sharp enough.

The Sri Lanka Tamil problem will continue to fester, with periods of civil war alternating with periods of "cease-fire," and the governments of both Sri Lanka and India will remain concerned and involved. If and when the requirement ever comes for India to become an active player again, India's national planners and strategists may well have forgotten history, or not even learnt the lessons of 1987-90.

## Chapter 10

# Afterword

Since the Sri Lanka Civil War still continues, it is useful to follow-on briefly from where the Indian military foreign-policy exercise left off, to understand broadly the trend of events as they continue.

During the next Indian Parliamentary election campaign, Rajiv Gandhi the former Prime Minister was assassinated on 21 May 1991, by a woman LTTE suicide bomber, Dhanu, who was introduced to him by party workers of his own Congress Party. He had been campaigning on behalf of his party's candidate in Sriperambudur, Tamil Nadu, 20 km from Chennai,. There was no guarantee that his party would have come to power again, and therefore that he would become Prime Minister again, but the LTTE bore a grudge against him for allegedly going back on his promises to Pirabakaran. The Government of India banned the LTTE in May 1992 after it was established through the Jain Commission of Inquiry that the LTTE, including Pirabakaran personally, had planned and carried out the killing, using a woman suicide bomber. Pirabakaran was declared a "proclaimed offender." A request to the Sri Lanka Government for the extradition of Pirabakaran continues to remain pending. The ban imposed in May 1992 is regularly extended for further periods.

Pirabakaran is also wanted in India for the murder of a former LTTE colleague and rival, Uma Maheshwaran, on a crowded street in Chennai city in 1982. He was arrested by the Tamil Nadu Police, but was released reportedly on the orders of the then-Chief Minister, the late M. G. Ramachandran. Predictably, he had jumped bail and returned to Sri Lanka.

Without ging into the political twists and turns and military details of the ongoing Sri Lankan Civil War, the next of the rare interviews given by Pirabakaran in 1993, to the Sri Lanka correspondent of the *Economist*, probably Mervyn de Silva, is also worth reading. Again, it has been put on the net for all to read by Sachi Sri Kantha:

*Top Tiger Talks about Talks*
[*Economist*, March 6, 1993]
from our Sri Lanka correspondent in Jaffna

"The leader of the Tamil Tigers, Vellupillai Prabhakaran, does not often give an interview to a journalist. So why now? During about three hours of talk with Prabhakaran, what emerged was a desire to negotiate once again with the government. He rejected any suggestion that this arose out of weakness. Victory, he insisted, was his for the taking.

Yet all is not well within the rebel group. The Tigers are finding it hard to recruit more fighters. Teenagers quickly become veterans. In January ten tigers were reported to have died when a ship said to be carrying arms was interrupted by the Indian navy. Among the dead was Sathasivam Krishnakumar, the Tigers' number-two and a close friend of the leader. Prabhakaran says he is too upset to talk about the loss. The Jaffna peninsula, the Tamil area where the Tigers have their stronghold, is a ruined place after ten years of fighting. There is no electricity and not much food. Thousands of people have fled. Those too poor to leave appear exhausted.

But the Tigers have been up against it before. The Indian peacekeepers invited to Sri Lanka in 1987 suppressed them for a time. A new president, Ranasinghe Premadasa, got rid of the Indians in 1990 and, in return, the Tigers talked peace. Nothing came of this talk, and many in the government believed that the Tigers used the pause in the civil war to rearm. They will be suspicious that this is what the Tigers have in mind now.

Even his enemies concede that Mr. Prabhakaran is a formidable leader. Despite the toll of the civil war, he appears to retain the support of the majority of Tamils in northern and eastern Sri Lanka, the area which the Tigers claim as the Tamil homeland. He is 37, on the small side, and a bit overweight. With his black hair and moustache and large eyes, he looks a little like the hero that turns up regularly in Tamil films. He dresses in army fatigues, and carries a gun. Around his neck is a black cord at the end of which is a capsule, presumably containing the cyanide which Tigers are supposed to swallow rather than be taken prisoner.

His house—at least, the house where he gave his interview—is small and modern, and a bit of a drive from the town of Jaffna. There are maps on the walls, but no radio or television or books, although Prabhakaran appears well informed about affairs outside Sri Lanka, especially wars, in Afghanistan, or in Indo-China. Much of the talk was over dinner: noodles and a soft drink. Prabhakaran's portliness does not seem to arise from over-eating. He appears to speak only Tamil. Interpreting was done by Anton Balasingham, a much-traveled man—he lived for a time in London—who has been the Tigers' principal negotiator in the past.

Is there anything the Tigers might offer than would encourage the government to open negotiations? The Tigers' demand has been for an independent Tamil state covering a third of the country and holding much of the coastline, a proposal that the government rejects totally. Some politicians in Colombo believe the way to peace is to turn Sri Lanka into a federal state.

The government is considering the idea, although the majority Sinhalese, who have dominated the government and army since independence in 1948, are believed to be against federalism. It would give the Tamils too much power, some believe. The Tamils would want a high degree of autonomy, particularly over law and order, land and education, all controversial themes. The size of a possible Tamil state within a federation is matter for endless argument. Although Tamils are in the majority in the north, there are sizeable other groups, including Muslims, in the east.

Prabhakaran talks of the possibility of a "reasonable" compromise, although it is unclear what compromise he would make. He did say, though:

"If a proposal which gives autonomy and satisfies the expectations of the Tamil people is put forward, we are prepared to consider it."

However, he talks of "extremists" in the government. President Premadasa, who has always favoured negotiation, might be willing to try it again, but the army, a growing force in Sri Lankan politics, would probably object. If its view prevails, the Tigers will fight on. Prabhakaran said:

"Victory in a war does not depend on manpower or weapons. Firm determination, valour and love of freedom are the factors that decide victory in a war. Our fighters and our people are full of these."

Sri Lanka's civil war could continue for a while yet."

The first of the two above-mentioned quotes from Pirabakaran in his 1993 interview disproves unequivocally the views expressed by Colombo, Chennai, London and New York pundits that he had down-graded his demand for separate state as a result of "post September 11" developments. The second of the two above-mentioned quotes shows his courageous and uncompromising stand, which has not wavered for the past ten years."

President Premadasa believed that it was possible to come to a political arrangement with the LTTE, but finally his talks with the LTTE broke down, and ultimately he was assassinated by an LTTE suicide bomber.

The USA declared the LTTE as a terrorist organization in 1997, thereby making fund-raising activities for it there illegal, and the UK banned the LTTE in 2001.

Today, the island of Sri Lanka is de facto partitioned into two "nations": the Sinhalas and the Tamils, with a military confrontation across a cease-fire line (CFL) established after the formal cease fire of 22 February 2002, and since broken. The LTTE having eliminated all its rival Tamil groups after the withdrawal of the IPKF, through murder, intimidation, and the most active resistance to the SLAF, unofficially rules the Sri Lankan Tamils with an iron hand, and continues to be a disturbing factor in the Indian state of Tamil Nadu. The merger of the Northern and Eastern Provinces, the major achievement of the ISLA, was declared constitutionally illegal by Sri Lanka Supreme Court in October 2006 on technical grounds, since it was ordered by a Presidential Decree under Emergency powers.

# APPENDICES

## Appendix-A

# The Organization and Rank Structure of the Indian Army

The Indian Army is very broadly divided into two main groupings: the "Arms," which do the actual fighting, and the "Services" which provide all the physical support which allows them to do so, such as providing the arms and ammunition, the food and fuel and other such requirements, the medical care, the maintenance and repair of all equipment, and so on.

The Arms consist of the "Combat Arms" and the "Supporting Arms." The Combat Arms are the Infantry and the Armoured Corps, plus the infantry who are routinely carried in and fight from "mechanized infantry combat vehicles," and generally support the tanks of the armoured corps, known as the Mechanized Infantry. The Supporting Arms, without which tactical operations by the combat arms would be very difficult, if not impossible, are the Artillery, who fire the field guns and the larger medium guns (such as the Bofors of political notoriety), the Corps of Engineers, who are the combat engineers, and the Corps of Signals, who provide the communications and much else.

The Services include a number of essential branches of the army. The Army Service Corps (ASC), which provides the food for the fighting soldiers and for everyone else, fuel for its vehicles, fodder for the mules used to carry stores in the remote mountain areas, vehicles and their drivers to carry all the goods of every kind needed by the army to fight and to maintain itself in the battlefield and in peacetime locations, clerical staff, the mules and their handlers, and other similar essential services. The Army Ordnance Corps (AOC) provides the fighting men with the arms, ammunition, explosives and other warlike stores necessary for fighting, which it procures, supplies, and maintains adequate stocks of. The Army Medical Corps (AMC) and its allied services, the Army Dental Corps and the Military Nursing Service, provide the health and emergency battlefield medical cover, including life-saving measures and surgery in the field, that are necessary to maintain the physical fighting efficiency of the troops, and the battlefield morale of the army. The Corps of Electrical and Mechanical Engineers (EME) inspect, maintain and repair all the weapons, vehicles, communications equipment, optical instruments, and all other electrical, mechanical and some of the electronic equipment of the army. There are some other highly-specialized smaller services, which all have their essential roles in the functioning of the army.

### *The Organization of the Combat Arms and the Supporting Arms*

The infantry is divided into social groupings known as "Regiments" which wear the same uniform details, such as the identifying cap badge, shoulder titles, and lanyard, and are generally drawn from the same area or social classes, or have what is known as a "fixed class composition." Examples are the "Madras Regiment," with men from all the communities of the four southern states, the "Bihar Regiment," of men from Bihar and Jharkhand states, the "Sikh Regiment" with Jat Sikhs, the "Punjab Regiment" with Jat Sikhs and Dogra Rajputs of Himachal Pradesh and the Jammu region, the "Maratha Light Infantry," the "Garhwal Rifles," the "Assam Regiment" with men from all the north-eastern states, the "Jat Regiment," the "Rajputana Rifles," the "Grenadiers," the "Parachute Regiment," the "Brigade of Guards," and various others. All these regiments have a training center of their own, at which the young recruits are trained to become soldiers, and imbibe the traditions and culture of their regiment. The fighting units of an infantry regiment are its "battalions," which are numbered, generally from 1 onwards, such as "4th Battalion, the Kumaon

Regiment" (or 4th Kumaon in spoken language), 3rd Dogra (3rd Battalion, the Dogra Regiment), or 20th Rajput. A regiment may have a large number of battalions. Gorkhas have seven different regiments, which are numbered, eg, 1st Gorkha Rifles, 4th Gorkha Rifles, or 11th Gorkha Rifles, so their battalions have two numbers, the first of the individual battalion, the second that of the regiment, for example, "2nd Battalion, the 3rd Gorkha Rifles" (2nd/3rd Gorkha Rifles or 2/3 G.R.). Since there are a number of Gorkha regiments, these regiments have fewer battalions than other infantry regiments.

Individual tank units are known as "regiments," as are individual artillery units and units of the combat engineers, which is the corresponding term to the infantry unit, the battalion. Regiments of armour have names such as "Skinner's Horse (1st Horse)," "3rd Cavalry," "Hodson's Horse," "7th Light Cavalry," "Scinde Horse," "18th Cavalry," "20th Lancers," etc, which are the names from the times when they were actually cavalry regiments with horses. Many regiments raised in the post-horse era have also been named "cavalry," such as "64th Cavalry," but many of the modern raisings have modern names, such as "70th Armoured Regiment."

Artillery units are individually called "regiments," such as "25 Field Regiment," "32 Mountain Regiment," or "223 Medium Regiment" even though the formal name of the artillery branch as a whole is the "Regiment of Artillery," this name corresponding to the names of infantry regiments, which constitute a social "family," while the artillery branch as a whole are informally called "Gunners." The Corps of Engineers, the combat engineers who are also called "Sappers," are grouped into three groups, each with its own training centre, the groups being the "Madras Engineers," the "Bengal Engineers," and the "Bombay Engineers," corresponding to the three separate armies of the British East India Company which raised them. The engineer units are named, for instance, "42 Engineer Regiment," or other similar names, such "101 Assault Engineer Regiment."

Informally speaking units of the artillery and of the engineers are referred to as "gunner regiments" and "sapper regiments."

All units of all of the arms and services are commanded by Colonels (earlier by Lieutenant-Colonels), and have a standard complement of officers, men, arms and equipment, ranging from some 550 all ranks for an armoured regiment, to the nearly 900 all ranks of an infantry battalion. Below the unit are its sub-units, which actually do the fighting, the "rifle companies," named "Company" of the infantry, the "sabre squadrons" named "Squadron" of the armour, and the "Battery" of the artillery. Sub-units are commanded by Majors or Lieutenant-Colonels, and are numbered alphabetically, the four rifle companies of an infantry battalion are 'A,' 'B,' 'C' and 'D,' the three sabre squadrons of a tank regiment are 'A,' 'B,' and 'C,' and the three batteries of an artillery regiment are 'P,' 'Q,' and 'R.' these are invariably spoken of in the phonetic alphabet; thus there are "Alpha" to "Delta" Companies in infantry battalions, 'Alpha' to 'Charlie' Squadrons in armored regiments, and 'Papa,' 'Quebec,' and 'Romeo' Batteries in every artillery regiment.

These sub-units are further broken down into smaller sub-units, "platoons" in the case of infantry, and "troops" in the case of tanks. An infantry rifle company has about 135 all ranks, and basically has three platoons of 35 men each, plus other elements. An infantry platoon has three smaller sub-units, the "sections." The infantry section of ten men is commanded by a Havildar, who wears three stripes on his sleeve, though earlier it used to be commanded by a Naik. Naiks wear two stripes on their sleeves.

For the actual business of tactical military operations, battalions of various regiments, and units of the other arms and services are grouped together into "field formations," the lowest of which is the brigade, commanded by a Brigadier. The basic brigade is the infantry brigade or mountain brigade of three infantry battalions, almost invariably from three different regiments. A normal infantry brigade would have about 3,000 all ranks. The corresponding formation of the armoured corps, also broadly called the "mechanized forces," is the "armoured brigade" or "mechanized brigade," with three or four units, such as two units of tanks and one of mechanized infantry for example, or vice versa. Artillery regiments are grouped together as an "artillery brigade." The next higher field formation is the "division," which could be an "infantry division," an "armoured division," a "mechanized division," or even an "artillery division." A division is commanded by a Major-General, the General Officer Commanding (GOC) or "divisional commander." An infantry division or mountain division would routinely consist of three infantry brigades and an artillery brigade, plus various other units of supporting arms and services. An infantry division would have between 15,000 and 17,000 all ranks, though some static infantry divisions in a defensive 'holding' role along the Line of Control in Jammu and Kashmir have much more, as a result of having more brigades, and more battalions per brigade.

Two or more divisions are grouped under a larger field formation known as a "Corps," each of which has a number, such as "16 Corps," and is commanded by a Lieutenant-General, the GOC of the Corps, or the "Corps Commander." An even larger fighting grouping is the "field army" of two or more Corps, which in India's case are the static territorial "commands," such as "Eastern Command" or "Northern Command." These are commanded by a Lieutenant-General who has other Lieut.-Generals who are GOC's under him, and so is a General Officer Commanding-in-Chief, or GOC-in-C of the command, but because it is the equivalent of a field army, he is also known as the "Army Commander." On an even larger scale, field armies of the Allies which were fighting overseas in the Second World War, were grouped together under "Army Groups" commanded by Generals, but the Indian Army is not likely to reach such a size. The largest field formation employed in or near India was the 14$^{th}$ Army on the eastern front against the Japanese in India and Burma during the Second World War, which was commanded by an Indian Army officer, Lt.-Gen. Bill Slim as GOC-in-C 14$^{th}$ Army, which had two Corps operating under it, XXXIII Corps and IV Corps *(as 33 Corps and 4 Corps, which continue today, were then written).*

## Appendix-B

# The Indo-Sri Lanka Accord

To establish peace and normalcy in Sri Lanka the president of the Democratic Socialist Republic of Sri Lanka, his Excellency Mr. J.R. Jayawardene, and the Prime Minister of The Republic of India, His Excellency Rajiv Gandhi, having met at Colombo on 29 July 1987, Attaching utmost importance to nurturing, intensifying and strengthening the traditional friendship of Sri Lanka and India, and acknowledging the imperative need of resolving the ethnic problem of Sri Lanka, and the consequent violence, and for the safety, wellbeing and prosperity of people belonging to all communities of Sri Lanka, Have this day entered into the following agreement to fulfil this Objective.

In this context,

1.1 Desiring to preserve the unity, sovereignty and territorial integrity of Sri Lanka,

1.2 Acknowledging that Sri Lanka is a "multi-ethnic and multi-lingual plural society" consisting, *inter-alia*, of Sinhalese, Tamils, Muslims (Moors) and Burgers,

1.3 Recognizing that each ethnic group has a distinct cultural and linguistic identity, which has to be carefully nurtured,

1.4 Also recognizing that the northern and the eastern provinces have been areas of historical habitation of Sri Lankan Tamil speaking peoples, who have at all times hitherto lived together in this territory with other ethnic groups,

1.5 Conscious of the necessity of strengthening the forces contributing to the unity, sovereignty and territorial integrity of Sri Lanka, and preserving its character as a multi-ethnic, multi-lingual and multi- religious plural society in which all citizens can live in equality, safety and harmony, and prosper and fulfil their aspirations,

2. Resolve that:

2.1 Since the Government of Sri Lanka proposes to permit adjoining provinces to join to form one administrative unit and also by a referendum to separate as may be permitted to the northern and eastern provinces as outlined below:

2.2 During the period, which shall be considered an interim period (i.e. from the date of the elections to the provincial council, as specified in para 2.8 to the date of the referendum as specified in para 2.3), the northern and eastern provinces as now constituted, will form one administrative unit, having one elected provincial council. Such a unit will have one governor, one chief minister and one board of ministers.

2.3 There will be a referendum on or before 31st December 1988 to enable the people of the eastern province to decide whether:

(a) The eastern province should remain linked with the northern province as one administrative unit, and continue to be governed together with the northern province as specified in para 2.2 or:

(b) The eastern province should constitute a separate administrative unit having its own distinct provincial council with a separate governor, chief minister and board of ministers. The president may, at his discretion, decide to postpone such a referendum.

2.4 All persons, who have been displaced due to ethnic violence or other reasons, will have the right to vote in such a referendum. Necessary conditions to enable them to return to areas from where they were displaced will be created.

2.5 The referendum, when held, will be monitored by a committee headed by the Chief Justice, a member appointed by the President, nominated by the Government of Sri Lanka, and a member appointed by the President, nominated by the representatives of the Tamil speaking people of the eastern province.

2.6 A simple majority will be sufficient to determine the result of the referendum.

2.7 Meetings and other forms of propaganda, permissible within the laws of the country, will be allowed before the referendum.

2.8 Elections to provincial councils will be held within the next three months, in any event before 31 December 1987. Indian observers will be invited for elections to the provincial council of the north and east.

2.9 The emergency will be lifted in the eastern and northern provinces by 15 August 1987. A cessation of hostilities will come into effect all over the island within 48 hours of signing of this agreement. All arms presently held by militant groups will be surrendered in accordance with an agreed procedure to authorities to be designated by the Government of Sri Lanka.

Consequent to the cessation of hostilities and the surrender of arms by militant groups, the army and other security personnel will be confined to barracks in camps as on 25 May 1987. The process of surrendering arms and the confining of security personnel moving back to barracks shall be completed within 72 hours of the cessation of hostilities coming into effect.

2.10 The Government of Sri Lanka will utilize for the purpose of law enforcement and maintenance of security in the northern and eastern provinces same organizations and mechanisms of government as are used in the rest of the country.

2.11 The President of Sri Lanka will grant a general amnesty to political and other prisoners now held in custody under

The Prevention of Terrorism Act and other emergency laws, and to combatants, as well as to those persons accused, charged and/or convicted under these laws. The Government of Sri Lanka will make special efforts to rehabilitate militant youth with a view to bringing them back into the mainstream of national life. India will co-operate in the process.

2.12 The government of Sri Lanka will accept and abide by the above provisions and expect all others to do likewise.

2.13 If the framework for the resolutions is accepted, the Government of Sri Lanka will implement the relevant proposals forthwith.

2.14 The Government of India will underwrite and guarantee the resolutions, and co-operate in the implementation of these proposals.

2.15 These proposals are conditional to an acceptance of the proposals negotiated from 4.5.1986 to 19.12.1986. Residual matters not finalized during the above negotiations shall be resolved between India and Sri Lanka within a period of six weeks of signing this agreement. These proposals are also conditional to the Government of India co-operating directly with the Government of Sri Lanka in their implementation.

2.16 These proposals are also conditional to the Government of India taking the following actions if any militant groups operating in Sri Lanka do not accept this framework of proposals for a settlement, namely,

(a) India will take all necessary steps to ensure that Indian territory is not used for activities prejudicial to the unity, integrity and security of Sri Lanka

(b) The Indian navy/coast guard will cooperate with the Sri Lankan navy in preventing Tamil militant activities from affecting Sri Lanka.

(c) In the event that the Government of Sri Lanka requests the Government of India to afford military assistance to implement these proposals the

Government of India will co-operate by giving to the Government of Sri Lanka such military assistance as and when requested.

(d) The Government of India will expedite repatriation from Sri Lanka of Indian citizens to India who are resident here, concurrently with the repatriation of Sri Lankan refugees from Tamil Nadu.

(e) The Governments of Sri Lanka and India will co-operate in ensuring the physical security and safety of all communities inhabiting the northern and eastern provinces.

2.17 The government of Sri Lanka shall ensure free, full and fair participation of voters from all communities in the northern and eastern provinces in electoral processes envisaged in this agreement. The Government of India will extend full co-operation to the Government of Sri Lanka in this regard.

2.18 The official language of Sri Lanka shall be Sinhala. Tamil and English will also be official languages.

3. *This agreement and the Annexure thereto shall come into force upon signature.*

*In witness whereof, we have set our hands and seals hereunto.*

*Done in Colombo, Sri Lanka, on this the twenty-ninth day of July of the year one thousand nine hundred and eighty seven, in duplicate, both texts being equally authentic.*

*Junius Richard Jayawardene*

President of the Democratic of the Socialist Republic of Sri Lanka

*Rajiv Gandhi*

Prime Minister Republic of India

*Annexure to the Agreement*

1. His Excellency the President of Sri Lanka and the Prime Minister of India agree that the referendum mentioned in

paragraph 2 and its sub-paragraphs of the agreement will be observed by a representative of the Election Commission of India to be invited by His Excellency the President of Sri Lanka.

2. Similarly, both heads of Government agree that the elections to the provincial council mentioned in paragraph 2.8 of the agreement will be observed and all para-military personnel will be withdrawn from the eastern and northern provinces with a view to creating conditions conducive to fair elections to the council.

3. The President, in his discretion shall absorb such para-military forces, which came into being due to ethnic violence, into the regular security forces of Sri Lanka.

4. The President of Sri Lanka and the Prime Minister of India agree that the Tamil militants shall surrender their arms to authorities agreed upon to be designated by the President of Sri Lanka. The surrender shall take place in the presence of one senior representative each of the Sri Lanka Red Cross and the Indian Red Cross.

5. The President of Sri Lanka and the Prime Minister of India agree that a joint Indo-Sri Lankan observer group consisting of qualified representatives of the Government of Sri Lanka and the Government of India would monitor the cessation of hostilities from 31 July 1987.

6. The President of Sri Lanka and the Prime Minister of India also agree that in the terms of paragraph 2.14 and paragraph 2.16(c) of the agreement, an Indian peace keeping contingent may be invited by the President of Sri Lanka to guarantee and enforce the cessation of hostilities, if so required.

*Exchange of letters between the Prime Minister of India and the President of Sri Lanka*

Excellency,

1. Conscious of the friendship between our two countries stretching over two millenia and more, and recognizing the importance of nurturing this traditional friendship, it is imperative that both Sri Lanka and India reaffirm the decision

not to allow our respective territories to be used for activities prejudicial to each other's unity, territorial integrity and security.

2. In this spirit, you had, in the course of our discussions agreed to meet some of India's concerns as follows:

(i) Your Excellency and myself will reach an early understanding about the relevance and employment of foreign military and intelligence personnel with a view to ensuring that such presences will not prejudice Indo-Sri Lankan relations.

(ii) Trincomalee or any other ports in Sri Lanka will not be made available for military use by any country in a manner prejudicial to India's interests.

(iii) The work of restoring and operating the Trincomalee Oil Tank Farm will be undertaken as a joint venture between India and Sri Lanka.

(iv) Sri Lanka's agreements with foreign broadcasting organizations will be reviewed to ensure that any facilities set up by them in Sri Lanka are not inimical to India's interests.

3. In the same spirit India will:

(i) deport all Sri Lankan citizens who are found to be engaging in terrorist activities or advocating separatism or secessionism.

(ii) provide training facilities and military supplies for Sri Lankan forces.

4. India and Sri Lanka have agreed to set up a joint consultative mechanism to continuously review matters of common concern in the light of the objectives stated in paragraph 1 and specifically to monitor the implementation of other matters contained in this letter.

5. Kindly confirm, Excellency, that the above correctly sets out the agreement reached between us.

Please accept, Excellency, the assurances of my highest consideration.

Yours sincerely,

*Rajiv Gandhi*

## Appendix-C

# History of Jaffna*

*Part 1: Jaffna Kingdom*

Ceylon gained independence in 1948. Though Ceylon obtained independence from the British, long before that foreign colonial powers had conquered the Jaffna Kingdom comprising the North and East and the Kotte Kingdom in South West, and the Kandyan Kingdom in the Center.

The Portuguese first set foot in Ceylon in 1505. At that time there were three kingdoms in Ceylon. They were the Jaffna, Kotte and the Kandyan Kingdoms.

First the Kotte Kingdom was captured by the Portuguese. Then in stages they brought the western territory of the Jaffna Kingdom under their control. Finally in 1519 they enslaved the Jaffna Kingdom by defeating the last king Sankili in the battle field. However, the defeat of Sankili didn't mean the end of resistance in Jaffna. Between June 1619 and February 1621 there were several uprisings against the Portuguese. Consequently the Portuguese lost many areas of the Jaffna Kingdom. However, the uprisings were put down due to Portuguese command of the sea which enabled them to bring in reinforcements from India and Colombo.

The Portuguese ruled Jaffna with a heavy hand. Christian missionary activity spread simultaneously with destruction of Hindu temples. In 1628 a small force from Kandy attacked Jaffna. The Tamil people who were waiting for an opportunity rose in revolt against the Portuguese. The Portuguese were forced to retreat inside the Jaffna Fort. However, the combined

*As placed on the Tamil Eelam web-site.

Tamil and Sinhalese forces were not equipped for a siege warfare. The Portuguese defeated the Tamil-Sinhalese forces by shelling them from the Fort. After that the Portuguese gradually regained control of the lost territory.

The Portuguese conquest of Jaffna was facilitated by several factors. Jaffna was easily accessible by sea. There were Portuguese outposts at Mannar and on Coromandel Coast. By the second half of the 16th century the Jaffna Kingdom had lost much of its power due to rivalry for the throne. Though the Jaffna King sought the help of Ragunatha Nayakkan who ruled Madurai it did not materialize. Above all the Portuguese used Sinhalese mercenary troops to defend the Jaffna Kingdom.

It should be observed that although the Portuguese landed in Ceylon in 1505 it took them another 115 years to conquer the Jaffna Kingdom. The Kotte Kingdom came under complete control of the Portuguese in 1597. The Kandyan Kingdom was ceded to the British in 1815. Sankili was captured by the Portuguese and taken to Goa where he was hanged.

Though the Jaffna Kingdom fell, the areas to the south called Vanni did not accept the rule of the Portuguese. It did not pay tribute to the Kandyan Kingdom or to any other kingdom. It functioned as an autonomous entity. However, the three Vanniamai in the East (Then Tamil Eelam) viz Kodiyaram Vannimai, Palugamam Vannimai and Pannamai Vannimai sought the help of the Kandyan Kingdom for their defense. But they still functioned as autonomous regions.

Although at different times the territory of Eelam came under foreign rule, it never lost its Tamil Identity. Even its borders remained intact till 1833.

The Jaffna Kingdom existed with Nallur as its capital from 1215 AD 1619 AD. The following are the names of the Kings and their period of rule of Tamil Eelam:

1. Kalingaman alias Koolangai Singai Aryan alias Kalinga Vijeyabahu (1215 to 1240)
2. Kulasegara Pararajasegaram (1240 to 1256)
3. Kulothungan (1256 to 1279)

4. Vikramnan (1279 to 1302)
5. Varothayan (1371 to 1380)
6. Marthanda Perumalan (1325 to 1348)
7. Kunapooshanan (1348 to 1371)
8. Virothayan (1371 to 1380)
9. Jeyaveeran (1380 to 1410)
10. Kunaveeran (1410 to 1446)
11. Kanagasooriyan (1446 to 1450). From 1450 to 1467 Jaffna Kingdom came under the rule of Kotte kingdom. Troops which came under the command of Chenpagap Perumal captured Jaffna. Later he become King of Kotte under the name of King Bhuvanekabahu (VI). Kanagasooriyan fled to Tamil Nadu and came back with an army and re-captured the Kingdom and again ruled from 1467 to 1478.
12. Pararajasegaran (1478 to 1519)
13. Sankili Segarajasegaran (1519 to 1561). He was born to the third wife of Pararajasegaran.
14. Pararasa Pandaram, Pararasasekaran (1561 to 1565). he is son of Sankili.
15. Kurunchi Nainar (1565 to 1570)
16. Periapillai Sekarasa Sekaran (1570 to 1582)
17. Puvirasa Pandaram II (1582 to 1591)
18. Ethirmanna Singa Pararasasekaran (1591 to 1615).
19. Sankili Kumaran (1615 to 1619).

In all the Jaffna Kingdom existed for 403 years.

*Part 2: Kalinga Magan*

We learnt in the last chapter about the arrival of the Portuguese and the capture of the Jaffna Kingdom in 1619. Also we learnt that the Jaffna Kingdom existed for 403 years and the names of the 19 kings who ruled during the same period. For over 200 years the Jaffna Kingdom remained the single most powerful Kingdom in Ceylon. The Jaffna Kings maintained close relationship with South Indian Kingdoms and later with the Portuguese. This we can glean from Sinhala historical books, some Sinhala inscriptions and through Sinhala literary works like Kokila Sandesiya, Paravi Sandesiya, Parakum Paciritha.

From the beginning of the 16th Century we can learn the history of the rulers of Jaffna lucidly and someway in detail from Portuguese sources.

There are some Tamil books, if not in great detail, but at least to some extent, that gives the history of the origin, rise and growth of the Jaffna Kingdom and the history of its rulers. One such book is the Yalpana Vaipavamalai. Others are the Vaiyapadal, Kailayamalai, Rajamurai and Parajasegaran Ula.

The Yalpana Vaipavamalai was written by Mylvagana Pulavar from Mathagal in the eighteenth century. From the forward to the book it can be understood that this book was written at the request of the Dutch authorities and the author based his written on books like Vaiyapandal, Kailayamalai, Rajamurai and Parajasegaran Ula. Both Rajamurai and Parajasegaran Ula are now extinct.

Vaiyapandal was written by Vaiyapuri Aiyar during the reign of King Segarajeskeran. This book describes events commencing from the first ruler of Jaffna. It also describes the names of the chieftains and social groups and how they came from Tamil Nadu and settled in Jaffna and Vanni. Like other Tamil works Vaiyapandal also does not give the events in chronological order.

In the thirteenth century (1215 AD) following the invasion of Kalingamagan (1215-1255 AD) the Polonaruwa Kingdom which was already in a state of decay declined in power. Magan ruled with Polonaruwa as his capital. He was then the most powerful monarch in Ceylon. After the fall of Polonaruwa the Sinhalese Kings shifted their capitals to Dambedeniya and Yapahuwa. The Vanni King Vijayabahu III captured Mayarata and ruled with Dambedeniya as his capital.

His son Parakramabahu II (1236-1270 AD) captured the hill areas and the southwest and strengthened his rule. He, like his father, entertained the ambition to capture Rajarata again and bring it under his rule. A number of Vanni chieftains are said to have been persuaded to shift their allegiance from Magan to Parakramabahu.

Following the fall of Polonaruwa there arose several minor kingdoms called Vanniars. Those areas ruled by these minor kings under the name of Vanniars were called Vannipattu or Vanni. Since some of the warriors consisted of Vanniars, the appearance of Vanniyars must have occurred during the Polonaruwa period.

The ancient Batticalo chronicle states that Magan captured Polonaruwa and then gave military control to the Vanniars.

The Konesar inscription states that Kulakkoddan appointed Vanniars as rulers of Trincomalee, Nilaveli, Kaddukkulam areas. Kulakoddan's real name was Cholkathevan.

The Chulavamsa and other chronicles say that Magan stationed troops at places like Trincomalee, Koddiyara, Kantalai, Padavia, Kaddukkulam, Illuppaikadavai, Kytes, Pulachery and ruled Rajarata from his capital Polonaruwa. Polanaruwa captured and ruled by Magan was later over-run by the Javanese.

*Part 3: Aryachackravathis...*

The King of Java by the name Chandrabanu twice invaded Ceylon from Malaya. On both occasions his invasion ended in failure. Later he raised an army from Chola Nadu and Pandiya Nadu and captured territory in North Ceylon ruled by Magan. After consolidating his position he again attacked the Dambedeniya kingdom ruled by Parakramabahu II. Chandrabanu demanded the surrender of Buddha's Tooth relic and the kingship to him failing which he informed Parakramabahu II to be ready for war. According to Chulavamsa Parakramabaku II refused to accede to the demands made by Chandrabanu and was successful in halting the invading Army which had penetrated upto Yapahuva and completely freeing him self from his (Chandrabanu) domination. Yet Chandrabanu's rule covered the Jaffna Peninsula, Vanni in the North and Trincomalee.

The place names such as Chavakachcheri, Chavankoddai and Chavakakoddai came into existence as a result of the rule of Chavakas in the 13th century.

Around this time the Pandian empire under the rule of Maravarman Sunderapandyan became very powerful. During his reign the domination of the Kingdom in North Ceylon by Pandias was further strengthened.

When Chandrabanu refused to pay tribute to the Indian empire, Maravarman Suderapandian defeated Chandrabanu and brought his Kingdom under his domain.

Among those chieftains who were left behind by the Pandias to rule over Jaffna one Pandimalavan emerged very powerful. After Chandrabanu, his son accepted the suzerainty of the Pandias and ruled for some time. After him, it is claimed that when there was no successor to the throne Pandimalavan who hailed from the village of Ponpatti went to Madurai and brought Prince Singairiyan and crowned him king of Jaffna. The rule by Aryachakravarthis were established in Jaffna as a sequel to invasion of Ceylon by Pandias under the leadership of army general Aryachackravarthi about A.D 1284.

According to inscriptions, during the rule of Maravarman Kulasegaran (AD 1268-1310), Aryachakravarthis served both as army generals and ministers under him.

According to the astrological book Segarajasekeramalai the ancestors of Jaffna Kings served as army generals and ministers under Pandias. They are said to be Brahmins who belonged to Kasyappa ancestry and descendants of five-hundred and twelve "Panchagrama Vethiyar" of Ramesvaram temple.

The Aryachackravarthis are not in fact Aryans in the ethnic sense, but they referred to themselves as such because of matrimonial relationship established with brahmins in Rameshvarmam.

The Chulavamsam referring to the invasion of Pandias following the death of Bhuvanakabahu 1 (AD 1272- 1281) states that Pandian Kings despatched troops under the command of a Tamil army general. Although he was not an Aryan he was considered both popular and influential. Further it states that the invading force destroyed the fortified city of Yapahuva and carried away the Budha's Tooth relic and other priceless valuables.

Consequent to the invasion by Pandias under the command of Aryachckravarthi the Sinhalese kingdom got further weakened. Yapahuva lost its status as capital city. Also there was infighting for the throne between Bhuvanakabahu II (son of Bhuvanakabahu I), and Parakramabahu III (son of Vijayabahu IV, AD 1271-1272) As a result the Sinhalese Kingdom got divided. Bhuvanakabahu made Kurunagala his capital and ruled from there. Parakramabahu III went to Madurai and retrieved the Tooth Relic that was taken away by the Pandian king and installed the same at Polonarwa where he established his rule.

The Aryachakravarthi mentioned by Chulavamsam or some other descendant of him must have by passage of time crowned himself king of Jaffna. The name Aryachakravarthi does not refer to real name but one denoting ancestry.

## Appendix-D

# Problems Faced by IPKF Soldiers' Families

*Problems Faced by IPKF Soldiers' Families*

What happens when a unit is suddenly asked to deploy from a peace station without the proper mobilization process? If they are suddenly pulled out without any warning? Chaos reigns supreme. The experience for the families of the IPKF was, to say the least, traumatic. Families of soldiers not only got no time to prepare mentally and formalize administrative details related to husbands going into active duty, but had to face a host of family and personal problems with sick wives and children. In some cases the authorities were insensitive to the situation by simply not taking adequate steps to handle the ill-tidings from the battlefield. This further demoralized the families and also the fighting troops who got to know of the situation back home. In most cases it fell to the lot of the CO's wife to take up immediate matters with the authorities who were often unresponsive and taken up with other matters like celebrations of a festival. To illustrate the scenario, an account by the Second-in-Command of 16 SIKH of 41 Infantry Brigade which departed Lucknow in haste, and whose wife happened to be the senior-most lady of the unit in station, should suffice:

"My wife had to keep pleading with the Army authorities, along with the unit's Oficer-in-Charge Rear, for withdrawing of the notice for vacation of family quarters of men killed in action, for helping make minimum administrative arrangements for the wives of the Other Ranks, and visiting the hospital along with the wives whose husbands were wounded. She had the very difficult job of consoling the growing number of widows and orphaned children. She tried to keep the morale of the families high by joining the worried families in prayer for missing husbands. No one from the army hierarchy appeared to be sympathetic to the plight of the families of the dead or wounded in action. It was a shame for the organization. They were instead busy in preparing for "Diwali". When our soldiers were dying at Jaffna due to LTTE fire the sound of crackers was in the air at Lucknow Cantonment as Diwali was being celebrated! But nobody had the time to meet these wailing ladies and at least ask them about the difficulties they were facing and what help they needed, even though their husbands had died obeying the lawful command of their superiors, having gone on duty to uphold the honour of the country."

# References, Bibliography and Source Material

The major bibliographical reference material and the standard reference works on both guerilla warfare and on counter-insurgency operations, as well as major internet resources referred to are given below:


Athale, Colonel Anil A., "The Genesis of the Sri Lankan Conflict," on internet at http://www.rediff.com/*The Rediff Special*, March 2000.

Bayo, General Alberto, "150 Questions for a Guerilla," 1960 (Translation: Hartenstein, Hugo and Harber, Dennis, 1963).

Bhaduri, Major Shanker and Karim, Maj. General Afsir, "The Sri Lankan Crisis," 1990.

Burchett, Wilfred G., "The Second Indochina War," 1970.

Cardozo, Maj. General Ian, "The Indian Army: A Brief History," 2005.

Das, Maj. General Chand N., OBE, "The Rajputana Rifles, Brief History," 1995

Depinder Singh, Lieut. General, "The IPKF in Sri Lanka," 1992.

Depinder Singh, Lieut. General, "There were Constraints," as told to Venkatramani, S.H., *India Today*, 15 November 1987, p. 36.

Dixit, J.N., "Assignment Colombo," 1998.

Dixon, Dr. Norman F. "On the Psychology of Military Incompetence," 1976.

Fall, Bernard B., "Street Without Joy," 1987.

Gabriel, Major Richard A. and Savage, Lieut. Colonel Paul L., "Crisis in Command," 1978.

Galula, David, "Counter-Insurgency Warfare, Theory and Practice," 1964.

Giap, General Vo Nguyen, "People's War, People's Army," 1962.

Guevara, Ernesto 'Che,' "Guerilla Warfare," 1960 (English translation, 1961).

Gunaratna, Rohan, "Indian Intervention in Sri Lanka, the Role of India's International Agencies," 1993.

Gupta, Shekhar, "Operation Pawan: In a Rush to Vanquish" and "Commando Assault: The Lost Offensive," in *India Today* magazine, 31 January 1988.

Harkirat Singh, Maj. General, "Venture in Sri Lanka," 2007.

Jain, Justice Milap Chand, Commission of Inquiry into the Assassination of Sh. Rajiv Gandhi, May 1991, Report, 1998.

Jaspal Singh, Brigadier, 'India's Land Forces: Structural Imperatives," 2003.

Jaswant Singh, "Defending India," 1999.

Joshi, Manoj, "Beyond Jaffna," *Frontline* magazine, 14-27 November 1987, pp. 17-22.

Kadian, Rajesh, "India's Sri Lanka Fiasco, Peacekeepers at War," 1990.

Kalkat, Lieut. General A.S., on internet at http://www.rediff.com/*The Rediff Special*, March 2000.

Kaul, Colonel, Anil, Vr.C., "Better Dead than Disabled," 2006.

Katyal, K.K., "A Slower Pace," *Frontline* magazine, 14-27 November 1987, p. 21.

Kautilya, "Arthashastra," ca. 300 BC.

Khanduri, Brigadier C.B., "History of the 1st Gorkha Rifles (The Malaun Regiment)," Vol. III, 1947-1990, 1992.

Kitson, Frank, "Low Intensity Operations," 1971.

Larteguy, Jean, "The Lost Command" (original in French *'Les Centurions'*), 1960.

Ludra, Lieut. Colonel Th. Kuldeep Singh, "Operation Pawan: A Critical Analysis of the Sri Lanka Imbroglio," 1999.

Mao Tse-tung (Mao Zedong), "On Guerilla Warfare," (Mandarin Chinese *"Yu chi chan"*), 1937 (English translation: Samuel B. Griffith II, 1961).

Mehta, Maj. General Ashok K., "Tackling the Tigers," *Seminar* 1999, on internet at http://www.india-seminar.com/1999/479/mehta.htm.

Michigan, Maj. General A.H.E., "Right of the Line: The Grenadiers, A Historical Record," 1995.

Mukherjee, L., "History of India," 27th Edition, 1963.

Narayan Swamy, M.R., "Tigers of Lanka: From Boys to Guerillas," 3rd Ed., 2002.

Nehru, Pandit Jawaharlal, "The Discovery of India," 1961.

O'Ballance, Major Edgar, "The Wars in Vietnam 1954-1973," 1975.

Palsokar, Colonel R.D, Military Cross, "History of the 5th Gorkha Rifles (Frontier Force)," Vol. III, 1858 to 1991, 1991.

Palsokar, Colonel R.D, Military Cross, "History of the Sikh Light Infantry," Vol. II, 1997.

Praval, Major K.C., "Indian Army after Independence," 1993.

Raza, Major Maroof, "Low-Intensity Conflicts," 1995.

Rediff.com, "The IPKF in Sri Lanka, 10 Years On," Parts 1 to 11, 2000.

Sardeshpande, Lieut. General S.C., "Assignment Jaffna," 1991.

Sodhi, Brigadier H.S., "Top Brass—A Critical Appraisal of the Indian Military Leadership," 1993.

Sri Kantha, Sachi, "The Pirabaharan Phenomenon," Parts 1-54, on internet at http://www.tamilnation.org, 2001-2003.

Sridharan, Commander K., "A Maritime History of India," 1965.

Subrahmanyam, K., "Lessons of History," *Frontline* magazine, 14-27 November 1987, pp. 23-24.

Subrahmanyam, T.G., "Famous Battles in Indian History, 1969.

Subramanian, T.S., "A Chain Reaction," *Frontline* magazine, 17-30 October 1987, pp. 6-11.

Sundarji, General Krishnaswamy, 'Of Some Consequence,' 1999.

Suryanarayan, V. (Ed.), "Sri Lankan Crisis and India's Response," 1991.

Swamy, Dr. Subramanian, "Sri Lanka in Crisis: India's Options," 2007.

Taber, Robert, "The War of the Flea," 1965.

Tamileelam News Service, on internet at http://www.tamileelamweb.com.

Tekwani, Shyam, "In the Tigers' Den," *India Today*, 15 November 1987.

Thayer, Charles, "Guerilla," 1963.

Trinquier, Colonel Roger, "Modern War," 1961.

Yousaf, Brigadier Mohammad and Adkin, Major Mark, "The Bear Trap, Afghanistan's Untold Story," 1992.

# Index